MARRIED TO THE WELL

(Including Three Volumes Of The Book)

The Shrine

(Volume 3)

Ata Servati

To obtain more or other books by this author go to:
www.loveata.com
www.ataservati.com

Registrations #
ISBN print: 978-1-0882-0565-5
ISBN eBook: 978-1-0882-0572-3

This book was released in 2022. This book was printed and bound in the United State of America

ALSO BY ATA SERVATI

I AM A LOTUS (Spiritual Poems from the Heart)
IN SEARCH OF HEAVEN (The Howard Baskerville story)
IN SEARCH OF LOVE
MARRIED TO THE WELL (INCLUDES 3 Volumes)
ASYEH (Volume 1)
THE SILENT BEGGER (Volume 2)
THE SHRINE (Volume 3)

=========

Plays (In Farsi)
OVER THE BRIDGE, BOTTOM OF THE RIVER
Windows

TABLE OF CONTENTS

Chapter 1 – When superstitions overwhelm and hinder human beings.... 7

Chapter 2 – In the cloak of night, darkness becomes the sanctuary for those who steal from religion. 22

Chapter 3 – When the thieves of faith and those who exploit religion slink into the shadows of the night.. 30

Chapter 4 – When wolves show their nature… 38

Chapter 5 – When the call of happiness and joy is overshadowed by the color and face of sorrow... 61

Chapter 6 – When the prescribed drug itself becomes the cause of the doctor's demise... 84

Chapter 7 – When a blind man sees clearer than all others and hopes to liberate people from superstitions... 100

Chapter 8 – When the blind man becomes the eyes of the bright... 117

Chapter 9 – After making some adjustments for clarity and coherence, here's the edited version… 133

Chapter 10 – What can be done when a person leaves the world, but the people of the world do not leave him?! 149

Chapter 11 – When politics force friends to be seen as enemies and enemies to be considered friends… 181

Chapter 12 – When a single event shatters the foundations of humanity and the world... 191

Chapter 13 – When superstitions supplant authentic religious convictions, and religion itself morphs into a platform exploited by deceitful individuals and unscrupulous groups... 207

Chapter 14 – When superstitions take precedence over religion and replace it… 217

Chapter 15 – When, rage, hate, knives, sword and gun replace love, peace, and affection in religion 248

Chapter 16 – When uninformed and naive individuals amplify trivial matters. A century has come and gone, yet... 260

Introduction

I always struggled with writing introductions in my novels and plays. I often left this crucial section to others, giving them complete freedom to write whatever they felt was appropriate for the three books in my trilogy. However, in this particular case, I felt compelled to write the introductions myself as they required some explanations.

Several years ago, I embarked on a month-long journey in San Rafael, California, with a new girlfriend. It was during this time that I wrote the first volume "Asyeh" of what would eventually become a trilogy. Unfortunately, as I completed volume 1, I realized that I lacked any emotional connection to her, and I ultimately made the difficult decision to leave and return to Los Angeles. This decision was made even though I was going through a six-month period of homelessness at that time. For a long while, I carried a sense of guilt, uncertain about what steps to take next.

However, following my departure, I came to the realization that the novel I had written was excessively long and incomplete. While still living in my car, it took me approximately two months to complete the remaining two parts and transform it into a trilogy. The trilogy now consists of three books: "Asyeh," "The Silent Beggar," and "The Shrine"

During my time at the College of Dramatic Art in Iran, I had the opportunity to travel extensively throughout the country with my best friend, Kamran Norad. These journeys provided us with countless opportunities to learn and experience the diverse cultures and customs we encountered. We were always on the lookout for stories during these trips, engaging in conversations and connecting with local people, including the elderly.

On one of these trips, I came across a story that deeply fascinated me: "Married to the Well." The story lingered in my thoughts for many years, until one day, while sitting alone in silence, it resurfaced in my mind. Inspired by its essence, I decided to write a short story based on it. However, as I delved into the writing process, the story expanded far beyond my expectations, eventually spanning over 900 pages. Realizing its magnitude, I made the decision to turn it into a trilogy, consisting of three distinct books. Through this trilogy, I aimed to explore how religions can influence and alter individuals' lives, especially when they are wielded by unscrupulous religious leaders driven by greed, power, and a lack of spiritual grounding. These leaders manipulate and deceive innocent individuals who blindly follow their lies, believing in promises of heavenly rewards and salvation after death.

Regrettably, the misuse of religion for personal gain extends beyond individuals, infiltrating governments, and institutions throughout history. This unfortunate reality has inflicted more harm than good upon people. The fundamental principles of all religions revolve around nurturing better human beings, fostering love, respect, forgiveness, and construction rather than destruction. They are meant to inspire individuals to help rather than harm others. Witnessing the manipulation of religion in such a manner deeply saddens me.

Note: To ensure clarity for English readers who may not be familiar with the names of the characters in the book, I included a description of the characters at the end of the book for reference. This will help readers better understand and connect with the characters throughout the story.

Yours Sincerely,
Ata Servati

Chapter 1
When superstitions overwhelm and hinder human beings...

The morning call to prayer by the old muezzin of Shourcheh's Mosque brought a glimmer of hope to the people of two villages, Shourcheh and its neighboring village, Tikken. It symbolized the arrival of light and peace, dispelling the terror and darkness of the night. However, as darkness blanketed the village, a mournful melody of reeds and flutes emanated from the nearby hill, overlooking Shourcheh and Tikken. Contrary to its expected joyous effect, this haunting sound only instilled fear and anxiety in the hearts and minds of the villagers, depriving them of peace and sleep.

For nearly four decades, this haunting tune persisted, a constant reminder that the mythical creatures, the Elves and fairies, were said to dwell on the slopes and behind the hills above the villages. It was believed that they still lurked in the vicinity, ready to strike and take away unsuspecting individuals, draining their blood and extinguishing their lives. Whispers and sporadic sightings of those who vanished without a trace served as chilling evidence of this grim reality.

As dusk descended upon the land, both villages transformed into desolate graveyards, devoid of life. Doors and windows were tightly shut, and meticulously checked to ensure no crevice remained open. Superstition and fear held the residents captive within their own homes. With the resounding melody of the reed coinciding with sunset, anyone caught outside had to hasten back before darkness engulfed the villages. Those who needed to venture out after nightfall, whether to tend to their fields or visit the farms, never went alone. They formed groups, armed with oil lamps, sturdy wooden sticks, or sharp knives to defend themselves against Elfish attacks. A brighter oil lamp provided a sense of reassurance, while prayers inscribed on talismans hung visibly, a deterrent to the mischievous creatures. The presence of goblins in the hills had disrupted the peace and harmony of the villages for years. Even the Law Men, responsible for upholding justice, dared not venture into the forbidden areas. The villagers had been repeatedly warned that seeking assistance from law enforcement would be futile if they found themselves ensnared by fairies in the forbidden territories.

Over the past few decades, numerous tales have circulated about a large mulberry tree located in a high mountain valley above two villages, and the ghostly presence that surrounded it. Some individuals even claimed to have witnessed these apparitions firsthand, insisting that they were indeed ghosts. According to their accounts, the eerie silence was occasionally interrupted by the faint sound of a man singing. There were rumors of a ghostly figure frequently seen beneath the mulberry tree, draped in tattered brown cloth from head to toe. Among the local population, there were superstitions about goblins inhabiting the area; it was believed that if someone found themselves alone there, these creatures would drain their blood and steal their soul, leaving no trace behind. In fact, there were even tales circulating among the villagers about a silent beggar, a wandering dervish, and Mashhadi Hassan Gorkan/the Grave Digger, who vanished after passing through that very region. These rumors instilled fear in the villagers, causing them to avoid the area altogether, deeming it a forbidding and ominous place.

As dawn approached, the muezzin of the village mosque in Shourcheh had only just begun his call to prayer when the shepherd prepared to leave his house, clutching the collars of his four dogs. The dogs, eager to be the first out, jostled and struggled at the old, weathered door, momentarily impeding their owner. After a brief pause, they managed to break free, rushing into the alley, competing with each other to take the lead.

Ali, a shepherd, was one of two shepherds in Shourcheh renowned for his storytelling skills, making him popular among the shepherds of the neighboring countryside. However, his propensity for stretching the truth had caused his fellow villagers to take his words with a grain of salt. Nevertheless, children delighted in his tales and eagerly gathered around to listen whenever he began his storytelling sessions.

The shepherds' task was to gather the villagers' sheep and goats and lead them to the hills for grazing throughout the day, only to return them home as the sun set. Thus, every summer morning, the villagers entrusted their livestock to the shepherds, reclaiming them in the evening. Payment for the shepherds' services was made annually, coinciding with the completion of the harvest, with fees determined based on the number of sheep and goats each villager owned.

In the pre-dawn darkness, the shepherd's dogs fearlessly navigated the secluded village alleys. Restless and eager, they strained against their leashes, which were tightly wrapped around Shepherd Ali's wrists multiple times. Accompanied by his young assistant, Asef, Shepherd Ali collected the sheep from various houses along their route. The number of sheep in their procession steadily grew. The dogs, driven by their innate sense of responsibility and duty, could detect the faint bleating of the sheep and goats, their excitement evident in the snarls emanating from their moist snouts. They understood their role in safeguarding the herd, and they excelled at it.

Along the way, sleepy village women emerged from their homes, clutching their water jugs as they hurried towards the water creeks. Their objective was to fetch clean water for their daily drinking and cooking needs before the arrival of the herd and other animals, which could potentially contaminate the water. Adorned in long, vibrant clothes and floral scarves, the women painted a beautiful picture in the twilight. The sound of sheep, accompanied by the presence of dogs and the rhythmic jingle of brass bells hanging from the goats and sheep, created a captivating scene at the break of dawn in the village.

Asef, while making his way from the other side of the village, joined the herd and Shepherd Ali, who had gathered the sheep. Now, the herd stood in front of the Village Public Bathhouse. In ancient times, each village housed two or three public bathhouses that served the community. At dawn, thick smoke billowed from the rooftops of these bathhouses. Mashhadi Hossein, who managed the village's general bathhouse, and his assistant Taghi, stacked dry bushes beneath a small pool inside the bathhouse to warm the water before customers arrived. The bathhouse roofs were situated only one or two cubits above the ground, as they were built underground to shield from the cold winter weather and maintain warmth during the day. Dry bushes were used as insulation underneath the bathhouse to heat the water. Men typically utilized the bathhouse from dawn until shortly after sunrise, while women bathed throughout the day. When Shepherd Ali and his herd reached the bathhouse, Mashhadi Hussein openly ridiculed him, his voice carrying over the noise of the passing sheep. "Shepherd Ali, for God's sake, please try to spare a few poor wolves today."

The villagers laughed along with Taghi as Shepherd Ali continued walking without acknowledging Mashhadi Hussein's irony. It was known that Hajji Amir, the wealthiest man in Village Shourcheh, also owned his own herds and shepherds. Simultaneously, another herd was making its way to the hills above the village on the opposite side of Shourcheh. This herd seemingly belonged to Kadkhoda. In principle, however, most of the herd belonged to Mullah Mahmud, the main preacher at the village mosque. Yet, people believed that only a few of the animals belonged to Mullah Mahmud, as he didn't want others to know about his wealth and monetary resources. This way, he could continue receiving donations intended for religious purposes and use them to sustain his extravagant lifestyle. Unfortunately, the villagers were unaware of this deception. Mullah Mahmoud maintained a facade of poverty to preserve his sacred image. Mullah Mahmoud's shepherd, Samad, and his assistant, Ghazanfar, were staunch adversaries of Shepherd Ali and Taghi. The animosity between the two pairs was evident, and they didn't hold back in their efforts to torment each other at every opportunity. However, only a few people were privy to this enmity, and those who knew wisely refrained from getting involved, leaving them to their own devices.

Before Shepherd Ali's herds reached the road, the path they needed to take to exit the village towards the hill, Ghazanfar stepped forward and blocked their way. Simultaneously, Samad's herd also arrived, heading towards the main road leading to the hill.

Asif, positioned in the middle of the herd with Shepherd Ali at the rear, encountered a tall wall obstructing their view. Unaware that

Ghazanfar had directed their herd towards a forbidden area, Asif pressed forward. Once he passed the obstructing wall, he suddenly spotted Ghazanfar. Realizing that a significant portion of their herd had gone astray towards the forbidden area, Asif raised his voice and confronted Ghazanfar. "What in the world do you think you're doing, you despicable, sorry excuse for a human being?" Asif exclaimed angrily.

In their encounter, they collided forcefully. Meanwhile, Shepherd Ali, still searching for the herd behind the wall, tightly gripped his dogs' collars, oblivious to the clash between Asif and Ghazanfar. However, the herding dogs, seemingly sensing the tension even from behind the wall, became agitated, their barks reverberating in the air. Their excitement caused them to pull Shepherd Ali forcefully, and he struggled to maintain his balance and avoid falling.

Shepherd Ali followed his frenzied and unruly dogs, circumventing the wall that had obstructed their view. It was then that his gaze fell upon Asif and Ghazanfar engaged in a violent fight amidst the flock, resembling two ferocious dogs. They wrestled fiercely, pummeling each other relentlessly. Shepherd Ali recognized Ghazanfar's advantage in size and strength. He observed Ghazanfar ruthlessly striking Asif's head with a stick. Before rushing to Asif's aid, Shepherd Ali's eyes locked with Samad's. In that momentary connection, they forgot about the herd and the ongoing fight and began howling at each other. Holding their dogs' collars, they sprinted towards each other through the herd, entering the battlefield and swiftly launching attacks against one another.

The sheep, startled by the clashes between Asif, Ghazanfar, Shepherd Ali, and Samad, scattered in fear, creating a path for Shepherd Ali and Samad to confront each other. Both shepherds released their dogs, commanding them to attack, but the canine packs disregarded their owners' orders, showing no interest in participating in the conflict. Similar to the sheep and goats, the loyal dogs prioritized their duty of safeguarding the herd. Frustrated by their dogs' disobedience, Shepherd Ali and Samad vented their anger, cursing at the animals. Shepherd Ali shouted in exasperation:

"Unfaithful dogs... After all the care and nourishment Asif provided for you, this is how you behave!"

Shepherd Ali managed to reach Asif and Ghazanfar before Samad could intervene. Taking advantage of Samad's delayed arrival, Shepherd Ali struck Ghazanfar on the head several times, exerting a force that caused him to lose his balance and collapse onto the ground. The blows from Shepherd Ali resulted in blood streaming from Ghazanfar's head, leaving him writhing in pain. Seizing the opportunity while Ghazanfar was distracted, the injured and enraged Asif attacked him ferociously, unleashing a barrage of punches to his head and face. Soon, Ghazanfar's head split open, and his previously pristine white shirt turned crimson in an instant.

Finally, Samad arrived at the scene, joining the fray against Shepherd Ali. The confrontation between Samad and Shepherd Ali intensified, with all parties engrossed in the heat of battle. However, their skirmish was abruptly halted when Mashhadi Hossein doused both shepherds with a bucket of icy water. As Mashhadi Hossein berated them and swung his empty bucket, raining insults upon them, he demanded they act like adults and put an end to their fight. None of the combatants dared to protest or disrespect Mashhadi Hossein, and as other individuals heading to the bathhouse arrived, they intervened, separating the brawlers and leading them away from each other.

The valiant warriors of the rural landscape, filled with escalating fury, yearned to continue their clash like fierce lionesses. They exchanged heated curses from a distance, while a few individuals, more concerned about their sheep than the bloodied heads, confronted Shepherd Ali, pushing him and demanding an explanation for leaving the herd unattended before insisting that he retrieve the scattered flock.

Shepherd Ali reluctantly made his way towards his scattered herd, while Asif, who suffered more severe injuries, lagged behind. As he walked along the detour where his herd had been directed, the surroundings grew eerily silent. The narrow alley was flanked by high walls, separating the road from the fields on both sides. There were no signs of his herd or any dogs. After a few minutes, Shepherd Ali suddenly realized that he had strayed onto the road leading to the cemetery and the forbidden area once inhabited by the elves. Memories of goblins and the forbidden territory flooded his mind, causing him to pause and contemplate his next move—should he continue forward or turn back and escape?

In that fleeting moment, he wondered if the absence of his herd meant that the elves had taken them all. Then, at the far end of the road, where it met the cemetery, he noticed fleeting shadows appearing and disappearing. Uncertain whether they were human or elf, fear gripped his heart, erasing all thoughts of his herd.

A few moments later, still trembling with fear on the empty road, Shepherd Ali began reciting a prayer, fervently beseeching God for courage. Clutching his prayer amulet, which hung around his neck and was visible to the elves beneath his shirt, he started walking and gradually broke into a run, heading towards the road's end in search of his herd. With every step he took, panic and anxiety grew stronger within him. He slowly began to comprehend the depth of Samad's treachery, realizing that Samad had deliberately orchestrated the plan to lead his herd into forbidden lands.

Unbeknownst to Shepherd Ali, a group of men hired by Samad swiftly drove his herd towards the cemetery and the forbidden area. As they caught sight of Shepherd Ali approaching in the distance, they hastily vanished behind the roadside wall, concealing themselves from view.

The air was crisp and Shepherd Ali's head continued to bleed slightly. Filled with fear, he hurried to the end of the alley and entered the cemetery overlooking the village. It was there that he spotted his herd in the distance, grazing on a hill that led to the forbidden area an unsettling sight he had hoped not to witness. His gaze shifted to the herd dogs, milling about the sheep, and emitting faint sounds. It seemed as though they had spotted Shepherd Ali and were beckoning him to join them with the herd.

Unlike the fearful and tense shepherd Ali, the dogs and the herd showed no fear of the goblins as they approached the forbidden area. Standing amidst the cemetery, Ali faced the hill, clutching his prayer bag tightly and whispering incomprehensible words. Lost in thought, he contemplated his next move and the consequences of leaving the head alone on the hill. How would he answer to the statesmen who had entrusted their property to him if he returned to the village? Doubt and uncertainty plagued him, but the piercing howl of one of his dogs snapped him back to reality. Turning around, he noticed the dog standing a few yards away, patiently waiting for him.

The dog ran towards Ali, while onlookers cast judgmental glances at the shepherd and his herd as if reminding him of his negligence in caring for them. This happened repeatedly as the dogs dashed towards the herd and then returned to him. Ali gazed at the dust stirred by his dog's movements, hesitating to act. The faithful dog challenged its owner, protesting as if it were something new to Ali. Anxious and suspicious, the shepherd looked around and eventually yielded, following his dog's lead.

The herd had now reached the slopes of a hill that bordered the forbidden area. The dogs' brisk pace compelled Ali to quicken his steps, sensing his fear though unaware of its cause. Desperate to protect himself from the Elves, Ali retrieved another prayer charm from his collar, hanging it over his blood-stained shirt for added security. Gripping his cane tightly out of dread, he heard the sheep's plaintive cries and the jingle of their bells drawing closer with each passing moment.

Finally, Shepherd Ali reached the herd, cautiously guiding them away from the forbidden area and towards the village. However, his attention was suddenly drawn to the forbidden area by the alarming sound of reeds rustling in the night. His eyes landed on a large berry tree, infamous in local stories. What surprised him the most was a hidden chamber built within the mulberry tree, constructed with lumbar stones. The chamber sat atop a high rocky hill, almost like a mountain, concealed from the view of the nearby villages of Tikken and Shourcheh. Shepherd Ali's heart raced, and fear washed over him, his face still stained with dried blood and his complexion pale and ashen. The horrifying tales he had heard about the forbidden area came alive in his mind, and his soul trembled with fear.

Among the intriguing stories Shepherd Ali shared with children was one about a weeping man who frequented the base of the mulberry tree. He had witnessed this man cry so intensely that he lost consciousness. Another tale involved a beautiful young woman who sang beneath the tree.

Yet, when Shepherd Ali approached her to compliment her and offer her some milk, she vanished without a trace. Though Shepherd Ali was known for his embellishments and storytelling, he didn't exaggerate much when recounting these specific accounts. He had heard them from a traveling beggar known as The Silent Beggar, and he passed them on to the people as his own courageous experiences. Shepherd Ali's fear overwhelmed him to the point where he forgot his surroundings.

Suddenly, his anger flared as he observed his herd dogs rushing towards the mulberry tree. He noticed a figure resting against the trunk, clothed in a tattered gray garment, appearing lifeless as if in a deep sleep. Shepherd Ali couldn't discern whether it was a person or an elf. He watched anxiously as his dogs crept closer to the tree and the mysterious figure. Just as they were about to reach him, seemingly to tear him apart, Shepherd Ali's mind convinced him that such an attack would awaken the goblins, who would swiftly slaughter not only his dogs but also his herd and himself. This new wave of fear surged through his soul, leaving him unsure of how to cope with it or how to stop his dogs.

He was consumed by fear, rendering him unable to control his own limbs. Nonetheless, he continued to observe in bewilderment as his dogs growled and sniffed the ground with fervor. The hounds steadily approached the berry tree, yet the stranger stood motionless, seemingly unaffected by the commotion surrounding him. Gradually regaining his senses, Shepherd Ali shouted at his dogs in a mix of confusion and fear, commanding them to protect him and the herd. However, to his astonishment, Shepherd Ali himself became rooted to the spot, compelled to gaze in astonishment at the mulberry tree. He rubbed his eyes repeatedly, opening and closing them to ensure he wasn't mistaken—that what he witnessed was indeed real. His instincts did not deceive him. Emerging from beneath the worn, gray cloak, the enigmatic figure abandoned his post near the mulberry tree and confronted the advancing hounds. He assumed a crouched position on all fours, locking eyes with the dogs from beneath his hood. Shepherd Ali stood dumbfounded, as his typically fierce and courageous hounds suddenly halted, cowering before the stranger. Like Shepherd Ali, who stood transfixed in bewildered fascination, his dogs began to sniff the ground and scan their surroundings, evidently unsure of their next move. They had been subdued by this unfamiliar presence without a single sound. Overwhelmed by his astonishment, Shepherd Ali bit his thumb repeatedly while murmuring another prayer, seeking guidance from God.

Suddenly, Shepherd Ali noticed a pack of wolves closing in on his flock, diverting his attention from his dogs. Concerned for his sheep, he momentarily disregarded his loyal companions. Without hesitation, he sprinted toward his herd, swinging his wooden stick wildly through the air. Along the way, he stooped down and gathered a handful of rocks. As he approached his flock, he turned his attention back to his dogs, urging them to come and defend the sheep. Yet, it was as if his dogs were completely oblivious to his calls, or perhaps they simply didn't care, as if they were under the influence of an unknown force, no longer recognizing their duty to protect the herd. They stood near the mulberry tree, fixated on the cloaked figure, their commitment to the flock seemingly erased from their minds.

Shepherd Ali, who was now losing his patience and becoming more frightened than ever, angrily began shouting curses at the earth, blaming time for not being enough, the ancestors of his dogs, the attacking wolves, Samad for leading his herd towards the forbidden area in the first place, and anyone else he could think of. It was as if the fear of the wolves had made him forget about the Elf by the berry tree. Suddenly, he spotted one of the wolves breaking away from the pack and rushing directly towards him. Fearing for his life, Shepherd Ali sought refuge in the middle of the herd, barricading himself among the sheep. He threw stones at the wolves while simultaneously calling out to his dogs for help.

The wolves had already reached the herd, and the sheep were fleeing in fear for their own lives. Shepherd Ali realized that he was now the target, as several wolves closed in on him. In a desperate attempt to avoid being devoured by the ferocious wolves, he began reciting another verse. However, he soon ran out of breath, leaving him with nothing left to do but tremble in fear. The wild and hungry wolves were closing in, their snouts dangerously near. At that moment, all he could do was fervently plead to God for help. And so, he did. He asked God for forgiveness for his sins and begged to be saved from the wolves. In return, he made a solemn promise never to lie or spread rumors again.

Just as one of the wolves was about to sink its teeth into Shepherd Ali's foot, everything fell silent. Disappointed by God's apparent absence, he lost all hope, the sound of death bells persistently ringing in his ears. But then, a mournful reed replaced the somber tolling.

Upon hearing the sound of the reed, Shepherd Ali's attention was captured, and his panic doubled. The mournful voice of the reed was hauntingly familiar. It was the same sound that goblins were rumored to play over the hill when preparing to attack the village. As the sound of the reed grew louder, he couldn't decide what he should fear more the wolves nipping at his heels or the potential destruction wrought by the goblins. With his eyes still shut tight, he was too terrified to open them.

But he felt, if not sensed, that something was swirling through the air around him, like a gust of wind. In his mind, he believed that goblins must be whirling around him. His eyes remained tightly shut in fear. He contemplated that being devoured by wolves would be preferable to being captured by the goblins. Despite his apprehension, he wondered why the wolves hadn't already torn him apart. His confusion grew, and he remained hesitant to open his eyes, fearing what might lie behind them. It was as if an unseen hand materialized and pushed him, accompanied by a whispered voice calling his name, "Shepherd Ali..."

Struggling to maintain his balance and avoid stumbling, he unwittingly opened his eyes out of a mixture of fear and bewilderment. His astonishment increased as he noticed the wolves had relaxed and were now resting peacefully, much like his own dogs. He then realized they were observing something akin to a shadow flitting about among them and Shepherd Ali. The sound of the reed abruptly ceased. He surmised that it must be a ghost drifting between the wolves and himself. Still in a state of confusion, the ghost approached him, and a voice whispered to him once more, "Shepherd Ali, tend to the herd."

For Shepherd Ali, the sight of the hut coupled with the ethereal dance of the whispering ghost and the immediate tranquility that enveloped his dogs at the melodious notes of the reed was overwhelming and perplexing. He observed even the sheep had grown calm, grazing without fear of the wolves. Some of them had even turned their heads skyward as if reveling in the reed's melody. The most unsettling aspect of it all was the revelation of ghosts dancing and soaring around him, particularly since he felt as if he were spinning in circles. Moreover, they addressed him by name. He was convinced that goblins and spirits had encircled him, ready to whisk him away. He had no strength or breath left to flee, and his courage had deserted him, rendering him incapable of uttering a prayer or making any movement; the situation was simply too overwhelming for him to handle.

As Shepherd Ali's body and soul trembled with terror, his mouth went dry. Finally, overwhelmed by fear, he abandoned the herd and the dogs, opting to flee instead. He turned tail and began his escape on foot, running so frantically and panicked that he didn't even notice the numerous times he fell to the ground. Each time, he swiftly rose up, oblivious to the injuries he had sustained from the rugged, rocky terrain, only realizing them once he reached the village.

Throughout his desperate run, Shepherd Ali felt as though ghosts and goblins were relentlessly pursuing him. In a futile attempt to ward them off, he clutched his prayer beads tightly between his palms, whispering prayers to God, desperately seeking mercy and assistance. His supplications, driven by his belief that the goblins were hot on his heels, never ceased.

Shepherd Ali took a shortcut, aiming to reach the cemetery above the village more quickly. Upon arrival, he noticed an eerie stillness—a lifeless zone devoid of any signs of human presence, which was far from ordinary. Typically, there would be a few people at the cemetery, visiting their departed loved ones and offering prayers for their souls. His gaze shifted from the cemetery to Kal Ahmad's house, situated at the main entrance of the village, facing the cemetery. He was well aware that Kal Ahmad always sat on the front porch, keeping an eye on those entering or exiting the village. Kal Ahmad never missed an opportunity to engage in conversation or share a joke with passersby. However, for the first time, Shepherd Ali couldn't spot Kal Ahmad either, further intensifying his unease. Consequently, he swiftly left the cemetery, barely taking a moment to think.

Continuing his frantic run through the village, Shepherd Ali grew increasingly frightened and concerned. Not a single bird soared overhead, and there was no sign of the villagers or any signs of life as if the entire population had perished. Even the animals—dogs, cats, and other creatures—seemed to have vanished. The sight of closed and sealed doors and windows heightened his fear. It was customary to secure homes during the nighttime, but this situation was different. Unbeknownst to him, the moment the villagers had heard the haunting sound of the reed emanating from the forbidden area, they had hurriedly sought refuge in their homes, sealing themselves inside. Their collective fear stemmed from the belief that the goblins would attack the village even during daylight hours.

A gentle breeze blew, caressing the sweaty face of Shepherd Ali as he staggered. At this moment, his eyes caught sight of a blurry shadow, resembling a ragged old dervish emerging from Shaykh Ahmad's house. " Shaykh in Islam is a person respected for their piety, religious knowledge, and their deep understanding of the unknown world. They are often seen as spiritual leaders and guides within the community. In Arabic, the nickname for such a person is "Ash-Shaykh" or simply "Shaykh." The beggar stumbled toward him, appearing intoxicated. Approaching Shepherd Ali with an air of calmness, the beggar's gaze locked with his, captivating him and rendering him motionless and speechless. Uncertain if he was dreaming or encountering a spectral figure disguised as a beggar, Shepherd Ali became increasingly perplexed by the events unfolding before him.

The familiarity of the beggar's gaze surprised and bewildered Shepherd Ali, who questioned whether this ragged old figure was a human or a demonic apparition manifesting itself. As confusion clouded his senses, the shepherd found himself debating his next course of action, contemplating the nature of the beggar's existence—a wretched elf or a mere mortal.

Lost in his thoughts and torn between decisions, Shepherd Ali's attention was abruptly diverted by the loud chiming of his flock's bells, accompanied by the barking of herding dogs from the nearby cemetery. His head instinctively turned toward the source of the noise, the bells growing louder as they approached. Yet, when he shifted his gaze back to the mysterious beggar, he had vanished without a trace. Anxious and terrified, Shepherd Ali scanned his surroundings, searching every nook and cranny, but the beggar had seemingly disappeared as swiftly as he had appeared. The desolate alleyways of Shourcheh stretched before him, leaving him in a state of bewilderment and confusion, compelled to continue his quest for answers.

In his state of disarray, Shepherd Ali found himself wandering aimlessly through the deserted alleys, unable to find his way back home. When his herd and dogs finally reached him, he remained oblivious to their presence, his mind consumed by his own confusion. He stared at them, unable to recognize the familiar sound of sheep bells or acknowledge the passing of his faithful canines. Unaware that his flock had safely returned from the forbidden area and reached the village, Shepherd Ali remained trapped in a state of utter perplexity.

The herding dogs dashed back and forth behind the herd, assuming Shepherd Ali's role. It seemed as if an enigmatic force was guiding the herd towards the village. In no time, the herd ventured into the narrow alleys of Shourcheh, with some sheep even lingering near the field gates where they typically resided. However, despite the cessation of the reed's melody and the audible presence of the herd and dogs, not a single soul dared to venture out of their houses. The villagers were well aware that the herd had inadvertently strayed into the forbidden territory that day. They also harbored a deep-seated fear that the sheep and dogs might actually be malevolent goblins in disguise, apprehensive that venturing outside would expose them to potential attacks and abductions. The only exception was Zulfiqar, who emerged from the mosque and positioned himself at the entrance, gazing skyward. Mard Ali, too, emerged from the mosque and raced towards the herd, weaving through the sheep in search of Shepherd Ali. Failing to locate him, he resorted to conversing with the sheep and dogs, desperately seeking answers. "It's as if the Elves have whisked Shepherd Ali away. Have they made him vanish?" He then turned to the sheep in disbelief and inquired, "Are your goblins or sheep?"

* * * * *

Chapter 2
In the cloak of night, darkness becomes the sanctuary for those who steal from religion.

The air grew progressively darker, prompting people to seek refuge in their homes out of fear of the lurking goblins in the hills above the village. Any stragglers caught outside would hastily sprint back to the safety of their abode, their fear so intense that they might even collide with a tree if it obstructed their path. Their sole focus was reaching home swiftly to shield themselves from potential goblin and demon attacks.

In this tense atmosphere, a man hurriedly traversed the alleys, his anxiety palpable. Draped in a robe and wearing a turban on his head, he clutched a small holy book—the Quran. He concealed his thick beard and mustache beneath the garments to the point where even his own eyes struggled to see. It was evident that he made great efforts to remain hidden from both the goblins and the townsfolk. His gaze darted between doors, windows, and his surroundings, whispering prayers to God, imploring that no one crossed his path. If he spotted or sensed someone approaching, he promptly sought cover, nestling within the shadows of walls, desperate not to be noticed. His constant glances back and forth betrayed his intense terror of encountering the goblins. Under his breath, he continuously muttered prayers, seeking protection from the malevolent forces and pleading for paradise. His behavior clearly indicated his strenuous attempts to evade public scrutiny, which led him to enter the village and travel under the cover of darkness, despite his profound dread of goblins and demons.

Finally, the newcomer reached Mullah Mahmoud's house, seeking sanctuary beneath the archway in front of the door. He cautiously surveyed the surroundings and neighboring houses, ensuring that no one was awake or peering through their windows in an attempt to catch a glimpse of him. Satisfied, he emerged from the shadowy recess, his gaze nervously scanning the area, and swiftly crouched down to feel for small rocks on the ground in the darkness. Once he gathered a handful, he silently hurled them with all his might onto Mullah Mahmoud's porch. To avoid arousing the attention of any nearby neighbors, he hastily retreated and concealed himself once again beneath the archway at the entrance of the house.

One of the rocks hurled onto the porch managed to roll up the stairs before tumbling down. It passed by Leila Mulla Mahmoud's daughter, who clutched an oil lantern while walking behind her father, Mulla Mahmoud. Finally, the rock came to a halt near Mulla Mahmoud's foot, just to the left of the last few steps.

As the rock landed in front of him, Mulla Mahmoud was frozen in surprise and mostly fear. He stared intently at the rock for a prolonged moment. Then, he turned his gaze towards his daughter, Leila, seeking answers. However, she was equally bewildered and had no explanation to offer. Both pairs of eyes then turned towards the alley's entry door, the presumed source of the thrown rocks.

Mulla Mahmoud, over 90 years old and somewhat unwell, usually refrained from venturing to the outdoor toilet out of fear of encountering goblins until daylight arrived. However, on that particular night, his stomach seemed to rebel as if a revolution was underway. Despite the darkness enveloping him, he had no choice but to make his way to the toilet situated in the yard's corner. Coincidentally, it happened to be the same night when an unknown visitor was attempting to enter his house.

Confused and overwhelmed, Mulla Mahmoud turned to face Leila, who stood beside him. They both anticipated the other to break the silence. "Girl, are you throwing rocks? Have you lost your mind?"

"I didn't do it! Didn't you hear? Someone threw a stone from the alley onto the porch," Leila replied. Hearing her words, Mulla Mahmoud nervously cast his gaze towards the entrance door, which opened to the alley. Leila followed suit. They couldn't discern whether it was elves or someone else hurling the rocks from within the alley.

Mulla Mahmoud was now in distress, desperately needing to use the toilet, but his fear had rooted his feet to the ground. So terrified was he that he failed to hear the faint whispers emanating from behind the door. It seemed that whoever stood on the other side had noticed the faint glow seeping through the door's cracks and sought to capture the occupant's attention. When no response came from within, the individual whispered Mulla Mahmoud's name while softly knocking on the door, attempting to gain his attention. "AShaykh... AShaykh is that you? I heard your voice, and I can see you. Open the door!"

"AShaykh" is a brief nickname used to refer to Mulla members in the Islamic religion.

Outside the door, the man trembled with fear. He had heard Mulla Mahmoud's voice and could see him through the cracks in the door. He whispered again, trying to keep his voice low so that none of the neighbors would hear him. "AShaykh, it's me, Moharram. I'm not an Elf. I am Asghar. Please open the door. I heard your voice, and I can see you through the crack. Open the door. It's Asghar."

Inside the corridor, Mullah Mahmoud and Leila stood frozen with fear, their eyes fixed on the door. Asghar's trembling voice came from behind, whispering to them once more. "I'm Moharram, not a goblin. AShaykh please open the door. AShaykh I'm Asghar. Why won't you open the door?"

Mullah Mahmoud was bewildered and unsure of what to do. It had been thirty years since he had heard anything about Asghar. After Moharram set fire to Haji Amir's son and their shepherd, burning them alive, and killing his accomplice Abouli, he vanished from the village of Shourcheh to avoid being caught and hanged. Suddenly, Mulla Mahmud was hearing his name whispered by him, indicating that he had returned—a possibility that had never crossed Mulla Mahmoud's mind. He believed Asghar to be dead by now, and the thought of never encountering him again brought him a sense of relief. To Mulla Mahmoud, Asghar was responsible for such a brutal act, and in fact, Moharram carried out his orders. Exposing Asghar would also put Mulla Mahmud at risk. And now, after thirty years, he had suddenly reappeared. Initially, he would occasionally visit Mullah Mahmoud at night, but he hadn't been heard from for the past twenty years. That's why Mullah Mahmud was at a loss. He suspected it could be Moharram behind the door or an Elf pretending to be Moharram, or perhaps someone playing a prank on him. "AShaykh hit's me, Moharram. Open the door. What are you afraid of?"

Mullah Mahmoud was utterly confused and forgot that he urgently needed to use the toilet. His daughter, Leila, was equally frightened and bewildered. They stood in front of the door, unsure of what to do, lost in their confusion. It was then that Mullah Mahmoud and Leila noticed a shadow moving in the yard, creeping towards them. "Has the Elf come, Shaykh?"

Mullah Mahmud and Leila, both of whom believed they had spotted goblins emerging from the darkness, became incredibly terrified. In his panic, Mullah Mahmud involuntarily relieved himself before even reaching the toilet, causing him to stumble and lose consciousness. Leila, overwhelmed by fear, also fainted. Unbeknownst to them, while Mullah Mahmud failed to open the door, Asghar, a highly adept thief skilled in scaling walls, seized the opportunity. With no hesitation, he effortlessly climbed the house's wall and stealthily entered from the shadows.

* * * * *

It was nearly midnight, and the haunting melody of the perpetual reed resonated from the hilltop above the Village of Shourcheh, as it did every night. Its harmonies intertwined with the rustling of the wind and the distant howls of wolves roaming the hills, while the village dogs orchestrated their own symphony of barks in response to the wolves' menacing calls. Despite these familiar sounds, the persistent notes of the reed penetrated the air, causing the villagers to retreat into the confines of their homes.

Mullah Mahmud found respite on a vibrant cushion, leaning against another, while his gaze fixated upon Asghar, who sat beside him, savoring his tea. However, Mulla Mahmud couldn't help but notice that the slurping of the tea grew increasingly intrusive, overpowering all other sounds. The melodies of the reeds, the wind's whispers, the dogs' chorus, and the wolves' lamentations faded into insignificance. In that moment, Mulla

Mahmud experienced an unfamiliar silence, a void where no sound reached his ears.

Asghar's sudden revelation bewildered Mulla Mahmud. After more than two decades of knowing him, Mulla Mahmud never expected such a surprising claim. Above all, he found it astonishing that Moharram now professed to have spent several years in the holy city of Qom, studying, and delving into the depths of the Quran under the guidance of Ayatollahs. Moharram further claimed to have pursued studies in the esteemed city of Mashhad. Mulla Mahmud, torn between belief and skepticism, found himself ill-equipped to judge Moharram's assertions. As a self-made mullah, Mulla Mahmud had attained his clerical status overnight, without formal education. He possessed no proficiency in reading or writing Arabic and remained illiterate in the Farsi language, having never attended school. Mulla Mahmud had taught himself to read and write, penning cuneiform prayers for the unlettered masses seeking solace in his simple yet heartfelt words.

In short, the return of Moharram had become a mystery to Mullah Mahmud himself, which even a cunning and deceitful man like Mullah Mahmoud couldn't solve. Naturally, Mullah Mahmoud had reasons to doubt Moharram's story and couldn't easily accept his words. Firstly, Mullah Mahmoud himself was known for his dishonesty and trickery. Secondly, he knew that Moharram was also a man. Thus, Moharram didn't disclose the truth about his sudden transformation into a Clergyman. He didn't reveal that one night, while attempting to rob a house, he was chased by the residents and narrowly escaped by fleeing into the hills. Aware that people had witnessed him, Moharram anticipated their eventual pursuit and the likelihood of being beaten and harmed.

As he wandered through the hills, luck favored him, leading him to a farm atop a hill overlooking the village. Approaching the darkness, he heard voices and discovered a small pond used for water storage. It appeared that a couple was enjoying a clandestine bathing session at this secluded farm. Moharram cautiously observed from the edge of the pond and confirmed his suspicions. The man in the water was dressed in a turban and a clerical robe, having brought the woman there to avoid public scrutiny. An idea struck Moharram—he could utilize the Clergyman's attire to escape the people's wrath if they encountered him. In the dark, he stealthily stole the unfortunate Clergyman's clothes and hastily departed. After a considerable distance, he exchanged his own garments for the stolen ones, burying his original attire in the ground, before heading towards the village.

However, before reaching the village, Moharram stumbled upon a group of men wielding sticks and oil lanterns, searching for the thief. Acting as a Clergyman, he began speaking in Arabic, despite having little understanding of the language. Unbeknownst to the villagers who were also unfamiliar with Arabic, Moharram's performance was convincing enough to make them believe he had been a Clergyman all his life. Intriguingly, no one questioned why a Clergyman was descending the hill in the middle of the night. Convinced by Moharram's actions and words, the villagers followed his lead as he informed them about a man fleeing towards the farm above the village with a woman.

Assuming it was the thief they were after, the villagers hurried towards the small pond and the farm. Soon enough, their oil lanterns illuminated the naked Mullah who had been searching for his clothing. Disgraced and exposed, the Mullah had no means to cover himself. Witnessing the sight of their village Clergyman naked with another man's woman, the villagers forgot about the thief and unleashed their fury on the naked and disgraced Clergyman, intending to beat him to death.

Meanwhile, Moharram, now dressed in clerical attire, arrived at the village graveyard. He encountered a few others who were also searching for the thief along the way. Feeling a sense of safety, he began reciting a short prayer at a grave to honor the deceased. He then proceeded to approach anyone passing by, pretending to be lost and informing them about a man who had fled to a small farm. Moharram's convincing performance earned him the trust and respect of the villagers. He relished the treatment and regard he received while adorned in the clerical garb, as though he had been wearing it for ages. In those moments, he discovered a new occupation and a more successful scam. It turned out that the clerical attire suited him perfectly, and luck was on his side as it fit him well. With this newfound confidence, he decided to return and seek out Mullah Mahmoud.

At that very moment, Leila, Mullah Mahmoud's daughter, entered the room, carrying a tray of food while holding her chador in her mouth to conceal her hair. Asghar couldn't help but gaze affectionately at her. Leila's mischievous smile, accentuated by her rosy lips, eyes, and cheeks, instantly evoked memories of their childhood and youth. Naturally, both Moharram and Leila recognized each other from the past. Moharram had worked for Mullah Mahmoud when Leila was born, and he was in his twenties at the time. However, Moharram disappeared when Leila was just ten years old. Mullah Mahmoud, observing their secretive glances, had a sudden idea. He contemplated the idea of Leila being the perfect match for Moharram. Mullah Mahmoud was now old and deeply concerned about his daughter's future. In the past, driven by greed, he had forced Leila to marry a wealthy landowner in the nearby countryside. However, Leila's husband was much older than her, and she refused to share his bed. Fed up, he had thrown Leila out and divorced her. For the past few years, Leila had been living with Mullah Mahmoud, caring for him. It wasn't a bad arrangement for Mullah Mahmoud either, as his wife had passed away, leaving him alone. Having Leila at home proved to be a great help. If Leila were to marry Moharram, they could all live together under one roof.

Mullah Mahmoud pondered the idea of offering Leila to Moharram. Given Moharram's new clerical status, he could assume Mullah Mahmoud's position seamlessly, ensuring that everything remained unchanged. Now, there were two remaining challenges in executing Mullah Mahmoud's plan. The first and most crucial was finding a way to introduce Moharram to the villagers in a manner that would secure their acceptance while keeping his true identity concealed. If the villagers were to discover that he was, in fact, Asghar, the fugitive killer, he would be expelled from the village and inevitably handed over to the authorities. After some time, news began to circulate among the villagers that Moharram was responsible for the burning of Haji Amir's eldest son and their livestock. However, the second challenge was less significant, as Moharram had already agreed to marry Leila. He knew there would be no issue in satisfying Asghar's desires, as he was growing older and seeking stability and a place to call home.

Unknown to Mullah Mahmoud, another dangerous scheme was quietly taking shape in Asghar's mind. A master manipulator and cunning con artist, Asghar had already surpassed Mahmoud in his deceitful plans. His sinister plot involved marrying Leila, eliminating her father, and ultimately inheriting all of Mahmoud's possessions. With such wealth, he could live a life of utmost comfort and luxury. As the two seasoned tricksters sat across from each other, sipping tea, their gazes locked, carefully assessing one another's motives. Meanwhile, Leila, overjoyed by Moharram's return, relished in the newfound security of having a place she could call her own.

Outside, the echoes of howling wolves, barking dogs, and the whistling wind grew louder, blending with the melodies of the lingering reed instruments. However, the three conniving individuals were so consumed by their treacherous thoughts, so deeply engrossed in plotting against one another, that even if a bomb were to detonate outside their very abode, they would undoubtedly remain oblivious, undisturbed by the chaos unfolding just beyond their reach.

* * * * *

Chapter 3
When the thieves of faith and those who exploit religion slink into the shadows of the night...

The stray dog cautiously walked along the stream of water that flowed in front of the houses of Shourcheh village, yearning for something to fill its hungry belly and enjoying the gentle breeze. Perplexed, the dog couldn't comprehend why the villagers would assault it with rocks and sticks as soon as they laid eyes on it. It longed for the ability to communicate with them, to understand the harm it had supposedly caused and why they harbored such animosity. The dog wished fervently that they could comprehend its loyalty and desire to protect them, rather than resorting to aggression and deeming it unclean and unhealthy. Contemplating the potential use of its own power against the villagers, it wondered if it would succumb to the same hostility. Would it, in turn, treat them as they had treated him?

Despite these thoughts, deep in its heart, the dog knew that if its power surpassed that of the villagers, it would remain kind and loyal, as it had always been. Kindness, loyalty, and the instinct to defend were ingrained in its nature. It simply yearned for the power to ask the villagers why they singled it out. However, it was a lamentable reality that they couldn't comprehend the language of the unfortunate dog. Even if they could, would they grant it a chance to speak? Most likely not. Before the poor dog could even utter a word, they would pelt it with stones and thrash it with sticks, forcing it to flee.

Regrettably, the dog eventually reached the house of Mullah Mahmoud, known as the village Clergyman and perceived as everyone's worst enemy. Before the dog could approach, it was jolted by an electric shock emanating from Mullah Mahmoud's house, rendering it paralyzed. Suddenly, its head, which had been scouring the ground in search of food, swiftly lifted. Its eyes, which had been scanning for sustenance, turned towards Mullah Mahmoud's dwelling. It was as if past experiences had cautioned the dog to depart promptly before the infidels attacked that particular abode and subjected it to severe beatings. The poor dog's intuition was not misguided. Before the dog's head had fully risen, and its eyes had fully fixated on the window of Mullah Mahmoud's house, Mullah Mahmoud's displeasing voice resounded from the second floor. "Go and beat that filthy dog outside the house. I don't know what it wants from us, but it must not be here."

Mullah Mahmoud's voice had not yet been interrupted when the dog's sixth sense felt the threat and prompted it to flee. Perhaps the dog also wished it could have a conversation with the God of the religion that Mullah Mahmoud preached, asking if the practice and ideology of his religion, which persecuted weak and innocent animals, aligned with the philosophy of love and kindness. However, the dog remained unaware that it had been a few days since Moharram surprised Mullah Mahmoud by showing up in the middle of the night, completely changing his life. Mullah Mahmoud now hesitated and had second thoughts about Moharram's presence in his house, standing at a crossroads and pondering his next move.

On one hand, Mullah Mahmoud considered the possibility of Moharram marrying his daughter Leila and eventually taking over his role as he was old and weak. However, he was also aware that Moharram shared his ruthless nature and lacked mercy towards God, His servants, and even his own mother. Moharram would not hesitate to do whatever it took to achieve his own goals, even if it meant betraying Mullah Mahmoud once he gained power. Ultimately, Mullah Mahmoud decided it would be better for Moharram to remain in his house and work alongside him, grooming him as the next Mulla. However, winning over Moharram's approval was not an easy task. They had to find a way to introduce him to the villagers without raising suspicions, as their acceptance was crucial.

Meanwhile, Mullah Mahmoud couldn't leave Moharram alone at home with his daughter. Leila had been unmarried for quite some time, and the thought of her being with a man again would not please any father. Especially considering that the man in question lacked morals and mercy, and would stop at nothing to seduce Leila.

Thus, Mullah Mahmoud had been meticulously observing them in the house for several days, watching their every move. This raised concerns among some people, and eventually, a couple of individuals came to check on him and inquire about his well-being. As the guests called out to Mullah Mahmoud while climbing the stairs to his room on the second floor, their voices echoed through the house, indicating that they would soon reach the porch leading to his main room where guests were entertained. Consequently, Moharram had no choice but to hurry and hide in Leila's room until the guests left.

The guests entered and sat near Mullah Mahmoud, who, as usual, had tea ready to serve. It was evident that Mullah Mahmoud was distressed and preoccupied. He knew Moharram's nature all too well, and he was even worse. Although not present in the room, Mullah Mahmoud sensed that if Moharram had a few moments alone with Leila, he would be all over her while she innocently attempted to prepare some sweets.

"I don't know if you remember, but when you were so young and I laid eyes on your beautiful face, my heart felt complete, as if I knew one day I would marry you," Mullah Mahmoud confessed, addressing Leila.

As Moharram flirted with Leila, charming her with his sweet words, Leila played coy intentionally. Yet, deep down, she felt elated by the attention. In a fleeting moment, she embraced Moharram closely and began leading him towards the closet. However, her father's voice interrupted their private moment. "Leila, what are you doing? Why haven't you brought something for our guests?"

Upon hearing her father's shout, Leila swiftly picked up the tray of treats she had prepared and entered the guest room. Just before leaving the room, she realized she had forgotten to wear her veil. Instantly, she turned to Moharram, who already had her veil in hand, ready to place it on her head. He whispered in her ear, "If you become my wife, I will bring light to the village of Shourcheh. I will make you the queen of the village!"

Leila, still beaming with joy, entered the guest room carrying the tray of goodies. Yet, she immediately forced herself to suppress her smile. Raising her voice, she said, "I was looking for my veil. I couldn't remember where I left it when I returned early this morning after collecting drinking water from outside."

However, nothing escaped Mullah Mahmoud's notice. Seeing even a brief glimpse of Leila's smiling face, he deduced that Moharram had already begun courting her. "I hope you can forgive me. I couldn't find much," Mullah Mahmoud explained. "My father hasn't been feeling well for a few days, so he hasn't been able to leave the house for shopping."

The stout, elderly man cleared his throat, his voice thick and raspy. "My daughter, this is already too much. We didn't come here to eat. We came because we were concerned about AShaykh's hand. We came to see if he is okay. It's clear that he is unwell. It seems as though he's completely out of touch with reality."

Leila, noticing her father's suspicious looks, interjected during the old man's speech. "Excuse me, sir. My father is not feeling well, and I'm uncertain whether I should divulge the details of his dream. He might not appreciate it, but considering you are his closest friend and one of the wisest individuals in the village, perhaps you should be informed. I fear that due to my father's modesty, he would not bring it up himself. As I was saying, a few nights ago, my father had a troubling dream that he was concerned about. In his dream, there was a rain of light descending from the sky, illuminating the mosque, village, and cemetery with shades of blue and green. Despite my attempts to reassure him that it was a good dream, a sign of blessings bestowed from the heavens, he remains unconvinced. I explained that one must possess a deep connection with God to experience such beautiful dreams, but he remains resistant. I believe he might heed your words, being his trusted and wise confidant." Leila then turned to her father and urged, "Dad, please share your dream with them."

Within moments, Leila left the room, leaving Mullah Mahmoud oblivious to Asghar's whispered words, which continued to linger in her mind. Although Leila's sarcastic remarks were audible enough for Moharram to overhear, her intention was to toy with him and send a discreet message. Unaware of Moharram's level of involvement in her father's affairs, Leila underestimated his mastery of manipulation and persuasive speech. As he ascended the pulpit to address his guests, Moharram felt a sense of authority as if he were sitting atop the mosque's podium. He proceeded to fabricate numerous falsehoods, claiming that God had appeared to him in a dream, imparting a divine mission that would soon be revealed to him.

As the guests lingered in the room, Mullah Mahmoud wasted no time in setting his plan in motion. He privately discussed the matter with Moharram, emphasizing that, based on Islamic beliefs, it would be impermissible for him to reside there unless he was considered Leila's concubine. To establish their cohabitation within the confines of Islam, Mullah Mahmoud sanctioned their arrangement, enabling them to be in each other's presence and even share a bed, much like a married couple. However, he clarified that physical intimacy between them was strictly forbidden. Mullah Mahmoud justified this decision as a means for Moharram to maintain a presence in the village without arousing suspicion, but his underlying motives were evident. His true objective was to gauge Moharram's thoughts and actions. Subsequently, Mullah Mahmoud engaged in a private conversation with Asghar, strategizing how they would introduce Moharram to the village in a manner that concealed his true identity, ensuring that people would perceive him as a respectable Clergyman.

After hearing that Mulla Mahmoud had a dream and witnessed a divine light shining upon the village of Shourcheh, several people were drawn to visit him and learn more about his extraordinary experience. In the eyes of many innocent and uneducated individuals, Mulla Mahmoud became revered as a holy man chosen by God. Conversations centered around his dream, and Mulla Mahmoud began discussing the presence of Goblins in the hills above the village. An elderly man raised a question, inquiring why the Goblins did not take or harm Shepherd Ali.

Another individual chimed in, suggesting that perhaps God had intervened to protect them, hence the divine light witnessed by Mulla Mahmoud. This belief further solidified Mulla Mahmoud's newfound status as a holy figure. People began kissing his hand, paying their respects. Suddenly, Mulla Mahmoud had become the anointed holy man, endorsed by God. With the support and trust of the people, Mulla Mahmoud wasted no time in summoning Zulfiqar. He knew that if Zulfiqar was aware of the events unfolding in both the village of Shourcheh and Tikken, he would want to be informed immediately.

Soon, Zulfiqar found himself seated with Mulla Mahmoud, sipping tea and enjoying sweets. Although Zulfiqar was advanced in age and not as sharp as before, he quickly grasped the purpose of his visit and could discern Mulla Mahmoud's intentions. Zulfiqar wondered why the Elves, if they had indeed taken refuge in the forbidden area, had not captured, or kept Shepherd Ali. Meanwhile, the discussion took place with Moharram silently eavesdropping from the adjacent room, where he played with Leila.

Unbeknownst to Zulfiqar, he had unwittingly become popular in Mulla Mahmoud's eyes. Though unsure of the reasons behind this sudden favoritism, Zulfiqar understood that if Mulla Mahmoud's affection had momentarily turned towards him, he should seize the opportunity. Mulla Mahmoud turned to Zulfiqar and said, "Mr. Zulfiqar, I have composed a special prayer for you. I believe you should not be deprived of God's mercy and blessings. This prayer will safeguard you from any harm, even if the Goblins in the hills are no more. And even if a few of them remain, this prayer will ensure your safety in the forbidden area."

Mullah Mahmoud had not finished speaking when Leila entered and interrupted him, raising her voice to repeat the same words about the dream of light falling from the sky. She continued, stating that Mulla Mahmoud had heard a voice telling him that God was sending someone to save everyone and that this person was on their way and would arrive soon. Just as Leila was speaking, there was a knock on the door, and she turned to Mulla Mahmoud.

"AShaykh please remain seated. I will answer the door," Leila said.

She went to open the door and greeted the visitor, saying, "Excuse me, sister. I have come from the holy city of Qom to serve Mulla Mahmoud. I have a message from Ayatollah Birjandi for the Shaykh."

"Please, come in... Mulla Mahmoud is here," Leila pointed to Mulla Mahmoud. However, what Mr. Zulfiqar did not realize was that no actual messenger entered the room. It was Moharram and Leila who were performing a play for him, with Moharram assuming the role of the messenger from the holy city of Qom and using a thick Arabic accent. Their act continued as Moharram pretended to greet Mulla Mahmoud and asked to kiss his hand, while Mulla Mahmoud, completely engrossed, was unaware of the game being played by Moharram and Leila. Oblivious to this, Mulla Mahmoud rose in surprise to welcome his unexpected guest, ensuring that Zulfiqar also stood up in honor of the supposed messenger from Ayatollah Birjandi.

Zulfiqar was taken aback upon hearing that a messenger had arrived for Mullah Mahmoud from Ayatollah Birjandi, a well-known and respected figure among Muslims in the country. Eager to find out what was happening in the room, he listened intently as Moharram continued.

"Shaykh, the reason for my presence here is that Ayatollah Birjandi had a dream indicating something significant happening in the Village of Shourcheh. He dreamed that there would be an illumination here, meant only for those who are true Muslims and chosen by God. For this reason, both Ayatollah Birjandi from the holy city of Qom and Ayatollah Samiei from the holy city of Mashhad are sending a representative to assist you and ensure that the people of Shourcheh do not miss out on this divine miracle. I have arrived ahead of the representative to inform you of their impending arrival."

Leila interjected and took over from Moharram, saying, "Indeed, as you rightly understand, the Shaykh who is coming here is Ayatollah himself. Is that correct?"

Moharram continued, "Certainly, sister, they are. Anyway, my esteemed Shaykh, I must return immediately. However, Mr. Ayatollah Birjandi and Samiei wanted to ensure a warm reception for the arrival of His Highness Shaykh al-Islam Ayatollah Asghari, as he is expected to become the Imam of the Muslims soon. They are also aware of the issue of goblins here and are confident in their ability to eradicate them."

However, Mullah Mahmud now found himself as confused as Zulfiqar, but he began to grasp Moharram and Leila's plan. He observed Zulfiqar, overwhelmed by the thrilling news he had just heard, unable to contain his excitement. Zulfiqar couldn't wait any longer and felt compelled to inform the people about this groundbreaking discovery. He envisioned it as a once-in-a-lifetime story that would generate substantial donations.

A few minutes after Zulfiqar had left, Mullah Mahmoud learned about Moharram's scheme. Anger surged within him, and he struggled to contain it. He realized he had fallen for Moharram's game. He was well aware of Moharram's overnight transformation into an Ayatollah and representative of the Imam. Mullah Mahmud seethed with anger and frustration at the prospect of bowing down to the new Ayatollah, who had elevated himself overnight. He despised himself for falling into this trap. Although he now panicked about the consequences of his actions and plans, he realized it was too late to undo what had been set in motion. Zulfiqar and Mard Ali had already been manipulated, and Mullah Mahmoud could only rely on their assistance when they required him to spread rumors in the village, using it as leverage against him.

Following the final part of their plan, which involved changing Moharram's name to Asghar to avoid arousing suspicion about his true identity, Asghar departed the village of Shourcheh at midnight. He knew that he would return under a new name and identity. Despite his fears of encountering goblins, he hurriedly left the village, even risking a heart attack. Their agreement stipulated that once Mullah Mahmoud deemed the time right, he would send a message to Asghar. The representative of the Ayatollahs from Qom and Mashhad would then enter the village of Shourcheh with honor and respect, assuming his new identity as Ayatollah Asghari. Zulfiqar and Mard Ali were to inform the ordinary people that Ayatollah Birjandi's representative was on his way to serve and enlighten Mullah Mahmud. This news would undoubtedly attract many sincere and adulating individuals seeking healing and guidance. And indeed, Mullah Mahmud soon found himself overwhelmed by an influx of people from all walks of life, thinking they will be seeking healing and enlightenment.

* * * * *

Chapter 4
When wolves show their nature…

The sun calmly set behind the mountains above the village of Tikken, casting a reddish hue on the tall poplar trees that stood throughout the village. Gradually, the villagers finished their daily tasks and gathered their farm equipment, preparing to return home before darkness enveloped the land. As the night fell, the villagers sought rest, ready to resume their work the following morning. Typically, the houses emptied of men in the morning, with everyone heading to the fields to carry out their daily tasks. The older men would often gather outside the general store, engaging in conversations, playing cards, and indulging in occasional gossip. Meanwhile, the women were occupied with their household chores. Interestingly, in ancient times, contentment prevailed, and complaints were rare, if not nonexistent. It was only with the rise of urban life that grievances began to surface. However, that day unfolded like any other, starting and ending with a sense of familiarity. The village remained as tranquil as ever, with the constant roar of the river echoing in the background. The dancing and singing of sparrows amidst the rustling poplar leaves accompanied the daylight and faded into the night. Without these two sounds, the village would feel lifeless.

On the outskirts of Tikken, near the border with the neighboring village of Shourcheh, two boys aged five and six played by the riverbank. Their relatives were working on the farm about a hundred yards away. The approaching sunset cast a somber note, signaling the impending arrival of the night, much to the disappointment of the children. Their hands and feet were covered in mud, similar to the women who adorned their hands and feet with Hanna. Oblivious to the events unfolding around them, the boys immersed themselves in play and laughter. Amidst their game, one of the boys noticed an ant carrying a load several times its own size. He marveled at how such a tiny creature could bear such a weight. The boy watched intently, expecting the ant to eventually tire and drop its load. Yet, to his surprise, the ant persisted, determined to transport the grain to its nest a few meters away before darkness descended. A wave of ants moved around the nest, their synchronized movements devoid of any collisions or commotion. It seemed as though they possessed an innate radar, avoiding accidental encounters with one another. The young boy's gaze shifted, tracing the path of the ants. As his eyes wandered, they caught sight of a stranger approaching in the distance from the right side of his teammate's shoulder. The boy's attention shifted entirely from the ant and its burden to the newcomer drawing closer. Though the traveler remained indistinct due to the distance, the movement of his cane revealed he was not from the village. The boy's teammate, following his gaze, also fixated on the stranger who had just arrived.

The new passenger was drawing closer, allowing the children to observe him more clearly. It was evident from his white, long gray shirt and his appearance that he did not belong to the farming community or the neighboring villages. His countenance did not resemble that of a farmer either. As he approached and the children recognized him as the newly arrived passenger, their faces lit up with joy and excitement. Swiftly, they rose to their feet and wiped their hands on their clothes. They realized that the newcomer was none other than the silent beggar, known for his inability to speak. The silent beggar communicated with people through eye contact, hand gestures, and movements.

Everyone, especially the children, had become accustomed to the silent beggar's means of expression: an old harmonica that served as his mouthpiece and a bell attached to his cane. He had fastened the harmonica to the top of a weathered wooden stick, and a ring dangled from his neck to ensure its safekeeping. An old bag hung from his right shoulder, where he stored whatever people gave him.

The silent beggar drew closer to the children, bringing the harmonica to his lips. As the sound of his harmonica filled the air, he began to dance. Laughter and joy enveloped the boys, and their spirits uplifted. Upon hearing the melodies, the farmers, who had been toiling in the fields, decided to pause their work earlier than usual. They joined the silent beggar, ready to return to the village. Passing by the children, the beggar continued on his way.

Lost in their jubilation, the children joined in the dance and followed the silent beggar, unknowingly crushing several ants on their path to the nest. Amidst this unintentional massacre, a near-fatal encounter occurred between an ant carrying a burden larger than itself and the legs of the children and the silent beggar. Miraculously, each time they narrowly avoided calamity. Whether the ants responded to the harmonica's melodies, the bell's ringing, or the children's joyful singing and dancing was unknown. The surrounding space seemed to envelop the carrier ant and its companions, rendering them forgotten. With the children and the silent beggar disappearing into the distance behind the garden walls, a sense of tranquility settled upon the lone ant.

Soon, there was an eerie silence as darkness began to descend. There was no sign of anyone, and even the faint sound of the silent beggar's harmonica had faded away. However, the ant persevered, reaching its nest while still clutching its burden. Upon arrival, the other ants rushed to assist, and they all disappeared into the nest, carrying the load with them. In this moment, everything changed abruptly. A reed was raised from the forbidden area, disrupting the atmosphere of dancing, chanting, and excitement. People became distracted, saddened, and frustrated by the forbidden area and the haunting sound of the reed. Despite growing accustomed to the sound after many years of being confined to their homes at nighttime, fear and unease still gripped their bodies and souls upon hearing it. What astonished them further was that the reed's melody always arose one or two hours after nightfall, yet this was the third time that it had been heard before darkness had fully fallen. It took the people some time to believe their own ears, but the silent beggar continued to beat his drum and dance as if unaffected by the reed's haunting sound, exhibiting neither concern nor fear of the Goblins.

The Silent Beggar's gaze shifted toward the forbidden area as if he could perceive a reality that was hidden from the villagers. He knew that the situation in the forbidden area was vastly different from what met the eye. The silent beggar understood that with the rising sound of the reed, the joy, happiness, and tranquility that had filled their moments abruptly transformed into sorrow, fear, and frustration. He was aware that the situation in the forbidden area was far worse than in the village itself. It was as if he could see the storm brewing, sweeping desert debris across the weeds. The wind blew fiercely from the slopes of the hills, reaching such heights that it appeared to touch the sun, obscuring the sunset that had yet to fade. The air became heavy with gloom and sadness. The wind whispered through the leaves of the mulberry tree, which stood like an umbrella over the beggar's hut, playing a heartrending melody that only deepened the somberness of the moment.

Near the mulberry tree, the snout of a weary and famished old wolf extended across the ground. It was evident that amidst the wind and storm, he searched for prey to state his hunger, scouring the scattered rocks and bushes. The wolves of the Tikken foothills were renowned for their ferocity and brutality. Such was their reputation that many shepherds abandoned their flocks, seeking alternative livelihoods to avoid confronting these fearsome creatures. The howling wind perturbed even the hungry old wolf, who seemed isolated from his pack. He stood up, lifting his head slightly, his eyes gleaming in the darkness, resembling two blazing orbs amidst the turbulent tempest. He followed the sound of rustling reeds, moving in its direction. After some searching, he cautiously emerged from behind a sizable stone slab. From a distance beneath a mulberry tree, his gaze fell upon a tattered gray cloth. It was as if he sensed someone concealed beneath it, playing the reed. The light gradually waned, though darkness had not yet fully enveloped the surroundings. The aged wolf stealthily hid himself behind a large boulder, akin to a nocturnal thief, and fixated his gaze on the weathered fabric.

Meanwhile, a dog named Majnoon, meaning "the wonder," slept on the porch of the hut, as was his routine. Majnoon, as if sensing or perceiving something unfavorable, awoke partially, raising himself slightly. However, this occurred every night, and the dog was accustomed to it. Yet, Majnoon also felt a tad perplexed as the sound of reeds had now arisen for the third time during daylight, contrary to the usual nocturnal hours. The wolf lurked behind the stone slab like a phantom, fixated on the noise emanating from beneath the worn-out cloth, pondering his next move.

Simultaneously, in the village of Tikken, as the silent beggar reached Assad Khan's mansion, his gaze fell upon Assad Khan standing on the second-floor balcony. The silent beggar abruptly fell silent and became overwhelmed, his harmonica's melody abruptly silenced. The eyes of the silent beggar and Assad Khan locked in a moment as if engaged in an unspoken conversation. For a while, no sound or reaction was observed from either party. Though Assad Khan tried to conceal his elation and maintain composure, the onlookers surrounding him sensed his sheer joy upon encountering the silent beggar. It was as if he yearned to take action, but was uncertain of what to do. It seemed as though he wished to speak, but for reasons unknown to him, his tongue refused to cooperate. Onlookers speculated that Assad Khan experienced the same sentiments he had felt upon encountering the silent beggar and hearing the haunting melody of his harmonica. It was as if an invisible force had bestowed upon him renewed life and hope, particularly given Assad Khan's advanced age, rendering him less active than before.

Although the silent beggar's appearance and soft-spoken voice always conveyed a meaningful message to Assad Khan, it seemed that this time it held a special significance solely for him. However, Assad Khan remained unable to comprehend its true meaning. On a few occasions, he had attempted to coax words from the silent beggar's mouth, hoping to interrogate him, but to no avail. The silent beggar steadfastly refused to utter a single word.

Yet, this encounter felt markedly different for both of them. The silent beggar was the only beggar who would elicit Borzoyeh Khanum's presence, Assad Khan's wife and Sattar's mother. Whenever she heard the sound of his harmonica, she would emerge from the mansion and personally bring him provisions, believing that the silent beggar's prayers might reach God and bring about the discovery of Sattar. However, this time was unlike any other for her as well. It seemed as though the silent beggar did not even acknowledge Ms. Borzoyeh's presence; his eyes were solely fixed upon Assad Khan. Borzoyeh Khanum, much older and burdened with sorrow, could barely walk. Assisting beggars and dervishes had become her regular duty. She believed that by aiding them, their benevolent prayers would accompany her son and aid in the search for Sattar. While she was still alive, Ms. Borzoyeh held onto the hope that Sattar, too, was alive and would one day return. For some inexplicable reason, she felt compelled to personally help the silent beggar, thinking him to be purer than the other beggars and hoping that his prayers would bring Sattar back. Every time she approached the silent beggar, she felt a special solace and a glimmer of hope, as if reuniting with her lost son, Sattar, was within reach. Borzoyeh Khanum referred to the silent beggar as "Dervish," her voice filled with a plea. "Dervish, I implore you to pray to God and beseech Him to bring my son, Sattar, back to me. Tell God that I have endured enough... Please, have mercy on this destitute mother. Ask Him if my son is still alive, and have compassion on this impoverished soul by reuniting us, even if only for a moment before my passing... Or at the very least, inform me of his well-being..."

She then placed a bundle of provisions into the silent beggar's begging bag, which hung over his shoulder. It was at that moment, upon hearing the anguished pleas of the bereaved mother, that the silent beggar regained his senses and realized she was standing beside him. As his gaze fell upon her, his entire being seemed to weaken, and for a prolonged moment, he merely looked at her in silence. Then, suddenly, she heard it. "Mother..."

Borzoyeh Khanum, filled with wonder and shock, turned to look at the silent beggar. She couldn't determine if she had truly heard the beggar's voice or someone else's, or if she had simply misinterpreted it as a call from her mother. The silent beggar approached her calmly and peacefully, and after a moment, his whispering voice grew louder.

"Mother... God has heard your pleas. God has confirmed that your son is alive and well, and he is on his way to see you now."

Upon hearing the silent beggar's whispered words, Borzoyeh Khanum became so overwhelmed that she lost consciousness. She could no longer discern whether the silent beggar was speaking or not. Her eyes fell upon an older dervish-looking man, clad in a long, worn-out gray shirt that reached his ankles. He walked barefoot and was approaching her from a distance. The old dervish passed by the silent beggar, reaching Borzoyeh Khanum and coming to a halt.

Observing the unfolding scene, the silent beggar sensed that the dervish's attention was primarily focused on the window of Assad Khan's room. Assad Khan was currently battling for his life. Although the dervish briefly regarded Borzoyeh Khanum with concern, his main intention was to be there for her and observe. As the dervish was about to pass Borzoyeh Khanum and proceed towards Assad Khan, she lost her balance and nearly fell. At that moment, the dervish reached out, grabbed her, and prevented her from falling. She looked at him with confusion and overwhelming excitement, rendered speechless and unable to respond.

Just then, her daughter Shahin Dokht, who had grown into a woman and married, appeared in the doorway. Upon seeing her mother, she hurried to her side, accompanied by a few other women who came to her aid.

Interestingly, only Borzoyeh Khanum, the silent beggar, and Assad Khan could see the older dervishes. Borzoyeh Khanum had lost her voice and was unable to communicate or take any action. She could only stare at the dervish with great anticipation, and no one else was aware of whom or what she was fixated on. They all wondered about the message the silent beggar had conveyed to Borzoyeh Khanum, a message that left her powerless and left her gazing blankly at the entrance of the mansion.

The crowd was taken aback, both entertained and concerned for Borzoyeh Khanum. They were so engrossed in her condition that they failed to notice the silent beggar following the older dervish into the mansion.

A crowd of women gathered around Ms. Borzoyeh Khanum and led her inside. They began assisting her in regaining her senses by offering hard candy and tea. Meanwhile, another commotion unfolded in Assad Khan's spacious room, where he would often stay, smoke opium, and entertain his friends. The sight of Assad Khan, deeply distressed and unable to speak or move like his wife Borzoyeh Khanum, astonished everyone present. His outstretched hands were directed towards the silent beggar, his entire being consumed by a spark of joy and happiness.

Although his lips moved, no sound escaped them. Rostam Khan, Assad Khan's son, now bald and aged, sat beside his father, embracing him, and pondered the situation with confusion. It became evident to Rostam Khan that his father had passed away, so he patiently clung to his father while his gaze shifted between him and the silent beggar. Unbeknownst to Rostam Khan and the others, an older Dervish approached and sat beside Assad Khan. All Rostam Khan could do was strain his ears to catch his father's broken and excited whispers, hoping to grasp some understanding. "My beloved son, you have finally come. I have caused you much harm, and you have come to forgive me."

Suddenly, Assad Khan convulsed, and his voice ceased. The audience stared at Assad Khan in astonishment, unaware of what was unfolding before them. They failed to notice the hand of the older Dervish, who was none other than the soul of his lost son Sattar, resting upon Assad Khan's face, with closed eyes. All they observed was Assad Khan peacefully closing his eyes, a serene smile gracing his face. It seemed as though he had slumbered for a hundred years, his soul departing, leaving behind only Assad Khan's lifeless body that fell into Rostam Khan's embrace. "God bless him."

Finally, it was the voice of the silent beggar that marked the end of Assad Khan's life, whispering a prayer. Hearing the silent beggar's prayer, Rostam Khan, still holding his father, regained his senses and accepted his father's passing. Tears welled up in the corners of his eyes. The room filled with the echoes of "La Ilaha Allah" and prayers, resonating so strongly that they could almost be heard throughout the village. As per custom, the crowd in the room turned towards the Qibla, the House of God in Saudi Arabia. A few individuals immediately took charge, removing Assad Khan from Rostam Khan's arms and positioning him towards the Qibla. Unbeknownst to everyone, the silent beggar and Sattar had quietly left the room. Soon after, a couple of people climbed to the mansion's rooftop and began announcing Assad Khan's death through the call to prayer.

Just as Assad Khan passed away, a large number of women surrounded Borzoyeh Khanum in a room on the first floor of Assad Khan's mansion. This was the room where she used to spend most of her time, entertain her friends, and do her work. However, the sound of the loud prayer from the upper floor and the rooftop caused Borzoyeh Khanum great pain and suffering. The sudden death of her husband, Assad Khan, and the unexpected reappearance of her son Sattar after all these years were too much for her to bear.

As the news of Assad Khan's death was announced, the people in the room with Borzoyeh Khanum suddenly forgot about her and her struggles. Their attention shifted entirely to Assad Khan and his passing. Although Borzoyeh Khanum wanted to get up and search for her son Sattar, whom she had seen outside the mansion but had disappeared before her eyes, she was physically and emotionally drained. She lacked the strength to move or speak. The grieving mother, feeling helpless and wounded, found herself sitting on the ground on the verge of fainting. Memories from her past flooded her mind, but the sudden death of her husband filled her with fear and weariness, making her worry that a similar fate might have befallen Sattar.

For several years, the grieving mother had not experienced a single day or night of happiness. It was only after her son Sattar disappeared that she started praying, a practice she had never engaged in before. Her daughter joined her in earnest prayers, both beseeching their God to keep Sattar safe. Borzoyeh Khanum made numerous contributions to charitable causes, including Zulfiqar and other beggars, particularly the silent beggar. Suddenly, a smile appeared on her face, and she began whispering so softly that others could hardly hear her. "So, my beloved son, my Sattar, you finally came? I knew you were alive, and you did not forget your mother."

Unbeknownst to Borzoyeh Khanum, she was only seeing Sattar's spirit and not him in the flesh. The rest of the people present could not perceive Sattar's spirit; they could only see Borzoyeh Khanum's hands reaching out through the bodies of the women surrounding her, extending towards Sattar as he appeared inside the room to comfort his mother. She longed for him to fit into her arms. Everyone was now astonished and perplexed, trying to comprehend whom Borzoyeh Khanum was talking to and whom she wanted to embrace. All eyes turned to the silent beggar, who had just appeared and stood at the doorway, looking inside with a cheerful expression. The confusion among the onlookers grew, thinking that Borzoyeh Khanum had lost her sanity by asking the silent beggar to come and hug her. They failed to perceive that Borzoyeh Khanum's hands were now in Sattar's hands, and like a willow, her entire body trembled with excitement. "I no longer need to live. My Sattar has come to see me... now I can die in peace."

However, the silent beggar watched as Sattar trembled and closed his eyes as if battling an unseen force. Astonished by the light and energy emanating from Borzoyeh Khanum's body and entering Sattar's, the silent beggar knocked on the door. It appeared as though the spirits of both were merging, ready to soar together. It was evident that Borzoyeh Khanum no longer wished to leave her son Sattar alone and intended to take him with her. People attributed the strange behavior of Assad Khan and Borzoyeh Khanum to the presence of the silent beggar.

While the silent beggar observed, lost in his thoughts, he suddenly noticed the ghost of a wild wolf emerging from among the women, attacking Sattar. However, no one else in the room seemed to notice or see it. The silent beggar's eyes were suddenly clouded.

The silent beggar's instincts were correct. Even with his eyes closed, he seemed to witness, in that very moment, on the hillside next to the hut, underneath the mulberry tree, two outstretched hands pointing towards the village of Tikken, with the sound of the reed now silenced. Someone whispered from beneath the tattered cloth, but it was indistinct. The entire cloth trembled as if wrestling with an unknown force, leaving the silent beggar detached and oblivious to his surroundings. Unlike the tranquil weather in the village, a fierce wind and storm battered the worn-out cloth, the outstretched hand beneath it, the mulberry tree, and everything around, rendering visibility scarce from a few yards away.

A few yards from the worn-out cloth and the mulberry tree, an elderly, hungry wolf inched closer toward the cloth. Sensing the imminent danger, Majnoon, the dog, led some passers-by toward the wolf and the cloth. However, before Majnoon could reach the scene, the elderly wolf leaped into the air, swiftly descended onto the cloth, and vanished from sight in an instant. The hands that protruded from beneath the cloth disappeared as a man beneath the cloth crashed down onto Asyeh's grave. Whoever was under the cloth engaged in a desperate struggle for survival against the older wolf. Gradually, the figure of the older Dervish, none other than Sattar himself, who had been hidden beneath the tattered cloth, became visible as he fought fiercely against the hungry wolf.

Meanwhile, inside the room, the silent beggar and Borzoyeh Khanum were taken aback as the wolf pounced. At that moment, Sattar stood firm on the stormy hill. His hands slipped away from Borzoyeh Khanum's grasp, and suddenly, Sattar's spirit vanished from the sight of both the silent beggar and Borzoyeh Khanum. Only Borzoyeh Khanum remained able to perceive the ongoing battle between Sattar and the wolf amidst the women clad in vibrant garments who encircled her. It seemed that none of the other women could perceive the events unfolding before them; instead, they stared in bewilderment at Borzoyeh Khanum's uncharacteristic behavior. Even in her final moments, when the destitute mother was engrossed in her own struggle with life and death, she disregarded her own well-being and rose to aid her son Sattar. However, Sattar abruptly disappeared from his mother's tear-filled eyes. Overwhelmed by the relentless onslaught of death's embrace, his mother finally succumbed.

Even after her passing, the grieving mother refused to abandon her son. Her spirit now soared through the tempestuous weather, around the humble abode and the mulberry tree, and lingered near Asyeh's resting place. She watched vigilantly, yearning to come to her son's aid as he fought for his life against the wolf. Unbeknownst to Sattar's mother and others, he had detached himself from society, leading a clandestine existence in the foothills above the villages of Shourcheh and Tikken. For years, he dedicated most of his time to sitting beneath a tattered cloth at Asyeh's gravesite, delving into hours of mysticism and prayer, beseeching her to reveal herself to him. During these intense moments, he often slipped into a state of ecstasy, gradually losing consciousness. Through practice, he had acquired the ability to separate his soul from his body, allowing his spirit to roam freely, particularly in the villages of Shourcheh and Tikken. He observed his mother and father from an unseen vantage point, unable to make his presence known. Whenever he emerged from this trance-like state, he returned to his normal self. Undoubtedly, Shaykh Ahmad, his mentor, played a significant role in this profound transformation. It was Shaykh Ahmad's soul that journeyed into the trance world to aid Sattar and rescue him from the clutches of the Law Men when he was captured. Throughout these years, it was Shaykh Ahmad who played the reed at night, facilitating Sattar's transformation and establishing a peculiar friendship with the wolf, as the creature grew fond of the haunting melody.

As Sattar emerged from the trance-like state, locked in a fierce battle with the wolf, he remained oblivious to the tragic demise of his mother. Unbeknownst to him, her spirit lingered, vigilantly observing and attempting to aid him. Wrestling with the ravenous predator, Sattar relentlessly hurled the wolf back and forth, but it swiftly rebounded each time, launching relentless attacks without relenting. Even Sattar's loyal dog, Majnoon, joined the fray, engaging the wolf in a desperate struggle. Amidst the tumultuous clash between Sattar and the wolf, fate took a sinister turn. The wolf, seizing an opportunity, lunged at Sattar and clamped its jaws around his hand with a ferocious bite. Its razor-sharp teeth pierced halfway through Sattar's flesh, sinking into his bones. Despite Majnoon's valiant attempts to fend off the wolf, it adamantly refused to release its grip on Sattar's hand, further embedding its teeth with every aggressive strike from Majnoon. However, Sattar realized the pressing need to vanquish the wolf swiftly. He understood that if their struggle caught the attention of the other wolves, who were not as amicable as those they had encountered over the years, his and Majnoon's survival would be in grave jeopardy, torn apart mercilessly. Thus, Sattar resolved to steer the battle towards his hut, where he intended to seek refuge with his faithful canine companion and barricade the door.

In the past, whenever wolves approached Sattar's hut, the melodic tunes emanating from the worn-out cloth would inexplicably cause them to retreat, sitting back to revel in the enchanting melodies. Over time, they had grown accustomed to Sattar's presence, considering him a friend and a familiar figure. Upon setting their gaze upon Sattar, they seemed to recognize him by his scent, acknowledging him as an ally rather than an adversary—a hefty prey to fill their hungry bellies. Consequently, they would venture elsewhere, minding their own business. However, it appeared that the wolf currently assaulting him hailed from a different territory. Alternatively, Sattar's aura and demeanor might have changed, his energy altered by the sorrowful demise of his parents, exuding a scent unfamiliar to the wolves. Sattar was acutely aware that this time was unlike any other. During his intense struggle with the elder wolf, he had lost his reed and could no longer play the familiar tunes that identified him as their longtime friend. Sattar comprehended that sooner or later, the other wolves would arrive, witnessing the battle, and upon catching a whiff of the blood now staining his body, they would fail to recognize him as their ally. Undoubtedly, they would abandon their perception of friendship and hasten to assist the elder wolf. In such a scenario, both he and his devoted dog would meet a gruesome demise, torn apart, lifeless.

In the midst of the struggle, Sattar, consumed by a fury like the very wolf he faced, unleashed a cacophony of noises and shouts towards the pack, mimicking their primal language as if he were one of them. Majnoon, the faithful dog, joined in, creating a tempestuous whirlwind of bodies amidst the howling winds and enveloping darkness. Their sounds merged with the storm, carried away by its gusts.

Amidst the chaos, Sattar seized every opportunity to arm himself, scouring the ground for rocks to wield against the ferocious wolf. Finally, his hand landed upon a sizable piece of debris, clutching it tightly. Summoning every ounce of strength, he struck the wolf's snout relentlessly, determined to free himself and reach the safety of the hut. Sattar knew that he had to secure refuge within its walls, along with his loyal canine companion, and shut the door tight, for otherwise the approaching pack would surely seal their fate.

Sattar's voice grew louder, echoing with untamed ferocity. Majnoon, his senses driven to madness, sank his teeth into the wolf's tail with a vice-like grip, forcefully yanking it away from Sattar. The dog's bite sank deep into the wolf's flesh, provoking greater rage and savagery, causing the wolf to retaliate by sinking its own teeth into Sattar's flesh, breaking through skin and bone. Throughout this violent struggle, the spirit of Borzoyeh Khanum revolved around them, filled with concern for her son.

After enduring a relentless exchange of blows, Sattar's strikes shattered the wolf's teeth, leaving them scattered on the ground. However, the aging predator refused to surrender. Both the wolf and Sattar were consumed by pain, yet they had no time to contemplate their own suffering; their focus remained fixed on defeating their opponent. The wolf was determined not to relinquish such a substantial prize, while Sattar was resolute in his determination to rid himself of the wolf and avoid becoming its prey. Sattar continued his assault upon the wolf's snout, persistently bellowing, as he struggled to draw nearer to the hut, dragging the wolf along with him.

Eventually, the wolf, whose snout and mouth had been shattered by Sattar's blows, and most of its teeth were broken, was forced to release Sattar's hand. However, some of the wolf's broken teeth remained embedded in Sattar's flesh, skin, and bones. The relentless battle between Sattar, the wolf, and Majnoon the dog continued amidst the heavy storm, growing more intense with each passing moment. They danced amidst the swirling dust and debris that crashed upon their heads and faces, locked in a life-and-death struggle. All three beings had transformed into untamed creatures. Sattar, imitating a wolf, crawled on all fours around the mulberry tree, desperately trying to reach his hut while evading the wolf. They tumbled and rose repeatedly, their bodies bruised and weary. Sattar's hands had grown weak and numb, unable to register the blood flowing from his wounds. Meanwhile, the distant howls of other wolves blended with the wind and managed to reach Sattar's ears, as if they were orchestrating their arrival, hastening towards a momentous event.

Gradually, the wild wolf overwhelmed Sattar, knocking him down, and now death loomed before his eyes. Yet, Majnoon the dog had become even wilder and stronger. Sattar, lying on the ground, battered by the wolf, could discern the shadows of more wolves approaching from the cliffs above, drawn towards him through the raging storm. He knew the wolf pack would soon converge upon him. Although he was just a few steps away from the safety of his hut's door, his injuries were severe, and the wolf refused to release its grip. Time was running out, but he mustered all his remaining strength, aware that his chances of survival were slim. Unconsciously, he began to pray, reciting his final plea. In the midst of despair, when Sattar believed all avenues of escape were closed and all hope had faded, he witnessed a remarkable transformation in his loyal dog, Majnoon. In an instant, Majnoon's madness transformed into a fearless lion. Sattar watched as Majnoon leaped into the air, briefly disappearing into the tempest, only to reappear, landing forcefully on the older wolf's head. With an inexplicable power that Sattar could not comprehend, he sensed himself merging with Majnoon's body and soul, engaging in a relentless battle against the wolf, vowing not to let it harm Sattar. To his astonishment, Majnoon managed to subdue the wolf, pinning it to the ground, proving to be an unmatched adversary. Sattar momentarily forgot about his own peril, captivated by the fierce clash between Majnoon and the wolf. However, as the two combatants crashed towards him, Sattar regained his senses, summoning every ounce of strength to rise from the ground. He gazed briefly at his dog's unwavering determination to fight against the wolf. Then, his eyes shifted to the other wolves, their snouts now only a few steps away from the ground. His mother's spirit hovered among them, consumed by worry for her son, yet powerless to intervene.

Sattar was torn with indecision. He found himself faced with two choices: on one hand, he could abandon his dog, Majnoon, who was bravely battling an older wolf, and quickly retreat into the safety of the hunt. He would have to shut the door behind him, leaving Majnoon to face the approaching pack of wolves alone, ultimately resulting in his dog being torn apart before his eyes. On the other hand, he could stay and attempt to aid his beloved dog, knowing that both of them would inevitably fall prey to the hungry wolves. They were simply no match for the ferocity and hunger of the pack. Time was running out as the pack closed in, and Sattar, aged and badly injured from his previous fight with a wolf, knew he had to make a decision.

In the midst of the fight, Sattar managed to reach the safety of the hut, leaning against the wall for support. The wolves were drawing nearer, leaving him with no choice but to enter the hut, close the door, and lock it before the pack could reach him. As he shut the door, the wolves desperately tried to force their way in, their relentless hunger driving them to seek him out and devour him. Despite their efforts, he managed to push the door shut and secure it.

Sattar's entire being was consumed by pain. He lacked the strength to move and could barely remain standing, relying on the wall for support. His vision was impaired, his eyes badly injured and struggling to stay open. The scene outside appeared blurry, like a tumultuous storm intertwined with numerous apparitions. Though hazy, he could make out the ghostly figures of the hungry wolves, now preying upon his loyal companion, Majnoon. Sattar knew that his beloved dog stood no chance against the overwhelming pack, witnessing the heartbreaking sight of his innocent and faithful companion being torn apart. The wolves relentlessly fought over every piece of Majnoon's flesh, his skin, his meat, and even his bones. Sattar was utterly helpless, unable to aid or save his devoted dog, forced to endure the torment and suffering from his vantage point.

In his weakened state, Sattar's knees gave way beneath him, and he sank to the cold earth. Sitting there, he could still hear the echoing howls of the wolves, envisioning the savage frenzy with which they fought over the remains of his loyal companion. Unbeknownst to Sattar, his late mother's spirit restlessly wandered the room, filled with worry and anguish for her wounded son.

Watching the battle between wolves and dogs was a hauntingly familiar sight for Sattar. It felt as if his past memories had sprung to life, playing vividly in his mind and soul. Just like the wolves that had torn his dog apart outside, he vividly recalled the horde of frenzied men who had mercilessly attacked and beaten his dog with sticks and rocks, surpassing the brutality of the wolves. The entire memory unfolded in his mind, parallel to the ongoing chaos outside the room, a memory from when he was merely fourteen years old—helplessly witnessing angry men brutally end his dog's life.

Now, for the second time, he found himself losing a beloved canine companion. Both dogs had sacrificed themselves, one to save Asyeh, and now his new dog sacrificing its life to protect him. Sattar was deeply lost in a whirlwind of past and present, consumed by the pain of losing his dog. In his turmoil, he momentarily forgot where he was, forgetting even the tragic loss of his parents. His eyelids unconsciously met, shrouding his vision in darkness, but suddenly they opened again. His bloodshot and weary eyes beheld the ethereal presence of his mother, standing a few steps away, smiling at him. The sight of his mother stirred such a profound longing in him that he felt his soul yearning to depart his body, ascending to join her in death. He recollected the agonizing moment he had witnessed his mother's passing, how he snapped out of his trance-like state when the wolf attacked him, his spirit no longer able to witness his mother's demise. And now, he gazed upon the ghostly manifestation of his mother's smiling presence, briefly doubting if she was truly gone.

At that moment, he wished for the silent beggar to enter and reveal the truth about his mother. He pondered why Asyeh no longer spoke to him as she once did. Outside, the fierce struggle between wolves continued, fighting over the last remains of his loyal dog, while the storm raged on with unyielding force. Sattar found himself consumed by inner and outer anguish, unable to keep his weary eyelids open. He blinked a few times, perceiving the hazy apparitions of his parents who had come to visit him. Whispers of their names escaped his lips, and eventually, his eyelids fluttered and closed once more, plunging him into darkness and a profound stillness.

* * * * *

With the sound of the cry of "Allahu Akbar" (God is Great) and the prayer of "La ilaha illa Allah" echoing from the village of Tikken, Sattar regained consciousness and opened his eyes. Light replaced the darkness once again. It took him a while to orient himself and comprehend what had transpired. The wolves were gone. Summoning all his strength, he propped himself up and sat against the wall. The wolf had inflicted severe injuries upon him, but the pain of losing his dog was even more agonizing and heart-wrenching. The echoes of "Allahu Akbar" and "La ilaha illa Allah" from the Village of Tikken served as a reminder of the events of the previous night and the tragic demise of his parents. Though his soul had traversed and witnessed their passing, the sounds informed him that people were now conveying his parents' bodies to the cemetery for burial. The sounds grew louder and louder. Sattar longed to be present, to share in the collective grief with the villagers, his brother Rostam Khan, and bid farewell to his loved ones. Gazing out of the small room's window towards the village and the road, he wondered if he awaited someone or something—a flicker of hope or a miraculous intervention. As he ruminated, he realized that a true friend and companion was the most precious blessing one could possess, surpassing all wealth in value, transcending any price tag. It seemed wiser to embrace friendship and connection rather than harboring hurt and animosity. For no apparent reason, his gaze fixated on the road, as if anticipating the arrival of someone who could bring solace to his weary countenance and burdened heart, yet he remained uncertain as to who it might be. The anguish of waiting proved to be as excruciating as his physical wounds. He prayed that the silent beggar, at the very least, would make an appearance. Though Sattar harbored no fear of death and longed to depart this world to reunite with Asyeh and escape the tribulations of earthly existence, he didn't wish to pass away in such a state. He believed it was necessary to confess to the people of Shourcheh and Tikken, revealing that for the past four decades, he had been the one depriving them of sleep and tranquility. He was the elusive presence haunting the village at night, instilling fear, and playing the reed instrument to mourn Asyeh and simultaneously torment them, reminding them that despite their role in the death of his beloved Asyeh and his dog, he should have forgiven them long ago and not carried such pain for so long. Before departing this materialistic and painful world, he desired to offer his apologies. Yet, even sitting up proved to be an arduous task. He yearned to rise but lacked the strength. He had lost copious amounts of blood, his fever raging, and his parched mouth struggling to utter words. He attempted to rise once more, but his body had been drained of all energy. He managed to fold his legs and settled back down. With closed eyes, he embarked on a recitation of prayers to God, seeking forgiveness for the wrongs he had committed throughout his life and beseeching divine mercy for his departed parents.

But his gaze remained fixed on the door, hopeful that someone would open it and enter. He knew that the only person who ever acknowledged his existence and frequented that place was the silent beggar. He had last seen him the previous night at his parents' home. Now, he eagerly awaited the arrival of the silent beggar. His body trembled like a willow, and pain consumed his entire being. The wolf had inflicted severe wounds upon him, rendering his vision blurry and distorting everything before his eyes. To him, everything appeared lifeless and devoid of meaning. He closed his eyes once more, plunging into a world of darkness and emptiness.

The creak of the door opening jolted Sattar from his slumber, and his eyes fluttered open. A figure resembling the ghostly presence of the silent beggar entered the room. Sattar's excitement surged upon seeing him, momentarily erasing his thoughts and fantasies. He stared intently at the silent beggar, who anxiously took a seat beside him, attentively assessing his condition. Never had Sattar been happier to lay eyes on the silent beggar. "Those cursed wolves... They've done a number on you. You're badly injured. Shall I take you to a doctor and fetch some medicine?"

Now, Sattar's focus was solely on the silent beggar. Without delay, the silent beggar kindled a fire and placed a kettle beside it, preparing hot tea. He then dampened a piece of cloth and gently wiped away the dried blood from Sattar's hands, feet, and face, searching for the wounded areas. "Did they bury the two of them?"

The silent beggar understood that Sattar was asking if they had buried his parents. He glanced at Sattar, but it seemed as though he couldn't speak or didn't want to, refusing to reveal that he had left the village of Tikken before dawn when it was still dark. The villagers had been reluctant to transfer Assad Khan and his wife Borzoyeh Khanum's bodies to the mosque during the night due to their fear of the goblins, particularly Sattar. Hence, the bodies remained indoors until morning. Throughout the night, prayers and mourning cries echoed loudly without respite. In the early morning, the bodies were finally taken to the mosque. However, Assad Khan was no ordinary person, so it was necessary to wait until word spread to the nearby villages and people from far and wide arrived at Tikken to escort his body and participate in the burial. Assad Khan's servants were dispatched to neighboring villages to inform every one of his deaths. It was only after the servants had relayed the news and the bodies had been transferred to the mosque that Rostam Khan had the chance to search for the silent beggar. He wanted to inquire about what had transpired with his parents the previous night and why they had both died simultaneously. Rostam Khan was perplexed since he had noticed that his parents were perceiving things that no one else could see, and their behavior was peculiar as if they were interacting with Sattar. Rostam Khan was convinced that the encounter with the silent beggar on the night of his parents' death had not been a mere coincidence. However, as he sought out the silent beggar, he discovered that the beggar had vanished from the mansion. Determined, Rostam Khan mounted his horse with a couple of servants and scoured the surroundings in search of the beggar, but he seemed to have disappeared without a trace. It was only when one of the elder servants spoke up that Rostam Khan relented. "There's no point in pursuing him, Rostam Khan. He must have left the village, maybe a few villages away. Besides, the silent beggar is like a ghost; he appears and vanishes at will. He could be right in front of you, yet you wouldn't see him if he didn't want you to. Let's return and attend to your deceased parents. It wouldn't be appropriate for you to be absent while people gather to pay their respects." Moved by the servant's words, Rostam Khan decided to turn back. On their way, they encountered Zulfiqar, who had just emerged from the village of Tikken. After exchanging greetings, Zulfiqar continued his journey back to the Village of Shourcheh to spread the news and, naturally, narrate his own version of how Assad Khan and his wife had died, aiming to garner donations from the people of Shourcheh. It wasn't long before Rostam Khan and his cavalry remembered that they hadn't seen Zulfiqar in the village. Doubts arose, and they wondered whether the person they had encountered was actually Zulfiqar or a goblin in disguise. Fearing the goblins once more, panic seized them, and they promptly turned back and headed for the Village of Tikken.

*****

Cloudy weather and the stillness of the empty road enveloped the people of Zulfiqar, creating a sense of suffocation. A gentle breeze began to blow, softly caressing Zulfiqar's face. Standing alone, he could feel the desert's silence on one side and the soothing sound of the wind on the other, comforting his weary mind. Zulfiqar ascended the nearby hills once again, gazing intently at the forbidden area. He recollected the stories of Shepherd Ali, who had ventured there and returned unharmed. Rumors circulated that even the quiet beggar had made his way to that place. Consequently, Zulfiqar contemplated embarking on his own journey there one day. He believed that by exploring the forbidden area, gathering information, and sharing the news with the neighboring villages, he could establish a lucrative position for himself, reaping the rewards that awaited him. In the midst of this contemplation, a wild bee flew past Zulfiqar's ear, its buzzing sound resembling the wind. The bee's presence abruptly awakened him from his reverie of forbidden adventures, reminding him of the mythical beings and spirits that resided in those lands. A sudden wave of fear and terror gripped his body and soul, for he believed that bees should not be found in such a place. Instantly, he set off towards Shourcheh Village, afraid to even cast a glance at the forbidden area.

*****

Sattar's hand rested on the silent beggar's, interrupting his thoughts, and bringing him back to reality. He remembered where he was and recalled Sattar's question about the burial of the two of them. "They must have already started working on it. Besides, they are already gone and free... we are the ones who should be concerned and await such a holy departure. You have lost a lot of blood."

The silent beggar, who had cleaned Sattar's face and hands of blood and sweat, went to the fire to prepare, and serve some hot tea. "You should eat something, maybe some milk or hard candy with tea... vegetables, I don't know. I'm not a doctor. Did you pray last night? Did God answer your prayers by sending these wolves to you?"

After filling the teapots with water and setting them on fire, the silent beggar returned and soaked a cloth in a bucket of water. He placed it on Sattar's face to reduce the heat and fever. He was extremely concerned and nervous, unsure of what to do for Sattar. Moreover, both of them had severed ties with the village, and people didn't even know Sattar was alive. If he took him back to the village, no one would recognize him or know how to react. Additionally, he couldn't carry him alone down the high rocky hill. He could barely move himself. Furthermore, since assuming the identity of the silent beggar, he had not spoken, so suddenly going back to the village, and asking for help or medicine seemed impossible. Besides, there was no medicine in the village; he would have to take him to the city, which was a day or two away on foot. The falling snow made it even more difficult to traverse the rocky hill. He had heard that wetting the patient would lower their body temperature and prevent them from falling asleep. The silent beggar prayed for Sattar's fever to subside so that he could go and find his brother, Rostam Khan, who could come and help. He feared leaving Sattar alone with such a high fever, thinking he might die before help arrived. Therefore, whenever Sattar seemed on the verge of falling asleep, he would shake him and rouse him, afraid he may never wake up. He began reciting and chanting Rumi's poems to help Sattar stay awake. Now he had undressed Sattar and periodically wet the cloth, rubbing it from his head to his toes, determined not to let him slip into slumber. He constantly fed him hot tea with hard candy and anything he could find around the hut. A few days later, the sound of prayer from the village of Tikken echoed through the air. Both Sattar and the silent beggar knew that it signaled the arrival of Sattar's parents to their final resting place.

The news of Assad Khan's death spread through the Village of Tikken and its neighboring villages like a raging storm, stirring mixed emotions among friends and foes alike. It didn't take much time for the people residing in the surrounding areas to catch wind of Assad Khan's demise, particularly due to the unsettling circumstances surrounding his passing.

* * * * *

Chapter 5
When the call of happiness and joy is overshadowed by the color and face of sorrow...

It had been a few weeks since Sattar was injured. During this time, the silent beggar had remained faithfully by his side, tending to his needs. His responsibilities included cleaning Sattar, attending to his wounds, and using wet clothes to cool his feverish body. The beggar's efforts were crucial, as Sattar's body emitted so much heat that the cloth would quickly dry. The silent beggar believed that leaving Sattar alone for even an hour or two would result in his demise. To keep Sattar from slipping into sleep, the beggar would instinctively play his old Harmonica. This not only occupied Sattar's mind but also helped the beggar himself stay awake. Occasionally, the beggar would succumb to exhaustion, and his eyes would involuntarily close, but within ten to fifteen minutes, he would awaken abruptly. Similarly, Sattar would experience the same, and it was the silent beggar who roused him. Sometimes, when the beggar failed to awaken on his own, Sattar would touch his hand, instantly bringing him back. It became a game between them, a strategy employed by the silent beggar to maintain their wakefulness. He would talk to Sattar incessantly, to keep them both alert. After weeks of sleep deprivation, the beggar eventually lost consciousness while caring for Sattar, alternating between sleep, and waking states.

Despite Sattar's critical condition and the beggar's concerns about his ability to save him, the beggar contemplated taking him to either of the nearby villages, Shourcheh or Tikken, to seek help. However, Sattar adamantly refused to go and insisted on remaining where he was. Consequently, the silent beggar had no choice but to do his utmost to aid him. Unfortunately, Sattar's condition did not improve; in fact, it deteriorated further. It was evident that he was fighting against death's grip. To cool his body, the silent beggar removed all of Sattar's clothes and diligently fanned him. Only a piece of cloth covered his genitals. The beggar could feel the intense heat radiating from Sattar's body to the point that touching him would scorch one's hand. Hallucinations had begun to plague Sattar, and he whispered incomprehensible words. Among the murmurs, the silent beggar could discern the name "Asyeh," the beautiful young girl both of them had loved in their youth, who had tragically been murdered. However, the rest of Sattar's whispers remained unclear. It had been nearly fifty years since Asyeh's passing, and Sattar had forgotten almost everything, except for the memories of their love, which remained vivid and alive in his mind and heart. Even as he teetered on the edge of death, the thought of Asyeh persisted, as if the events had transpired only a few days ago. It was as if Asyeh had been the center of Sattar's religion and faith throughout his life, constantly present in his dreams and waking moments. Sattar yearned for death, longing to reunite with his beloved Asyeh on the other side. However, it seemed as though death eluded him. His breaths grew labored. Struggling to keep his eyes open, he strained to see the blurred image of the silent beggar. Pure silence enveloped them, stretching across time and the earth. Involuntarily, the weary voice of the silent beggar rose, chanting philosophical words about life, death, and the afterlife. His chant served as medicine, ointment, and solace for Sattar's soul.

The sound of the Dohol/Large drum resonated from outside, reaching the Village of Shourcheh and stirring the silent beggar from his slumber. It took him a moment to gather his senses and determine his surroundings, as well as the origin of the melodic instrument. He had collapsed from exhaustion beside Sattar and was unsure how long he had been asleep.

The clamor of instruments, drums, and trumpets reverberated so loudly that it seemed to deafen the ears of both the silent beggar and Sattar. The silent beggar's gaze involuntarily shifted towards the village, drawing his attention away from the window. His voice was drowned out amidst the instrument's cacophony and the commotion stirred by the villagers in Shourcheh. Puzzled, the silent beggar wondered what could be happening and what it signified. It was evident that the events were taking place along the roadside, beyond the village and near the graveyard. Knowing it was not the wedding season, he questioned why there would be celebrations at the cemetery. If someone had passed away, mourning rather than merriment would be expected. For a brief moment, the silent beggar's thoughts and imaginings diverted from Sattar, consumed by the melodies of the instruments and the rhythmic chants emanating from the village.

Simultaneously, inside the hillside hut, Sattar wrestled with the clutches of death. Outside, on the road leading into the Village of Shourcheh, a crowd of people made their way towards the cemetery. A group of musicians accompanied them, playing drums and trumpets. A spirited elderly man orchestrated the festivities, and an air of jubilation permeated the atmosphere. Nearly everyone joined in the dance, chanting joyously. The elderly man took hold of the young men's hands, initiating the dance, and soon others joined in the revelry. The musicians and singers harmonized their melodies and lyrics with the movements of the dancers. The children formed their own group, seemingly competing with the adults.

Among the stream of people rushing out of the village and converging on the road and the growing crowd was Zulfiqar, who, as usual, had his head held high, gazing up at the sky. Though older now, Zulfiqar lacked the agility and energy of his youth, causing him to walk at a slower pace. Despite his efforts to keep up with the others and reach the roadside crowd as quickly as possible, it proved challenging, unlike in his earlier years. Everyone swiftly overtook him, leaving him behind, which did not bring him any joy. Eventually, Zulfiqar arrived at Kal Akbar's house, situated just outside the village, adjacent to the cemetery and the road beyond. Kal Akbar's house stood approximately a hundred meters away from the road leading to the cemetery. As usual, Kal Akbar sat on the porch of his house, observing the people passing by his laughter and jests still intact. Time had aged him significantly, with only a tooth or two remaining in his mouth, rendering him less active. Occasionally, his daughter or son, who lived with him, would lend a hand, assisting him onto the porch. This simple act brought him joy, as he could observe and engage in conversations with those who passed by. "Mr. Zulfiqar, your horse is lagging behind the others... Hurry up! They're serving free food. Bring some for me too," he exclaimed jokingly.

Then his infectious laughter filled the air. However, Mr. Zulfiqar was so absorbed in his own thoughts that it seemed as if he couldn't hear the words and voice of Kal Akbar. Lost in his reverie, he inadvertently passed Kal Akbar and continued on his way towards the gathering crowd. Just a few steps away from Kal Akbar, a young man on a donkey emerged from the village, swiftly riding past him, followed by a group of hurried individuals eager to join the gathering. Kal Akbar's gaze fell upon these riders, each clutching a sheep that struggled and bleated, desperately attempting to break free from their captors. Their cries were drowned out by the sounds of instruments and chants echoing through the road, suffocating amidst the vibrant atmosphere. Some people chased after the donkey, vigilantly ensuring the sheep remained secure in their captor's grasp. Everyone was in such a rush that Kal Akbar didn't even have a chance to utter a word or engage in jest with them.

Kal Akbar, who seemed somewhat disheartened at the sight of the distressed sheep, watched with a heavy heart as the donkeys and their captive animals reached the crowd. As the group of donkey riders carrying the sheep approached the gathering, the crowd erupted in greetings and blessings, their jubilant voices reaching the sky and echoing for miles. The sheep were promptly taken down from the donkeys, and while they struggled fervently to escape their captors, several kind-hearted individuals rushed forward to assist, collectively taking control of the unfortunate animals. Together, they guided the sheep towards a group of seasoned butchers, who were meticulously sharpening their knives. It was as if these innocent and defenseless creatures somehow sensed the impending fate awaiting them. Their instincts kicked in, compelling them to resist with all their might, desperately trying to evade their captors and preserve their precious lives.

Just like a roadside brawl between a butcher and a helpless sheep, a struggle for life and death unfolded inside Sattar's humble hillside hut. The butcher continued sharpening his knife, preparing to sever the poor sheep's head from its body and end its life. Pilgrims, nobles, and their followers had gathered, chanting, and eagerly awaiting the outcome. Some individuals were digging a large hole near the road that led to the forbidden area where Sattar's hut stood. The crowd grew as more people arrived.

As the butcher removed his coat, ready to take the sheep's life, several people tried to snatch the coat from him, but his assistant quickly intervened and took hold of it amidst the uproar of prayer. Amidst the growing clamor of prayers, Kal Akbar emerged from the front arch of his house, gripping the wall for support, as he sought to understand the commotion unfolding on the roadside. Unaware of the reason for the gathering, nobody paused to inform him, as everyone was in a hurry.

While the butcher rolled up his sleeves, proudly and gleefully preparing to take the life of the helpless sheep, prayers merged with dancing and the sound of musical instruments and drums. Although Kal Akbar was now advanced in age and no longer as sharp-witted, his senses remained focused enough to recognize that it was neither wedding season nor a time for mourning and condolences. He wondered why people were playing music, chanting, and dancing, and he desired to uncover the truth.

It didn't take long for Mullah Mahmud, riding a black donkey and followed by a sizable crowd, to approach Kal Akbar. The people greeted Mullah Mahmud as they headed towards the roadside. Upon seeing Kal Akbar, Mullah Mahmud averted his gaze, aware that Kal Akbar's jests would belittle him in front of the crowd. Kal Akbar harbored no fondness for Mulla or faith. However, amidst the throng of Mullah Mahmud's entourage, this did not matter. At that moment, Mullah Mahmud felt elevated, as if seated atop the highest mountain, untouched by any disturbances, including the sweet-toned voice of Kal Akbar.

"Mullah, are you in such a hurry to find a bathroom?" Kal Akbar's voice called out, but it was drowned out by the multitude's greetings and blessings upon sighting Mullah Mahmud approaching. Nonetheless, Mard Ali, a fifty-year-old passerby amidst the bustling crowd and the cacophony of instruments and prayers, heard Kal Akbar's voice. He responded with his customary laughter, "The Mullah's armed, the Imam is paying him a visit, and he's filling the villagers' minds... The Mullah has become an Imam himself!"

Now, Mullah Mahmoud's caravan was several yards away from Kal Akbar, and he was safe from Kal Akbar’s teasing. However, before he turned his gaze back, his eyes fell upon Haji Ghazanfar, who was also rushing from the other side of the cemetery with his caravan and followers, determined to reach the crowd before Mulla Mahmud did. Accompanying them were two donkey riders carrying sheep, which had been gifted by Hajji Ghazanfar to be sacrificed for the incoming Imam. Haji Ghazanfar, a resident of the upper part of the village, was the son-in-law of the late Kadkhoda, the village mayor, who was one of Mulla Mahmud’s former partners in crime.

Upon Kadkhoda's passing, Haji Ghazanfar inherited all of his wealth, instantly becoming one of the wealthiest individuals in the village. This sudden change in fortune transformed him from a humble man to an arrogant and ignorant individual. While both Haji Ghazanfar and Mullah Mahmoud were among the richest men in the village, there was an underlying enmity and fierce competition between them. However, in public, they pretended to be friends, showing respect, and flattering one another, while secretly harboring desires for each other's demise and even contemplating murder. Their ultimate goal was to seize leadership in the village, though they concealed their true intentions from the public.

Now, as they spotted each other, they engaged in a silent race to reach the crowd first. They knew that the one who arrived first would garner more attention, respect, and admiration from the crowd, satisfying their egos. Both Mullah Mahmoud and Haji Ghazanfar and their followers shouted and urged their donkeys to move faster, each vying for the lead. However, in this clandestine competition, it was Mullah Mahmoud who emerged victorious, reaching the crowd with his caravan just a few steps ahead of Haji Ghazanfar.

Along the way, Mullah Mahmoud would shout loudly, urging the people accompanying him to raise their voices in prayer. He understood that the louder their voices, the more visible and noteworthy he would be to the crowd. By doing so, he aimed to divert attention away from Haji Ghazanfar. Mullah Mahmoud sought to captivate the crowd's interest and blessings for himself and his caravan, leaving no room for Haji Ghazanfar.

With the arrival of Mullah Mahmoud, followed closely by Haji Ghazanfar, and the convergence of the three groups of people, the sound of greetings and prayers intertwined with the beats of drums and trumpets, creating a commotion that could be heard miles away. The two sheep brought by Haji Ghazanfar were carefully taken down from the donkeys, and the executioners and their assistants began to prepare the victims, watering them and sharpening their knives. As the innocent and helpless sheep gazed upon the gleaming blades, it seemed as if they understood their impending fate sacrificed for the greater cause.

For some reason, people were increasingly gathering around Mullah Mahmoud. There was a rumor circulating in the village about Mullah Mahmoud having a dream where a radiant light showered upon their village. A few days after his dream, news arrived that an Imam's representative was on his way to bless the village. Interpreting Mullah Mahmoud's dream, some individuals, mostly paid followers, started referring to him as the Imam of the village, and others followed suit. People from all directions began approaching him, kissing his hands and feet, while Mullah Mahmoud remained seated on his black donkey, unaffected. The competing sounds of instruments, drums, and trumpets grew so loud that the voices of people praising Mullah Mahmoud got lost amidst the noise. Frustrated, Mullah Mahmoud raised his voice in anger.

"You non-Muslim unbelievers! If you attend a wedding celebration, you should lower the volume of those instruments playing religious music to seek blessings from God. It appears you are blind and unaware that the Imam's representative is approaching."

As Mullah Mahmoud's protest echoed, Mard Ali, riding his wooden horse, echoed his words, serving as his loyal follower. Mullah Mahmud's paid followers quickly intervened, instructing the musicians to silence their instruments. The music abruptly stopped, and a sense of sorrow and mourning replaced the previous joy and happiness. Now, Mard Ali, like a parrot, repeated Mullah Mahmoud's words and added his own thoughts, imagining himself as a warrior fighting against the enemies of Islam while riding his wooden horse.

"Non-Muslims, if you dare attend the wedding, yes, Mullah! They think they're attending a joyful occasion, oblivious to the fact that the Imam's representative is coming to lead them to hell. Play the religious drums and trumpets, Mullah! Get another drum and give it to someone else to play. They are as foolish and ignorant as we are."

Upon hearing Mard Ali's derogatory remarks, Mulla Mahmoud swiftly swung his cane, striking Mard Ali on the head while he stood beside Mullah's donkey. This act triggered a chain of events, with Mulla Mahmud's men and paid followers launching an attack on Mard Ali, as they had done numerous times before. As a result, Mard Ali lost both his respect and his position among them. The familiar dance between Mard Ali and Mulla Mahmud's men ensued, with Mard Ali attempting to escape while enduring the beatings. Nevertheless, he persistently voiced insults directed at Mulla Mahmud, viewing himself as a valiant warrior against the enemies of Islam.

After some time, the chase and the back-and-forth between Mard Ali and Mulla Mahmud's followers concluded, with Mard Ali emerging as the victor, managing to elude his pursuers and find refuge on a small hill. There, Zulfiqar sat alone, observing the scattered crowd, as he habitually did, with his head held high, attentively listening to the events unfolding. Mard Ali, still uttering chants and astride his wooden horse, grew weary and eventually approached Zulfiqar, taking a seat beside him, while continuing to lament his circumstances.

"Oh, if I had only spoken differently! How can someone be a Clergyman if they can't distinguish between a drum and a trumpet?" Mard Ali moaned.

However, Zulfiqar remained silent, his gaze fixed upon the hill where the road disappeared. It seemed as though he possessed a keen vision, as just then, several boys emerged on the road atop the small hill, running towards the crowd, shouting to announce the imminent arrival of the Imam's representative. Unfortunately, the sincere people were so deeply immersed in Mullah Mahmud's flattery that they neither saw nor heard the boys' proclamation. Desperate to make themselves heard, a couple of the boys cupped their hands around their mouths, straining their vocal cords as they shouted toward the oblivious crowd. Yet, their efforts proved futile.

Witnessing the presence of these children, messengers of the Imam, Mard Ali was spurred into action. He resolved to inform the people by shouting and gesturing towards the hilltop where the children stood.

"Oh, if you are deaf and blind, look at the children! Your Imam is coming! Enough with flattery for the Mullah. The Imam is right there! What are you doing, flattering the Mullah? You should go and pay homage to the Imam, for he surpasses the Mullah!"

And finally, the people became aware of the children who were rushing and shouting, pointing towards the hill and the road, announcing the arrival of the representative of the Imam. Upon hearing the children and their announcement, a thunderous roar of greetings, blessings, and the exclamation "Allahu Akbar-which means God is great" erupted from the crowd, deafening everyone present. The breathless boys had not yet reached the crowd when a man and a Clergyman appeared on the hill and at the top of the road. As soon as the men, women, young, and old caught sight of their Imam's representative, excitement surged through them, and they could not contain their anticipation. They all set off in a frenzied race to reach him, driven by a mixture of eagerness and reverence, as if God Himself had brought them the highest paradise. Not a single person remained in the village, not even the dogs and cats. The air resonated with fervent prayers from every direction. Meanwhile, the plaintive cries of the sheep protested against their impending sacrifice, but their voices were drowned out by the clamor of the impassioned crowd. It was as if they sensed that death was imminent. Amidst the escalating sounds of prayers, drums, and trumpets, the executioners, who were seated on the sheep, struggled to restrain them as they squirmed and wriggled on the cold ground. The pressure and punishment inflicted by the executioners intensified, causing great pain and agony for the sheep. They were not mistaken. Now the executioners attempted to force their heads into the water container, as custom dictated that they should drink the last water before being executed. However, the sheep, with all their strength, resisted the urge to dip their heads into the container and refused to partake in the water that served as their final medicine before the merciless executioner's blade. It was as if the unfortunate sheep were fully aware of their impending fate.

The dispute between the sheep and the executioners persisted, with the sheep refusing to back down. It seemed as though the sheep, like Sattar, sensed death looming before them. Despite their mouths being forcibly closed by the executioners, they persisted in their struggle, moving their limbs desperately, pleading with the humanoid figures to release them. It appeared as if they questioned why they had to sacrifice their lives for the comfort of others. However, their desperate cries and pleas fell on deaf ears, as not a soul heeded their calls. In fact, other men, bolstered by a sense of superiority, callously rushed to aid the executioners, each vying to demonstrate their dominance over the sheep. They reveled in the opportunity to exert control, firmly pressing their hands against the poor sheep's necks, reminiscent of a victor's pose with hands submerged in a bowl of water.

In their struggle, the men sought to showcase their power over the helpless, innocent sheep. Hence, they relentlessly pressed and held the sheep's snouts in the water. Under the unrelenting pressure of these merciless executioners, the sheep's necks teetered on the verge of snapping, their mouths and noses submerged, robbing them of the ability to draw breath. Despite the dire circumstances, the valiant sheep refused to yield, battling with their claws and teeth to free their snouts from the water, determined to avoid suffocation. However, the might of the executioners of death prevailed, and the snouts remained submerged. With every forceful push, every moment the executioners kept the sheep's heads submerged, the sheep grew more resolute in their fight for survival, adamantly refusing to ingest the lethal concoction before meeting their demise. Although aware of their impending doom, they defied their oppressors, declining to drink the elixir of death, thereby denying their executioners the satisfaction they sought.

Simultaneously, as the sheep's heads emerged from the water, their cries reverberated towards the heavens. It seemed as though they were attempting to beseech the executioners' deity, the very god to whom they were being sacrificed, hoping to earn his favor or perhaps secure a place in his paradise. Yet, the executioners of this god remained deaf, blind, and devoid of empathy. Their hearts, shrouded in darkness, remained unmoved by the sheep's anguished cries. Undeterred, the sheep refused to surrender to their tormentors, adamantly rejecting the deathly potion. They persisted in their cries, even as their oppressive executioners callously ignored their pleas.

With the representative of Imam drawing closer, the executioners grasped their knives with great force and callously seized the defenseless sheep by its limbs. Lifting the helpless creature as if they were hefting Mount Uhud itself, they slammed it forcefully onto the ground near the hole, creating a tremor akin to an earthquake. A morbid competition ensued among the executioners, each vying to be the first to sever the innocent sheep's head and end its life.

The suffering of the sheep appeared excruciating, its cries reverberating so loudly that they seemed to permeate Sattar's body and soul, causing him to tremble uncontrollably. Seated beside Sattar, the silent beggar puffed on his pipe while observing Sattar, lost in deep contemplation. However, he noticed that Sattar's gaze remained fixed on the window, directed towards the village of Shourcheh from where the commotion emanated. The silent beggar's eyes shifted back and forth between Sattar and the window several times until he finally rose from his seat and peered out towards the village. It was evident that he, too, sensed the unsettling events unfolding on the roadside, which disturbed both him and Sattar.

Sattar witnessed a distressing scene on the roadside, where an executioner's cruel actions were evident. Knees and hands pressed down upon innocent sheep, awaiting their brutal fate. Despite their desperate struggles, the sheep refused to surrender to their merciless captors and fought fiercely to break free. In response, additional individuals rushed to assist the executioners, grasping the sheep by their limbs in an attempt to restrain them. The sheep's cries and protests reverberated loudly, causing a commotion among them.

Amidst this chaos, a few individuals approached with a small brass container containing red fire. They tossed dry beads onto the flames, producing a crackling sound and billowing smoke. The container was then moved around the sheep's heads, believed to purify them and rid their souls of any lurking elves or demons. The thick smoke from the burning beads caused the sheep's eyes to tear up, adding to their plight. The individuals wielding the container moved on, convinced that they were purifying people and banishing elves and demons, while musicians continued to play with their remaining strength.

As the scene unfolded, people took on the role of purifiers, spraying rose water on one another and on the innocent sheep, symbolizing purification, and continuation of their actions through the crowd. Following this, another group of individuals distributed small white hard candies over the heads of the people. They held the belief that this act would also purify individuals and rid them of their inner demons. However, this particular aspect of the ritual became a playful game for children. Eagerly chasing after the candies tossed in the air, they risked being inadvertently kicked by indifferent individuals in the crowd.

Throughout this spectacle, all eyes remained fixed on the arrival of the Imam's representative, who steadily approached from a distance. As anticipation grew, some individuals could no longer contain their excitement and began rushing towards him, competing to be the first to greet him. A flood of people quickly congregated around the Imam's representative, exerting all their efforts to reach him and show their reverence by kissing his hands, feet, and any part of his body they could reach.

The poor sheep's eyes stared helplessly as Mullah Mahmud sat alone on his black donkey, surrounded by the brutal executioners who ruthlessly manipulated and contorted the innocent animal's body, nearly shattering its bones. Mullah Mahmud found himself surprised and displeased by the fervent reception the Imam's representative, known as Moharram but now adopting the name Asghar, received from the people. Little did they know what Mahmud knew—that this so-called representative was actually a murderer, responsible for the deaths of several individuals, who had now assumed a new identity.

Mullah Mahmud felt a sense of confusion and resentment as he observed the false adoration bestowed upon the imposter, yearning for such reverence himself. More importantly, he harbored a deep jealousy that consumed him, fully aware that Asghar's deceptive acts were part of the many manipulations he had orchestrated over the years, exploiting Islam and religion to deceive people. However, this time, Mahmud was not satisfied with his own actions. In fact, he entertained the thought of exposing the imposter's true identity. Alone on his black donkey, Mahmud despised himself for his deeds, even fantasizing about seizing Asghar by the throat and strangling him to death.

Meanwhile, the executioners continued their gruesome task, forcefully gripping the sheep by their throats, their eyes fixed on Asghar, eagerly awaiting his signal. Soon, their knives would touch the innocent creatures' throats, ending their lives. The strangled sheep were then dragged towards a dug hole by the roadside. As the self-proclaimed representative of the Imam, Asghar walked calmly among the crowd, avoiding eye contact with anyone, fearing that someone might recognize his true identity. He was now surrounded by several individuals acting as his bodyguards, some of whom were on the payroll of both Mullah Mahmud and Asghar. Among them, a few wore white turbans and robes, while the primary guard who walked alongside Asghar was known as Mullah Omar.

The knives were now positioned beneath the sheep's throats, causing slight cuts. Drops of blood slowly dripped from the unfortunate animals. All attention and anticipation were focused on Imam Asghari, waiting for his arrival. It seemed as if the presence of suffering sheep, with their throats nearly cut by sharp knives, went unnoticed. The executioners grew impatient, eager to swiftly decapitate the sheep and fulfill their Imam's wish by sacrificing them. After killing the animals, like others before them, they would proceed to kiss their Imam's hands and feet, perhaps hoping to secure a place in heaven.

Imam Asghari was nearing them, followed by a crowd. The executioners' gaze shifted between him and Mulla Mahmoud, awaiting their master's command to kill the helpless sheep. However, they failed to notice that their self-proclaimed Imam had completely abandoned his role, and their attention was solely focused on the newcomer. Imam Asghari was lost in regret, contemplating the self-destruction he had brought upon himself. Even Mulla Mahmoud could hardly believe his eyes, witnessing how people would bow and submit themselves before their supposed Imam, willing to do anything to touch or kiss his hand. It was particularly surprising for Mulla Mahmoud to hear his own fabricated religious figure being called "Imam" and witnessing Asghar's sudden success in representing the Imam. Some individuals even used their coats and hats instead of brooms to sweep away pebbles, thorns, and debris from the path of the Imam, ensuring not even a single pebble would harm his feet. Dust filled the air as people swept in front of him. Imam Asghari kept his gaze lowered, avoiding eye contact with anyone. He would occasionally raise and lower his hand, tenderly touching the blessed children. If he ever lost control and lifted his head to look at the crowd, he quickly averted his gaze back to the ground. Mullah Omar, the Imam's assistant, constantly urged the guards to protect the Imam, pushing people away to ensure his safe passage. The guards diligently followed his orders, clearing a path for the Imam to continue his journey.

In short, the crowd rushed forward, competing, and pushing to kiss Imam Asghari's hands and feet so forcefully that he almost lost his balance and fell. Haji Ghazanfar quickly ordered his companions to protect the Imam. Following his command, several men surrounded Imam Asghari, preventing anyone from approaching him, thereby putting an end to the act of kissing his hands, feet, and touching his body and clothing. Meanwhile, the excursionists eagerly awaited Mullah Mahmoud's order to sever the heads of the sheep. One of them, now praying aloud, sought to ensure that his voice reached the new Imam, establishing himself as the caller to prayer. It seemed as though the butcher was striking a deal with God and Prophet Mohammad, seeking to demonstrate that he was sacrificing the sheep to appease them, or perhaps requesting their permission to carry out the slaughter. The other butchers followed suit, raising their voices to keep pace with their comrade, their attention shifting between the new Imam Asghari and Mullah Mahmud, who seemed distracted and oblivious to the fact that the butchers awaited his order. Mullah Mahmoud remained deep in thought and consumed by jealousy, still mounted on his donkey. On the contrary, Haji Ghazanfar, who had eagerly approached the Imam with his staff, radiated a joyful and contented smile. Finally, it was Haji Ghazanfar who commanded the sheep to be slaughtered upon the arrival of Imam Asghari. Thus began a race among the excursionists, wielding bloody and malevolent knives in one hand and holding the heads of the unfortunate sheep, their blood dripping onto the ground, in the other. They offered these severed heads one by one to their Imam as if proclaiming to God that through the beheading of innocent sheep, they believed they were purchasing paradise for themselves. The voices of the excursionists and the people shouting prayers grew increasingly louder and overwhelming. The wooden pedestals, thick and sturdy, were placed in dug pits and now drenched in the blood of the sheep's heads and bodies. These pedestals, serving as a display of welcome to Imam Asghari, still bore the struggle of the dying animals. Joy and elation filled the onlookers as they witnessed the slaughter of the helpless sheep. They continued their frenzied race to kiss, flatter, beat drums, dance, and chant prayers in honor of their new Imam Asghari.

As several people waited for the blood of innocent sacrificed sheep, they gathered around the dug pits. With great enthusiasm, they began filling the pits, signifying the official start of the event. Haji Ghazanfar and his successor Kadkhoda joined in, pouring dirt around the foundations, while others swiftly filled the base of the sign with stones, soil, and a mixture of water and sheep's blood. The perpetrators, now filled with pride and arrogance, acted as if they had returned from a victorious battle, reminiscent of the famous religious war, the Battle of Uhud. They washed their hands at the edge of the pits, as a show of their accomplishment.

Amidst the fervent prayers of the crowd, their voices resonated for miles, even reaching Sattar's hut, approximately a mile away. Sattar, engaged in his own battle against the devil, paused to listen. The sound of drums and trumpets from the roadside overpowered his pain, capturing his heart and evoking tears. It was as if Sattar empathized with the fate of the innocent sheep, experiencing their struggle with death firsthand. For a moment, everything seemed still and lifeless to Sattar, as if silence had engulfed the room. His gaze fixated on the window, although his vision was blurred. He yearned for someone to appear or enter, yet no movement occurred.

The silent beggar continued to chant passionate poems by Rumi, his voice rising above the sounds emanating from the roadside. Observing Sattar's expression, a gentle smile of contentment spread across his face. Concerned, the silent beggar followed Sattar's gaze and discovered the source of his joy. A smile formed on the beggar's lips as well, increasing his excitement. In that instant, an indescribable sensation filled the air, as if the room became warm and filled with a pleasant aroma. The more Sattar smiled, the more the atmosphere transformed into one of tranquility, serenity, and peace.

The silent beggar noticed that Sattar's gaze, fixed on the mulberry tree outside the window, suddenly shifted towards the door, his eyes locked on its entrance. In an instant, a surge of joy ran through Sattar's body, his face lit up like that of a child who had just spotted candy. The pain seemed to have vanished completely. The silent beggar continued his chant, observing Sattar's behavior intently, trying to discern what had caught his attention. Yet, he couldn't see anything out of the ordinary. All he could perceive was the scent of perfume lingering in the room. Suddenly, he noticed the entire space bathed in vibrant, colorful light. However, what eluded the silent beggar was that Sattar was beholding the spirit of Asyeh, now manifesting in the room, dressed in a flowing green silk shirt. As Asyeh appeared, radiance filled every corner. Surrounding her were several angels adorned in pale green and sky-blue garments. Asyeh had grown even more beautiful than before and had come to greet her beloved Sattar, wearing a magical smile. Sattar stood speechless, unsure of what to do. He couldn't distinguish between dream and reality, life, and death. "Sattar, arise! You are finally liberated, my love. I have awaited this moment for so long. Get up and join me... You needn't worry about people any longer; I have forgiven them, and you should too. Emancipate your soul, for you are now free... Come with me."

Sattar rose without hesitation, walking towards Asyeh, and together they exited through the door, heading towards the mulberry tree and the nearby water well. The silent beggar continued to chant, his voice growing louder and louder, finally comprehending the unfolding events. It was as if the silent beggar had glimpsed Sattar's soul separating from his body, merging with Asyeh, and departing together. However, an invisible force restrained the silent beggar, rendering him motionless and muting his voice. A serene breeze enveloped him, drowning out the clamor of the roadside. "May God bless you, how blissful you must be to depart."

Then he began playing his harmonica. Meanwhile, there were no more sheep wandering on the road. The sheep lay lifeless on the ground, drenched in their own blood, yet their eyes remained open, fixated on the signboard. The sign read: "Congratulations to the Imam." It seemed that their companions had forgotten about them, engrossed in approaching the Imam to kiss his hand and feet, so as not to miss out on his blessings. Other musical instruments joined the drums and trumpets once again as if the arrival of their Imam had granted permission, and the resounding music reached several villages beyond. The fervor of kissing hands, feet, showering flattery, and offering compliments to their Imam, combined with their chanting and dancing, reached its peak, erasing any memory of the date. Mullah Mahmoud was astounded and bewildered, witnessing the reception bestowed upon the now Imam Asghari, seeing how Asghar, once a rootless murderer and swindler, had overnight become an Imam. Mullah Mahmud seethed with anger, mostly at himself, contemplating the creature he had unknowingly nurtured. He was so consumed by fury that he lost track of his surroundings. In a state of shock and astonishment, he observed his counterfeit Imam standing before him, awaiting the gesture of respect, but Mullah Mahmud did not budge; he glared at him, burning with anger inside. Of course, Asghar was no better than Mullah Mahmud. He, too, was taken aback by the unfolding events. He never imagined that people would be so naïve and gullible. However, he remained cautious, maintaining his silence, and lowering his head, ensuring his eyes would not meet anyone else's, fearing they might recognize him. Finally, Mullah Mahmoud turned angrily to the musicians playing the instruments and shouted, "Oh, you godless nonbelievers! It appears you have mistaken this gathering for a wedding. Cease the music!" With Mullah Mahmoud's outburst, the instruments fell silent. "AShaykh," he continued, addressing the Imam, "they are not playing for mere pleasure or a wedding celebration, as it is forbidden in our religion. They are rejoicing in their faith. Let them continue."

Now, for the first time, the people heard the voice of their own Imam, Imam Asghari. They were delighted by his speech, prompting an immediate and joyous response. The sound of the musical instrument resumed, growing louder with each passing moment. Imam Asghari's words, spoken over Mullah Mahmoud's, resonated deeply with the people, who greatly appreciated his interpretation. For the first time, they disregarded Mullah Mahmud and instead followed their new Imam. Mullah Mahmud realized he had lost control and considered revealing the true identity of their Imam, but inexplicably, he lacked the courage to do so. Perhaps it was because he would have to confess to deceiving the people, admitting that everything had been a lie orchestrated by him to exploit their beliefs. Consumed by anger and confusion, he was emotionally numb, impervious to pain or bleeding, as if stabbed.

The situation continued to worsen for Mullah Mahmud. Observing his distraction and distress, Haji Ghazanfar seized the opportunity to provoke him further. With a broad smile, he loudly addressed Imam Asghari, ensuring Mullah Mahmud would hear. "Our esteemed Imam, it appears Mullah Mahmoud is so overjoyed and awestruck by your arrival that he is rendered speechless and motionless. If he could, he would dismount his donkey and offer it to you."

Hearing Haji Ghazanfar's words, Mard Ali echoed them, as was his habit. "Haji speaks the truth! Come down from the donkey, Mullah Haji. Let the Imam take your place. Don't you realize the Imam is above you? Haji is perplexed."

Encouraged by Haji Ghazanfar and Mard Ali, a few individuals who had silently disapproved of Mullah Mahmud but lacked the courage to express it, now found their voice. They approached Mullah Mahmud and requested that he step down from his donkey, allowing the Imam to take his rightful place. However, Mullah Mahmud remained motionless, displaying no reaction. Seizing the opportunity, the enthusiastic supporters of the new Imam wasted no time. In the presence of Mullah Mahmoud's astonished gaze, they lifted him from his donkey and respectfully installed Imam Asghari in his stead, showering him with honor, respect, and blessings. Mullah Mahmud was so disoriented and bewildered that he failed to hear the voice of Haji Ghazanfar, who, elated by Mullah Mahmoud's removal, raised his voice once again, this time even louder. "Imam, the people eagerly await your blessings. Let us proceed to the mosque, where they long to witness your grace."

Then Haji Ghazanfar turned to the people and commanded them to move. Immediately, a few guards began to guide the donkey towards the village and the village mosque, followed by a congregation of people offering greetings and blessings. They rushed and competed to be closer to their Imam, shouting their prayers louder than others. Imam Asghari took the saddle from Mulla Mahmud, who had held it for over seventy years and left him standing alone. Some individuals carried the sheep carcasses on their donkeys to the village for cooking and feeding the people. They rode past Mulla Mahmud, seemingly oblivious to his presence. The blood from the headless necks of the sheep carcasses continued to drip onto the ground. Soon, only Mullah Mahmoud remained, along with a sign welcoming the Imam. With Imam Asghari's arrival, the people no longer recognized their old Clergyman of seventy years, Mulla Mahmud. If one were to stab Mullah Mahmoud, he wouldn't bleed. He longed to cry but found himself motionless, speechless, and powerless.

"Shaykh, whatever befalls a person, he himself is responsible. As they say, when a new cloth arrives in the market, the old one becomes less desirable and is thrown away in the garbage... it's heartbreaking."

Mulla Mahmud could see Zulfiqar walking calmly behind the crowd until he reached and stopped near him. He heard Zulfiqar's voice and stared at him as he continued walking after the crowd towards the village. Mulla Mahmud was now the only soul remaining. However, Zulfiqar's words of wisdom and advice didn't bring comfort to Mullah Mahmud; they only plunged a more poisonous dagger into his wounded heart and soul.

Finally, Mard Ali's voice emerged. He had returned and noticed Mullah Mahmud standing alone. He shouted towards the departed crowd, "What about Mullah Mahmoud? Did your godless people leave him behind? If he is no longer considered human..., is it not a sin to abandon him?"

"These people? Is it a sin for them to acknowledge his presence?"

Then Mard Ali returned and rushed towards Mullah Mahmud. "These people, Mulla... they lack faith... they have completely forgotten about you... let's go, Mulla."

Mullah Mahmud, who had no expectations and couldn't fathom that Mard Ali, whom everyone deemed crazy, was the only one who remembered him, was so shocked that he didn't even realize Mard Ali had taken his hand and was leading him away.

* * * * *

A black crow soared through the village, its piercing cries capturing the attention of the residents. It eventually perched on a white mulberry tree standing proudly within the mosque courtyard. These white mulberry trees held significance in Islamic religious practices and were commonly found near mosques and religious gathering places. Despite the crow's persistent cries, it seemed as though its important message went unheard. Instead, a few individuals responded by throwing stones in an attempt to drive it away. Left with no choice, the crow reluctantly flew off, avoiding further insults and threats.

Meanwhile, an extraordinary ceremony was taking place inside the mosque led by Imam Asghari. It was an event that the village had never witnessed before. The Imam's sermon captivated the audience gathered in the courtyard and spilled out into the alleys surrounding the mosque. His words seemed to carry great weight, even to the extent that he singled out

Mullah Mahmoud, a renowned orator and speaker in the area. Mullah Mahmoud was astounded by what he witnessed. Although he recognized that Imam Asghari was utilizing the same techniques and rhetoric as many other mullahs, including himself, there was no denying the Imam's exceptional skill. Mullah Mahmoud couldn't help but acknowledge that Imam Asghari surpassed him in every aspect.

Imam Asghari's preaching followed a familiar theme, yet he excelled at it like no other. He even managed to evoke genuine emotions in Mullah Mahmoud, compelling him to shed tears alongside the rest of the congregation. Mullah Mahmoud knew deep down that the stories they were telling were fabricated and used to manipulate people's emotions, perpetuated by the organized religious institutions to maintain control, and exploit the masses. However, as he listened to Imam Asghari's compelling narratives, even Mullah Mahmoud himself began to believe them. It dawned on him that with the arrival of this charismatic imam, his own influence would wane and his time in the spotlight would come to an end.

The village had flocked to witness Imam Asghari, bringing him directly to the mosque with unwavering devotion. The entire community gathered inside and outside the mosque, eagerly awaiting the voice of their revered Imam. It was a sight that Mullah Mahmoud had never imagined or thought possible.

The crow reappeared; this time accompanied by its companion. Their growls were so piercing that even the blind and deaf could not help but notice, urging them to open their eyes and ears to heed the warning. However, it seemed that nobody possessed an open mind or the willingness to perceive the truth. Instead, the number of attackers multiplied, hurling stones and spewing insults. Regrettably, the crows realized that the people were just as blind and deaf to their attempts to reveal the truth, and in their frustration, they claimed the lives of a few more sheep, a sacrifice to their false Imam.

Meanwhile, behind the mosque, a flurry of activity ensued as many worked tirelessly to prepare food, aiming to provide sustenance for several villages. Among the chaos, Zulfiqar sat patiently, a few yards away, waiting for his turn to be fed. His ears were keen, capturing every sound within a hundred-yard radius. And for the first time, he witnessed tears welling up in Imam Asghari's eyes, his voice quivering with emotion.

Eventually, the ceremony concluded, and the crowd eagerly vied to bring Imam Asghari to their homes. Haji Ghazanfar also yearned to host the Imam and had promised three sheep to capture his attention. However, Imam Asghari, aware of the circumstances, chose to stay with Mullah Mahmud. He expressed his desire to spend a few days alone with him, granting Mullah Mahmud the joy of hosting him. To ensure their Imam's safety, the bullies of the village surrounded Mullah Mahmud's house, guarding its front and sides.

From the moment Imam Asghari entered Mullah Mahmud's house, groups of people from the village gathered, patiently waiting, and wandering around for hours. They hoped to catch a glimpse of their beloved Imam at the window, if only for a fleeting moment, to experience a surge of happiness and perhaps find their path to paradise by beholding his countenance.

* * * * *

Although the crow had not been able to communicate the game played by Mulla Mahmud and the fake Imam to the deaf, blind, and mentally disabled people of Village Shourcheh, a large flock of sparrows had gathered over the hill above the village. They congregated around Sattar's hut, both inside and around the mulberry tree, creating a joyous atmosphere with their songs accompanied by the melodies of a harmonica played by the silent beggar. This gathering served as a celebration of life and a farewell to Sattar, who had embarked on his eternal journey.

Throughout the silent beggar's solemn task of digging Sattar's grave, cleaning his body, and dressing him in fresh clothes, the sparrows never ceased their flight and song. They remained devoted to the silent beggar, not leaving his side even for a moment. Several days had passed since Sattar's burial next to Asyeh. Finally, the silent beggar sat on their grave and played his harmonica, seeking solace for the departed souls of Sattar and Asyeh. The sparrows joined him, harmonizing their melodies with the gentle notes of the old harmonica.

Although a couple of crows perched on the surrounding trees, they did not sing like the sparrows, nor did they emit any mournful cries. It appeared as though they had no sorrowful news to share with the silent beggar. Instead, they seemed to mourn in silence, paying their respects to Sattar's memory.

* * * * *

Chapter 6
When the prescribed drug itself becomes the cause of the doctor's demise...

The dancing and radiant sun, accompanied by the gentle caress of the wind, breathed new life into the village, banishing the chill of winter and infusing it with vibrant colors and an uplifting atmosphere. During the cold and snowy days, people sought refuge in their homes, rarely venturing out into the alleys. However, with the return of the warm sun and the gentle breeze, nature came alive, and so did the villagers. The birds, invigorated by the rising sun, frolicked among the branches, filling the air with joyful melodies that celebrated life.

Yet, amidst this rejuvenation, a peculiar presence disrupted the tranquility. A multitude of black crows encircled the trees and perched on the rooftops near Mullah Mahmoud's house, their raucous calls disturbing the serenity. It seemed as though the crows were determined to reveal a hidden truth, relentlessly attempting to awaken the slumbering villagers of Shourcheh to the schemes orchestrated by Mullah Mahmoud and Asghar. Their purpose: to expose the true nature of their newly appointed Imam, Asghari.

The choice of the trees and rooftops surrounding Mullah Mahmoud's house by the crows was deliberate and straightforward. Asghar, now known as Imam Asghari, had taken up residence in Mullah Mahmoud's abode. Days after his arrival, groups of people continued to flock to the house, seeking blessings and favor from the Imam. However, only a select few were granted permission to enter and catch a glimpse of their revered leader. Secluded in a spacious room, the Imam remained distant from visitors, his gaze fixated on the ground, avoiding direct eye contact, and seldom uttering a word.

Nevertheless, the Imam would make occasional appearances at the center of the tall window in Mullah Mahmoud's house. With a wave of his hand, he blessed the masses gathered outside, prompting a chorus of greetings and prayers that reverberated for miles. Some fortunate individuals, privileged enough to be in his presence or have connections or means to donate, found solace in serving Imam Asghari, briefly kissing his hands, feet, and even his garments, claiming that their touch emitted a divine fragrance. They believed that the very air in the room carried a heavenly scent, evident the moment they entered.

Unbeknownst to them, every morning and sporadically throughout the day, the Imam's clothing was discreetly sprayed with fragrant substances. As always, there was a competition among devotees to bring the most impressive gifts or make substantial donations. Upon leaving Mullah Mahmoud's house after their encounter with the Imam, these individuals were consumed by an overwhelming sense of pride, an inflated ego that surpassed that of an entire army regiment. Their chants and the newfound vitality on their faces became a testament to their self-importance.

But what the people did not know was that behind closed doors, while they were busy with their work, a hidden war of politics and deceit was raging inside Mullah Mahmud's house between Imam Asghari and Mullah Mahmud. Asghar, who used to be Mahmud's subordinate, now commanded more attention, pushing Mahmud to the brink of madness. Overwhelmed by jealousy, Mahmud found himself reduced to obeying Asghar's orders in front of the people. He had become insignificant in their eyes, while Asghar had become the revered Imam. This sudden reversal of roles was unbearable for Mahmud to accept.

The most agonizing part was that Mahmud had brought this situation upon himself. He felt so isolated that nobody cared to listen to him or pay attention to his words. He couldn't voice his thoughts, trapped in his own misery. Every passing moment filled Mahmud with increasing anger, eroding his patience and endurance. The empire he had meticulously built over the years was now destroyed, leaving him in a state of madness. Sleep and food became elusive, as the people's indifference added to his suffering.

Yet, it was not just the people's disregard that troubled Mahmud; it was also Asghar's actions and ruthlessness that pierced his heart. This pain was even more poisonous than the people's behavior. It tormented him deeply.

To make matters worse, Asghar genuinely believed he was the true Imam, oblivious to the fact that Mahmud had orchestrated the entire scheme to present him as the Imam's representative, only to be usurped overnight. Asghar no longer cared about Mahmud. Furthermore, Mahmud's daughter, Leila, had fallen in love with Imam Asghari. If Mahmud ever dared to object to Asghar, Leila would silence him. She, too, had been captivated by Asghar's charisma and considered him the rightful Imam, seeing herself as his wife.

The most agonizing realization for Mahmud was that he was responsible for all the misfortunes befalling him. His years of deception had finally caught up with him, suffocating him. He had created a monster that he didn't know how to eliminate. The poison he had once administered to the people was now gradually consuming him from within.

Therefore, as soon as Mullah Mahmoud's house was empty, his voice rose, reminding Asghar of his identity as Mulla Mahmud's loyal servant. He emphasized that he had elevated Asghar to his current position, providing guidance on what to do, what not to do, what to say, and what not to say. Mullah Mahmud threatened Asghar, warning him that if he failed to listen, act according to his wishes, and prioritize Mulla Mahmud's desires, he would expose Asghar's true nature to the public. This would result in the downfall of Asghar's authority and the destruction of the empire he had built with Mulla Mahmud's help. However, Mullah Mahmud soon realized his threats fell on deaf ears. He understood that his attempts to manipulate and intimidate Asghar were futile. Mulla Mahmud knew that if he were to expose Asghar's true identity, he would only be exposing his own lies and manipulations to the people. This would lead to his own exile from the village. Therefore, Mulla Mahmud had no choice but to stick to his plan, waiting for the right opportunity to assert his control over Asghar and reclaim his position of power. However, Asghar remained unfazed by Mulla Mahmud's threats, especially considering his alliance with Mulla Mahmud's daughter, his own wife. The two individuals, both cunning and strategic, had their own plans in place, ready to strike at the opportune moment. Asghar knew that sooner or later, Mulla Mahmud might lose his patience and reveal Asghar's true identity to the public. Therefore, he understood the urgency of eliminating Mulla Mahmud from the equation. Asghar convened a meeting with a select few of his men who had now aligned themselves with him, recognizing that their best opportunity lay with Asghar rather than Mulla Mahmud. Together, they shared their thoughts and devised a plan to rid themselves of the man who had once been their leader, Mulla Mahmud.

Their plan consisted of a few steps. Asghar knew that the first step was to officially marry Leila, Mulla Mahmud's daughter, in order to bring her to his side. He successfully accomplished this and they publicly announced their marriage, portraying Leila as the respected wife of the Imam. Furthermore, Asghari understood the importance of having Zulfiqar and Mard Ali on his side. Recognizing their ability to spread rumors and his message throughout the village, he took great care of them, to the point where they seemed to have forgotten or no longer recognized Mulla Mahmud.

The second part of the plan was for Asghari to distance himself from Mulla Mahmud, as long as the people still accepted him as their Imam. He needed to seize every opportunity to establish his independence and gradually break away. He realized there was a chance that his true identity might be revealed, so he made sure to secure his financial stability. If that day ever arrived, he intended to escape with enough wealth to live a comfortable and pleasurable life.

Therefore, the plan was to inform the people, during their visits, that there was a representative of the Imam from the holy city of Mecca. Being in Mulla Mahmud's house would be an insult to Islam and the representative. It was imperative to prepare a proper place for their Imam before the arrival of the representative from Mecca.

With the plan in motion, one day a few people had the opportunity to visit their Imam. If anyone had any questions, Imam Asghari, as always, had answers to satisfy them. In case of any doubts or skepticism, one or two individuals present, who were loyal to the Imam, would immediately dismiss the doubter as a non-Muslim or someone against religion. They would silence and, at times, even remove the person from the room. Additionally, those who questioned or protested privately would face attacks and harm from Asghari's hired men, ensuring that no one dared to express doubt openly. The situation escalated to the point where, even in broad daylight, if the Imam claimed it was nighttime, no one would dare to contradict him.

One day, a group of individuals gathered around Imam Asghari. Some of them began suggesting that the Imam should meet and bless more people, claiming that there were individuals eager to see him, kiss his hand, and seek his blessings. They proposed that he should leave the house and visit the villagers to bring them happiness. Among those present was Haji Ghazanfar, who had become a devoted supporter of Imam Asghari. However, his support stemmed not from his belief in the Imam or Islam, but rather from his desire to torment Mulla Mahmud. Zulfiqar and Mard Ali were also invited to be in the presence of the Imam, as they were known to spread news throughout the village. When the suggestion arose for the Imam to venture outside, he remained silent, leaving the people puzzled. Unbeknownst to them, the Imam's confidant discreetly whispered to Haji Ghazanfar, "Haji, as a respected and trusted figure in the village, you should be aware that the Imam has received information about one or two individuals from Mecca and Medina who are en route to visit him. The Imam is hesitant to receive them at Mulla Mahmud's house."

Haji Ghazanfar's gaze shifted towards Mulla Mahmud, who sat next to Imam Asghari, smoking a hookah. Then, turning his head closer to Haji Ghazanfar, the confidant continued manipulating and persuading him, "Haji, you know very well that Mulla Mahmud is no longer of sound mind. There is a possibility that he might disrespect the esteemed representative of the Imam of all imams, who is soon to arrive from Mecca. Such an act would not only insult the people of Shourcheh and tarnish the reputation of our village but also reflect poorly on you, the respected leader of the village. It is clear who holds authority here, Haji Ghazanfar, for you are now the elder and master of the village."

Before the message from Imam Asghari could be conveyed in its entirety, Haji Ghazanfar spoke up, his voice raised, "Imam, I am amazed that you kept the greatest news of all time hidden from us. This is the most sacred honor for us, the villagers, and they must be informed that the representative of the Imam of all imams is on his way to see you. It demonstrates the holiness and respect that surrounds you. Therefore, such significant news should not be concealed from the people. We must ensure that you are transferred to a more suitable and dignified place before the representative of the Imam of all imams from Mecca arrives. After all, he is a guest of the Imam and the village of Shourcheh. Your reputation is intertwined with that of our village, Shourcheh."

One or two others immediately snatched the ball from Haji Ghazanfar because they didn't want to lag behind. Haji Ghazanfar had spread a piece of flattering news, and these individuals wanted to demonstrate their honesty and loyalty to Imam Asghari by expressing their flattery and agreement with Hajji Ghazanfar. Now, everyone had an opinion, and all the flattery was in favor of Imam Asghari. A few suggested raising funds to build a court for Imam Asghari and made similar proposals. However, it didn't take long for the parliament to grapple with the differing views on how to support their Imams.

Amidst all this, Mullah Mahmoud, who remained unaware of Asghar's new politics and hypocrisy, observed silently, patiently waiting to learn about it later when everyone had left. At the same time, Imam Asghari continued to gaze at the ground silently, awaiting the outcome of the people's debate. Throughout this time, Zulfiqar squatted at the entrance of the room, maintaining silence. As usual, his head was held high, his ears sharper than ever, listening attentively, while his mouth moved as he ate. Nothing could escape Zulfiqar's ears; it was as if he had many open eyes, able to see everyone and everything.

The people had not yet reached a resolution, and the dispute on what to do and what not to do persisted. The verbal war between them escalated, and no one's comments or suggestions had been accepted. It was in this heated moment that Mard Ali's voice rose. "Why are you shouting so much? This is very simple... Why don't you crazy people think properly? Why not settle him in Kal Abbas's old mansion? No one lives there except mice and fleas. It's also spacious... Just remove the mice and beetles, and let the Imam reside there. Don't you people have brains? It also has large stalls where many donkeys and cows can be accommodated, and the whole village can visit."

As always, some took Mard Ali's comment as an insult towards the Imam, and he was harshly attacked from behind. Mard Ali swiftly got up and chose to run away, but he hadn't stopped speaking yet. "Oh, did I say something blasphemous? Well, I didn't lie. Its stables are large enough to accommodate the entire village if they come to see the Imam... You can all fit in there."

Mard Ali was forcefully removed from the room, but his impassioned speech had a profound impact on the parliament, leaving them all speechless. All eyes turned to Imam Asghari, curious about his suggestion and intrigued by Mard Ali's ideas. Surprisingly, it seemed that everyone suddenly found themselves in agreement with Mard Ali.

Imam Asghari raised his head, casting a brief glance at Haji Ghazanfar before averting his gaze. In a hushed tone, he whispered his thoughts to him, with only Haji Ghazanfar able to hear. The room fell into a deep silence as they awaited their Imam's decision, desperate to know the contents of his whispered words.

Mulla Mahmud, however, despised witnessing this secretive exchange between Asghari and Haji Ghazanfar, growing increasingly uneasy about their concealed conversation.

* * * * *

A day had passed since the meeting at Mullah Mahmoud's house, where Mard Ali had suggested that Imam seize Kala Abbas's old mansion. The sun shone brightly on the village, casting its light through the branches of the mulberry tree inside the mosque. The cawing of a few black crows could be heard, their calls muffled by the sounds within and outside the mosque's courtyard. In a corner of the yard, the ragged old man sat alone, deep in thought, cigarette in hand. His mind wandered everywhere except to the activities inside the mosque. No one else seemed to notice or care about the crows, nor did they throw stones or curse at them. The people had become so engrossed in Imam Asghari's nonsensical preaching and lies that they appeared oblivious and lost, as if they had forgotten who they were.

Mullah Mahmoud sat on the platform, delivering his sermon. This time, he was pleased that Imam Asghari had entrusted him with a mission and an opportunity to address the people. For a few hours, he enjoyed their respect and adoration as they eagerly awaited the announcement he was meant to make. However, he took his time, intentionally making them wait, and indulged in speaking nonsense. "I wonder why our Supreme Leader, Ayatollah, hasn't come himself," he pondered aloud.

Meanwhile, within the mosque's yard, the ragged old man continued to be lost in his thoughts, smoking his cigarette. It seemed he was the only one who had no interest in listening to Mullah Mahmoud's words or had purposefully blocked out his voice. As Mullah Mahmoud grew more fervent, the old man muttered to himself, "I still don't understand who these Mulla are. Are they mullahs? Shaykhs? Ayatollahs? Supreme leaders? Or perhaps they will soon claim to be God Himself?"

Before the old man could finish his question, one of the two zealous supporters of Imam Asghari interrupted and rebuked him, saying, "Oh, your godless old man and faithless non-Muslims, you should be ashamed! Do you not know that insulting the Imam is punishable by death? If you are not a Muslim, we are."

Just then, the sound of fervent prayers erupted from inside the mosque, and the voices outside joined in the chorus. The name of Imam Asghari was added to their prayers, and the people began pouring out of the mosque, shouting, "Allah Akbar! Imam Asghari is our leader!" In the blink of an eye, everyone had left, except for the ragged old man, who remained lost among the unheeding masses. It was as if he were invisible or didn't belong to the village of Shourcheh at all.

As Imam Asghari exited the mosque, in a flash, everyone followed him, leaving the elderly ragged man alone in the mosque's courtyard. He wondered where they were going and what their beloved Imam Asghari had planned for them. Soon after, he realized he wasn't the only one left behind. Mulla Mahmud emerged from the mosque, speechless, and passed by the older ragged man without a word, leaving him to his solitude. The elderly man pondered the unpredictable nature of life, witnessing Mulla Mahmud, who was once a powerful figure and desired by the people, become insignificant within a few days of Imam Asghari's arrival. It seemed as if nobody recognized or acknowledged him anymore.

As Mulla Mahmud wandered alone through the alleys outside the mosque, consumed by anger and frustration, he could hear the resounding cries of the people proclaiming, "Allah Ho Akbar... Imam Asghari is the leader." Despite his rage, he felt powerless and unable to change the situation. It suddenly dawned on him that he had lost his position of authority and control.

Meanwhile, a few blocks away, people eagerly pursued their Imam Asghari, unaware of their destination. They fervently chanted, "Allah Ho Akbar... Imam Asghari is the leader," as if echoing the Imam's own plan.

The clamor of the crowd disturbed the peaceful harmony of the birds, which had always brought tranquility with their melodious songs. The sparrows, sensing the disturbance, rose from the branches and distanced themselves from the tumultuous crowd. They refused to be part of or witness such unwarranted and unjust actions by humans. However, a group of black crows flew ahead of the crowd, perching on tree branches and rooftops, continuing their raucous cawing. As the crowd approached, they took flight again, only to land a few hundred yards away and repeat their game. Their cawing grew louder and more persistent. It remained unclear whether the crows were guiding the crowd's direction, protesting their actions, or attempting to convey a message of truth, urging people not to blindly follow Imam Asghari's will in order to please their Imams. They exposed the deceptive shepherd who led them astray. Whatever their motive, the crows persisted in their task, observing as more people emerged from their homes and rushed from all directions to join Imam Asghari and the crowd. Before reaching the crowd, they too began to chant, "Allah Ho Akbar... Imam Asghari, the leader." A competition arose, with everyone vying to shout the loudest slogan to demonstrate their devotion to Imam Asghari. Except for a few individuals dependent on

Imam Asghari's provisions, most of the newcomers were clueless about their destination and the purpose behind it all.

It appeared as though the crows possessed a greater understanding than Imam Asghari's soldiers. They seemed to be attempting to reveal the true intentions of the self-proclaimed Imams and the soldiers of the faith. Their intention was no different from that of a cunning fox. They wanted the people to realize that they were blindly following a fox, just like a flock of sheep following the Shepherd and his herding dogs. Unfortunately, their efforts were in vain. The people neither listened nor observed. It was as if every one of them was both deaf and blind.

Despite the crows' persistent attempts to deliver their message, the people remained oblivious. The crows cried out, desperately hoping to awaken those who were blindly following the fox, even if it disguised itself as a Shepherd. However, the people's senses and intellect were blocked, preventing them from hearing the crows' cries. Regardless of how loud and impassioned the crows became, their efforts were futile. They could only watch as these ignorant individuals followed a fox, lacking the insight, sight, understanding, or awareness to perceive the truth. Yet, they held an unwarranted sense of self-satisfaction, believing themselves to possess superior intellect, while their ego soared.

Simultaneously, they behaved like a flock of sheep that mindlessly followed the learned black goats. They stood obediently in front of the herd, ready to be directed by the shepherd's wooden stick and the herding dogs circling them. They would follow wherever they were led. If any of them made an independent choice or strayed even slightly from the shepherd's intentions, the shepherd would summon his wild and ferocious dogs to regain control. These people would grow fat enough to be slaughtered for their meat, filling the shepherd's stomach, while their fat and bones would be fed to the herding dogs. It was disheartening to witness that Imam Asghari played the role of the shepherd, his followers were the obedient dogs, and the people were mere sheep.

Observing Imam Asghari's treatment of these individuals, it became clear that anyone who dared question his will would be punished and intimidated by his hired henchmen. They would go as far as branding them as godless atheists and enemies of Islam and God, asserting that they must be punished. Fear would be instilled in their naive hearts, convincing them that failure to follow blindly would result in eternal damnation in Hell. Consequently, they remained obedient, much like sheep in a flock. Astonishingly, they claimed to act in the name of Islam and for the will of God. The sorrowful reality was that these individuals, possessing their own senses and intellect, failed to comprehend that if the entire flock united against the shepherd and his few wild dogs, their collective will would overpower them, leading to their eventual liberation.

The crows' thoughts, regrets, and longings lingered among the herdsmen as the crowd reached the alley where the old Kal Abbas's mansion stood. As they approached, Imam Asghari's men, who were already aware of their destination, began scaling the mansion's walls. Soon, the door swung open, and they stormed into the mansion, loudly invoking prayers to seek divine permission for their seizure of someone else's property—claiming it was justified by the law.

It was at this moment that the followers of Imam Asghari comprehended the nature of their mission. Without questioning, they joined his paid staff and set to work repairing and preparing Kal Abbas's long-abandoned mansion, which had been home to rodents and overgrown with wild weeds for years. Their relentless chant of "Allah Ho Akbar... Imam Asghari is the Imam..." echoed continuously. Throughout the mission, Mard Ali remained with them, passionately engaging in his own war dance and war chants to entertain Imam Asghari's soldiers, fully engrossed in his own world.

Nightfall brought the discussion of religious donations and zakat, the religious tax, to support Imam Asghari and fulfill God's will. Naturally, Mard Ali, caught up in his act, began echoing the Imam's words. Under the guise of religious duty, they took possession of Kal Abbas's mansion, turning it into Imam Asghari's residence. Although Zulfiqar occasionally felt skeptical, particularly regarding the appropriation of Kal Abbas's mansion—someone who had helped him in the past when he was young, needy, and unmarried—he recognized the need to stand united with the villagers, as he relied on their support, especially now that he was married.

In just one or two days, Imam Asghari's new court was ready, marking the promised day for his transfer from Mullah Mahmoud's house to the stolen mansion of Kal Abbas. The entire village, young and old, men and women, poured out to be with their beloved Imam. All work in the village came to a halt as they rallied around him. Religious trumpets blared, drummers played, and even the musicians, previously banned from playing at religious ceremonies, were allowed this time.

It seemed that this time the religious ceremony had transformed into something resembling a wedding party. The solemn religious rituals and fervent prayers had become intertwined with the lively atmosphere. The clamor of the crowd, shouting "Allah Oh Akbar... Imam Asghari the leader," mingled with the sounds of religious and wedding instruments, echoing for miles as the masses escorted their Imam Asghari to his new court.

There was an intense competition among the people, each vying for a chance to approach their beloved Imam, hoping for a stroke of luck to kiss his hands and feet or even touch his garments. Even the blind Zulfiqar was astonished and taken aback by the fervor. Mard Ali, too, used his stick to play his part, occasionally joining other men in clearing the path for their Imam and sweeping the road in front of the donkey that carried him, using his wooden staff.

Rose water was sprinkled upon everyone's heads, and the villagers offered special fruit syrup and water to the masses as they passed by. Hard candies were thrown over the head of their Imam, sparking a spirited competition among the children to collect them as they fell to the ground. Imam Asghari, seated atop a black donkey adorned with a large green cloth, reached out and placed his hand on the heads of the people, as was his custom, imparting his blessings. Some even lifted their babies up towards him, seeking his touch for their little ones.

Throughout the entire procession, however, Imam Asghari's gaze remained fixed upon the ground, devoid of any signs of laughter or emotion.

Finally, the multitude reached Kal Abbas's old mansion, which had been adorned even more splendidly than before by the Imam's followers and volunteers, continuing their prayers, music, and chants. And at long last, Imam Asghari entered his new usurped court, taking his place in the forty-room chamber of Kal Abbas's mansion. The room was dubbed the "Forty-One" because it boasted forty-two French windows, each with a balcony that could accommodate two or three individuals. The main room itself could hold up to five hundred people.

Kal Abbas's mansion had undergone an astonishing transformation, having been renovated and adorned within a remarkably short period of time. The floors were now adorned with vibrant and luxurious Persian rugs, while the walls were covered with Persian tapestries. Even several stables in the fifty-thousand-square-foot yard housed cows, goats, sheep, donkeys, mules, as well as numerous chickens and roosters. All of this was made possible through the donations, known as zakat, primarily contributed by the unfortunate and impoverished class who struggled to provide for their own families. Despite their own hardships, they possessed pure hearts and good intentions, believing that by doing so, they could secure their place in God's heavenly abode.

Sitting in his luxurious new mansion, Asghar couldn't believe the dramatic turn his life had taken. Having endured a lifetime of misery, displacement, theft, murder, and evading the law under various aliases, he now found himself as the Imam of the Muslims, and the owner of the once coveted property that belonged to the village's wealthiest and most powerful man, Kal Abbas. It was a dream come true, one that he never thought possible, achieved through manipulation and exploiting people's religious beliefs. Now, he held control over both the people and the village, solely by exploiting their faith.

Asghar couldn't help but reflect on his past, when he was known as Asghar Bogundo, a young man with a foul odor, working as one of Mullah Mahmud's henchmen. He was infamous for his involvement in gruesome murders, including burning two individuals alive and mercilessly killing his partner. Deception and harm were all he knew, yet now he found himself in the position of being the most trusted Imam among over two billion Muslims, all because of his ability to deceive and manipulate.

Proud of his achievements, Asghar was constantly on edge, fearing that his true identity would be exposed, and he would lose everything he had gained. His wife, Leila, the daughter of Mullah Mahmud, entered the room, calling his name. At that moment, fear gripped Asghar, worrying that he might lose his newfound power and face the wrath of the people who would discover his true nature.

As he looked at Leila, all he could see was a reminder of Mullah Mahmud and the potential threat he posed. As far as Asghar knew, the only individuals aware of his dark past were Leila and Mullah Mahmud. While he had control over Leila, knowing she was just as unscrupulous and determined to protect her own interests, he feared that Mullah Mahmud's jealousy and madness would eventually drive him to expose Asghar's true identity. This concern intensified, particularly as Mullah Mahmud grew older, sometimes losing his grip on reality.

Imam Asghar now considered Mullah Mahmud, who had lifted him from obscurity to greatness, as his primary adversary. With a sense of urgency, he immediately set out to devise a plan to eliminate Mullah Mahmud, regardless of the cost or consequences it would entail.

To execute his plan, he welcomed Mullah Mahmud into his house with utmost dignity and respect, employing flattery to gain his trust. Unbeknownst to Mullah Mahmud, he orchestrated a village-wide rumor, suggesting that Mullah Mahmoud had dreamt of his own demise. This fabricated tale served as the pretext for escorting him to the Imam's house and his daughter's residence, where he could find solace.

After a week or two, Mullah Mahmoud found himself seated on a cushion near the window, leaning against the bed and clutching a hookah. From the adjacent room, the Imam, Asghari, entered with a bowl to his lips, seemingly relishing ginger syrup. However, Mullah Mahmoud failed to perceive that the bowl was only half-full and the syrup never even grazed Asghari's lips—he merely feigned the act of drinking. Before Asghari could reach Mullah Mahmoud, the bowl was withdrawn from his lips, and with his other hand, he simulated the motion of wiping his moistened lips, pretending to have enjoyed the syrup. It was then that Mullah Mahmud unwittingly consumed the fatal sweet concoction. In those days, corpses were not subjected to forensic examination to detect potential poisoning, which allowed him to evade suspicion, particularly as Mullah Mahmud was elderly, prompting many to believe it was simply his time to depart. Even Leila, Mullah Mahmud's daughter, remained oblivious to the truth, shrouded in darkness.

Following Mullah Mahmoud's demise, Imam Asghari found himself in an unrivaled position of power. He plotted to eliminate the remaining individuals who possessed knowledge of his true identity, ensuring his peace of mind. With his political acumen, astuteness, and cunning akin to Mullah Mahmoud's, if not superior, he knew precisely how to proceed. Initially, he extended his benevolence to a few destitute men in the village, aiding them when they had nothing to their name. These individuals eventually became his trusted associates, acting as his enforcers to punish and silence those who opposed him, all the while concealing his involvement. Whenever someone dared to voice dissent or oppose Imam Asghari, they were promptly labeled as non-Muslims, and accused of insulting the Imam, Islam, and the Qur'an. This tarnished their reputation and provided a pretext for punishment, thus eliminating obstacles from the Imam's path.

Unlike Mullah Mahmoud, who consistently undermined Haji Ghazanfar in public, Imam Asghari held great respect for him, deliberately elevating his status in front of others. This tactic aimed to prevent any rebellion from Haji Ghazanfar, who remained unaware of Imam Asghari's true intentions. As anticipated, Haji Ghazanfar became a devoted disciple of Imam Asghari, and nobody dared to criticize or speak ill of Imam Asghari in his presence.

Importantly, Imam Asghari, a cunning manipulator, understood that as long as he maintained the support of a few influential individuals in the village, he would remain secure. He was also aware that keeping the law enforcement officials at a distance was crucial. He knew that if they arrived in the village, they would undoubtedly seek to learn about the new Imam, and his paid henchmen would be unable to attack, punish, or silence the law enforcement personnel.

Therefore, whenever conflicts or disputes arose among the villagers, Imam Asghari promptly intervened and resolved the issues, even if it meant offering substantial bribes to the parties involved, ensuring that the matter did not escalate to formal complaints and police involvement. On rare occasions when the police accidentally arrived in the village, Imam Asghari would feign absence, claiming to have traveled overnight to the holy city of Qom to confront Mullah Omar. Another time, he would leave the village, citing an invitation to lead prayers in a neighboring village.

During his absences, Haji Ghazanfar, and a few others, who were under Imam Asghari's influence, spoke highly of their Imam to the law enforcement officials, subsequently becoming followers and disciples themselves.

* * * * *

Chapter 7
When a blind man sees clearer than all others and hopes to liberate people from superstitions...

Some time had passed since Imam Asghari assumed the position of Imam presidency, and he began to manipulate the beliefs of the people and exploit their wealth for his own gain. Immersed in his new role, he even started to convince himself that he was the true Imam of the Muslims. However, among all the challenges Imam Asghari faced and successfully resolved, none proved more important or difficult than dealing with the issue of the forbidden area.

Every time people approached him, they would inquire about the presence of elves in the forbidden area, as if they believed their Imam possessed the power to confront and vanquish these creatures. It seemed that as soon as Imam Asghari arrived in the village of Shourcheh, luck was on his side. Coincidentally, Sattar's death coincided with his arrival, and with Sattar's passing, the haunting sound of reeds from the forbidden area ceased. This was enough for the people to attribute the silencing of the reeds to Imam Asghari's arrival and his spiritual power, suggesting that his closeness to God had caused this phenomenon.

Imam Asghari did not remain idle. Through his followers, he spread a rumor that he had prayed to God, specifically requesting the cessation of the reeds' sound, and that God had answered his prayer. They propagated this as one of Imam Asghari's miracles and a testament to his legitimacy. However, their plan backfired when people started to believe that Imam Asghari had the ability to eradicate the evil elves from the forbidden area once and for all, bringing peace and tranquility to their lives after many years. They yearned to travel at night without fear.

Despite the disappearance of the reeds' sound, people continued to confine themselves at night, fearing that the goblins had not truly vanished and could potentially invade the village. Consequently, requests poured in from the people, seeking help from Imam Asghari to permanently rid them of the goblins.

Imam Asghari was well aware that he had to keep people entertained from dawn till dusk and listen to their incessant requests, all of which revolved around the goblins in the forbidden area. He understood that no matter what occurred in the village, their daily plea remained the same and grew more fervent with each passing day. He also recognized that sooner or later, he would have to address the people's problem with the forbidden area; otherwise, they would lose faith in him, and he would risk losing his position.

In an attempt to divert people's attention from the forbidden area, Imam Asghari orchestrated various events and incidents, but his efforts proved futile. The only thing that occupied the minds of the people and their sole desire from their Imam was to witness one of his miracles, resulting in the eradication of the goblins from the forbidden area.

However, it was not easy for Imam Asghari. He was much more frightened by the goblins than by people, but he couldn't reveal this fear to anyone. After all, he claimed to be the Imam and had direct connections to God. It was believed that his miracles extended beyond just getting rid of the sound of the reeds; he should be able to rid the village of goblin attacks as well. However, his constant delays in addressing the people's requests and the different excuses he gave made some people doubt his ability to perform miracles or even question his true identity.

Even Mard Ali and Zulfiqar, who were strong believers in Imam Asghari's faith, occasionally had doubts. Mard Ali even accidentally referred to him as Asghar Bogundo, but he immediately retracted his words, fearing that the Imam's power might harm him. Despite these doubts, both Mard Ali and Zulfiqar continued to stand by Imam Asghari, enjoying the heavenly life he provided for them. They did not want to lose the comforts and blessings of being in the Imam's presence.

Imam Asghari had singled out Zulfiqar as one of his closest disciples and often referred to him as a man of God. However, Zulfiqar was unaware of the private agenda the Imam had for him. The Imam planned to encourage Zulfiqar to venture into the forbidden area, using his trust and admiration to manipulate him. He falsely claimed that the Muslim holy book, the Qur'an, stated that goblins and evil creatures would not harm a blind person. He assured Zulfiqar that he would be safe from harm.

Meanwhile, the villagers were so captivated by the presence of Imam Asghari that they had completely forgotten about the shepherd and his journey to the forbidden area. Shepherd Ali concluded that he no longer needed to fulfill his duties as the village shepherd or even speak about his experiences in the forbidden area. He chose to withdraw from the people and remain silent. People interpreted his silence in different ways. Some believed it was a result of him learning a lesson from his own lies and becoming a truthful man of God. Others thought that something significant must have happened to him in the forbidden area, causing him to fear speaking about it.

Time was passing, and the village had undergone noticeable changes since Imam Asghari's arrival. The villagers yearned for a miracle to rid themselves of the goblin menace. Little did they know that the game Imam Asghari had played with Zulfiqar was gradually starting to yield results. Zulfiqar found himself engaged in a mental debate, questioning whether Imam Asghari possessed valuable knowledge or if he was simply fabricating tales. He pondered the possibility that this could be a once-in-a-lifetime opportunity to seize and make the best of it. Determined not to fall short this time, Zulfiqar mustered the courage to venture into the forbidden area, aspiring to become the village's hero.

However, approaching Shepherd Ali for information proved more challenging than Zulfiqar had anticipated. Shepherd Ali remained silent, as if his voice had been muted, resembling the enigmatic beggar who resided in silence. Despite occasional disappointments, Zulfiqar refused to give up. It felt as though a persistent voice was whispering in his ear, urging him to embark on the forbidden journey. Consequently, day after day, for countless hours, Zulfiqar patiently awaited Shepherd Ali by the water creek. He would position himself near the spot where Shepherd Ali emerged from his house to collect fresh water and cleanse his hands and face. Each time Shepherd Ali appeared with a water jar in hand, Zulfiqar's voice would erupt with a barrage of questions, undeterred by silence or any lack of response.

Finally, Zulfiqar's unwavering determination paid off. Shepherd Ali broke his silence and turned to face Zulfiqar. "The people may perceive you as blind, but I believe they are the ones who truly lack vision. I see a brightness within you that far surpasses theirs. Blindness is not confined to the physical senses or the ability to discern colors. Mr. Zulfiqar, true enlightenment, and the ability to distinguish the truth stem from seeing with your mind, heart, and soul. That is why you persistently seek my attention, even when I ignore you. I am convinced that an unseen force is communicating with you, enticing you to explore the forbidden area and uncover the truth."

With those words, Shepherd Ali rose to depart but halted abruptly, turning back to face Zulfiqar. "And I am certain that, in due time, you will indeed fulfill that calling."

Then Shepherd Ali walked away and entered his house, leaving Zulfiqar alone with his head held high and his ears sharper than ever, still waiting to hear more from Shepherd Ali. It was as if he didn't realize that Ali had gone into his house and was no longer there. The words of Shepherd Ali had ingrained themselves so deeply in Zulfiqar's mind that from that moment on, all his thoughts and senses revolved around what he had heard from Ali about the forbidden area and the urge to explore it.

Zulfiqar stood up and set off aimlessly. Unbeknownst to himself, he soon found himself outside the village. He stopped at the cemetery, his head held high as usual, his ears open wide, and gazed at the nearby hills where the goblins resided, as well as the direction of the forbidden area. Taking a few steps towards the hills, he paused once more. Lost in his thoughts, he didn't even realize that he had arrived at Kal Akbar's house. Akbar, who usually sat on the platform in front of his house, observing everyone and engaging in jovial banter, noticed Zulfiqar's peculiar behavior. Wondering what had happened to him, Akbar kept a close eye on him.

For some unknown reason, that day Akbar decided to remain silent and refrained from starting a conversation or cracking jokes with Zulfiqar.

Instead, he observed him in confusion, curious about Zulfiqar's intentions. Even after Akbar's patience wore thin and he attempted to greet Zulfiqar jokingly, Zulfiqar remained so lost in his own world that he seemed oblivious to Akbar's voice. Akbar knew without a doubt that the Zulfiqar he was observing was not the same person he had known before. It was as if Zulfiqar existed in another realm, completely detached from this world, and lost in the unknown.

From that day forward, Zulfiqar would sit on a stone slab by the roadside near the cemetery, close to Kal Akbar's house, every day. He would stare at the adjacent hills, where the goblins resided, for hours on end. He neither spoke nor paid attention to anyone around him. His mind and senses were consumed by thoughts of the forbidden area and his determination to uncover the truth, becoming the hero of the village. Each day, he took a few steps closer to the forbidden area, but fear overwhelmed him, causing him to stop and find solace on another permanent stone slab, where he would continue to gaze at the hills. Nevertheless, with each passing day, he inched closer to the forbidden area.

Now, Kal Akbar had a singular responsibility: to sit on the platform in front of his house every day, fixating his eyes on Zulfiqar and meticulously calculating the number of steps Zulfiqar took and how close he came to the forbidden area. This newfound hobby and game delighted him immensely. His thoughts were consumed by a constant internal debate: would Zulfiqar ever summon the courage to venture into the forbidden territory? Such was his captivation with the game that he would stubbornly resist assistance and refuse to retire indoors even as darkness descended, persisting until Zulfiqar's return from the mosque at dawn.

It became evident that the story and grand spectacle of Zulfiqar's expeditions to the forbidden hills lacked excitement in the absence of Mard Ali. Mard Ali, too, would appear daily, occupying the stone board near Zulfiqar, infusing his presence with laughter and honeyed words, adding a distinct flavor to Zulfiqar's epic performance. His laughter resounded continually, growing louder with each passing day. "He is frightened! Zulfiqar is nothing but a coward. What are you waiting for, coward? Just go! Well, what do you have to say? What do you fear from those goblins? You cowardly fool, just go!"

Subsequently, Mard Ali would depart for the village, relishing his amusement as he rode his wooden horse, spreading news of Zulfiqar's daily exploits and the incremental steps he had taken towards the forbidden area throughout the village. Naturally, the followers of Imam Asghari would observe Zulfiqar from a distance, waiting for his return to the village, seizing the opportunity to engage in their game of encouragement, coaxing Zulfiqar to venture into the forbidden territory.

The story of Zulfiqar venturing into the forbidden area was quite the anecdote itself. There was no place where people wouldn't discuss it—whether it was in corner stores, the general store, or even the bathhouses. Zulfiqar's name was on everyone's lips, and conversations revolved around him. The discussions ranged from absences filled with laughter and jokes about Zulfiqar to the creation of their own stories. Some claimed that Zulfiqar was a goblin himself, consumed by their essence and no longer human. To add spice to their tales, they would even weave in Shepherd Ali, drawing parallels between the two. Playfully, anyone passing by Kal Akbar would jokingly inquire about how many steps Zulfiqar had taken that day, finding their answers from Kal Akbar himself.

As time went by, Zulfiqar's exploits lost their novelty in the Village of Shourcheh, disappointing the people who wondered why he hadn't ventured into the forbidden area yet. Gradually, the number of Zulfiqar's spectators dwindled. Only Kal Akbar and Mard Ali remained loyal to Agha Zulfiqar, faithfully coming to watch him every day. Additionally, Imam Asghari's men observed him from a distance. However, their wait was short-lived.

One day, Kal Akbar left his house earlier than usual, taking his seat on the platform and fixing his gaze on the stone board where Zulfiqar always sat, anticipating his arrival. However, Zulfiqar was nowhere to be seen. Kal Akbar contemplated whether Zulfiqar had given up and decided not to show up that day, or if he had already made his way to the forbidden area before Kal Akbar had even left his house. Despite his difficulty in moving, Kal Akbar managed to step out and search for Zulfiqar, but there was no trace of him. Instead, he noticed that Mard Ali, who had arrived early in the morning and occupied his usual spot, was also searching for Zulfiqar. Mard Ali's behavior indicated his discontent with Zulfiqar's absence, as his usual laughter had vanished from his face. "Cowardly coward scared and ran away," Mard Ali repeated constantly.

Just as Kal Akbar was about to fall asleep, he suddenly witnessed Mard Ali springing up, his hand pointing towards the village. A radiant smile lit up Mard Ali's face as if he had spotted something in the distance. Instantly, Kal Akbar's head leaned out of the platform, directed towards the village. To his astonishment, he saw Zulfiqar making his way, leaning on his cane. Joy engulfed Kal Akbar, and a rosy smile painted his face.

Zulfiqar, using his old cane, reached Kal Akbar, and passed by him without greeting, his head raised, fixated on the nearby hills where the forbidden area lay. Kal Akbar's greeting went unanswered as if his voice failed to reach Zulfiqar's ears. Confused, Kal Akbar watched as Zulfiqar walked past the cemetery, ignoring Mard Ali, who stood just a few feet away as if he were invisible. Zulfiqar continued towards the forbidden area, while tears of joy welled up in Mard Ali's eyes, followed by laughter that escaped his lips. "Zulfiqar is not a coward. Zulfiqar is brave."

Mard Ali's voice gradually faded away, leaving only a faint smile on his face as he stared at Zulfiqar's relentless march towards the forbidden area. Kal Akbar, still stunned and perplexed, took a few steps towards Zulfiqar, who showed no signs of stopping. Neither of them could believe what was unfolding before their eyes. Even as Zulfiqar vanished into the distance, beyond the small forbidden hill, they struggled to comprehend the reality of his departure. Now, Mard Ali and Kal Akbar faced the empty desert ahead, devoid of any trace of Zulfiqar.

Minutes passed since Zulfiqar had disappeared behind the hills, heading towards the forbidden area. Finally, Mard Ali's voice broke the silence. "Allah Oh Akbar, (God is great) ... he is gone... he has become a goblin... the goblins have taken Zulfiqar."

Little did Mard Ali and Kal Akbar know that the silent beggar had appeared to Zulfiqar while he slept in the mosque at night. Startled awake by the voice, Zulfiqar looked around the empty, silent, and dark mosque with fear and trembling. The voice of the silent beggar whispered in Zulfiqar's ear, "Zulfiqar, you must go to the forbidden area. They want you there, and you have no choice. They will not harm you. Go, for you have no choice."

Zulfiqar was abruptly awakened by a whispering voice near his ear, seemingly emanating from the silent beggars. Uncertain whether he had truly heard the silent beggar's voice or if it was the ghost or goblin mimicking it, he found himself sitting in confusion and fear. His gaze fixated on the entrance door, where he believed he saw an apparition resembling the silent beggar's ghost, or perhaps the spirit he had encountered in his dream, radiating with a white glow. This sight further intensified his confusion and fear, causing his speech to stutter as he attempted to communicate with the spirit of the silent beggar.

"D-dervish... th-they want me... why... dervish," he managed to stammer.

"You have no choice, Zulfiqar. You must go and see for yourself," replied the spirit in a calm tone.

As suddenly as the silent beggar's ghost had appeared, it vanished along with the ethereal white light, leaving Zulfiqar in darkness once again, alone and enveloped in silence. Overwhelmed by fear, it took him some time to regain his composure. The mosque returned to its gloomy state, and despite calling out to the silent beggar with trepidation, he received no response. From that moment onward, Zulfiqar's soul and spirit were inundated with thoughts, fantasies, fears, and shivers that he had never experienced before. He lacked the courage to even budge from his position. It wasn't until the morning light started to seep through that his weary eyelids began to close, and he succumbed to exhaustion and fell into a light slumber.

Several hours later, he was abruptly awakened by a dog barking outside. As he opened his eyes, still gripped by the fear of the events that unfolded during the night, he unknowingly called out to the silent beggar's name. "Dervish...? Dervish...?"

Zulfiqar used to refer to the silent beggar as a dervish.

"Zulfiqar, are you daydreaming? Whom are you calling for? The goblin's dervish?" came a voice in response.

"No... Darwish... the silent beggar," Zulfiqar replied, only to watch a disheveled man exit the mosque without uttering a word. Zulfiqar waited in silence, fixated on the doorway where the raggedy man had departed, but there was no sound. "Darwish?! Who are you?"

But no matter what Zulfiqar was waiting for, there was no response from anyone. Unbeknownst to Zulfiqar, a passerby who had spent the night in the mosque out of fear of the Elves was awakened by Zulfiqar's voice. Thinking that Zulfiqar must be an Elf and not Zulfiqar himself, the passerby exited the mosque. Lost in thought about his dream, Zulfiqar stood up and looked around. He realized that several hours had passed since morning, and the mosque was now empty and silent. Without realizing it, he found himself heading towards the hill where the goblins resided.

On the other hand, Zulfiqar had convinced himself that his only occupation was gathering and distributing news throughout the villages. However, fabricating false news and reporting it often caused him headaches and problems. Despite this, it had been his means of survival, relying on donations for his work. The appearance of the silent beggar in his dream must have held a special message, especially considering his admiration, respect, and trust for the beggar. Zulfiqar also recalled Imam Asghari's words about the Elves not harming blind and deaf people. These thoughts fueled his growing conviction to follow the silent beggar's suggestion, despite being unaware that he was venturing into the forbidden area.

Now, Zulfiqar found himself above the village, walking along an unfamiliar and desolate path amidst rocky hills. The silence of the deserted landscape and the gentle wind against his face occupied his thoughts and imagination. His mind was consumed by thoughts of the Elves and their rootless and dangerous nature. The stories he concocted and heard about the Elves, the mulberry tree, and the reed player were brought to life and then faded away. These stories had been his source of income and survival, as he would perform and entertain others with them. The silence of the desert troubled him the most. Fear kept his head raised, and in an attempt to dispel the negative thoughts and his fear of the Elves, he continuously offered blessings to God, Prophet Muhammad, the Imams one by one, and called upon Shaykh Ahmad and the silent beggar for help.

An hour had passed since Zulfiqar set out on his journey. However, as he crossed the border between the roadside and the hill, fear began to consume him. He became afraid of his own shadow and even the sound of his own breath. His senses were heightened, with his ears acting as his eyes and his hearing sharper than ever. He would stop and investigate every sound he heard, fearing it could be an animal snorting or someone following him. Fear caused him to halt frequently. He was certain that some living creature was trailing him, but he couldn't determine whether it was a demon, a human, or wild animals like wolves and jackals.

Fear consumed Zulfiqar's entire being, leaving him confused and paralyzed. Every sound sent shivers down his spine, even the gentlest breeze filled him with terror. His obsession with the unseen creature following him kept his head in constant motion, scanning his surroundings. Overwhelmed, he lost his balance and tumbled, crashing his head and face into a short wall of jagged rocks and mud. He lay on the ground, momentarily oblivious to the pain and blood oozing from his injured face. Gathering his strength, he grasped his cane and struggled to his feet. The presence of the lurking animal felt suffocatingly close as if it stood right beside him. With his head held high, Zulfiqar scanned the area, his mind racing for a solution.

"Shaykh? Darwish?" he called out, his voice trembling with fear and panic, unknowingly seeking help from Shaykh Ahmad and the dervishes. But no response came, not from Shaykh Ahmad, not from the dervishes, nor from anyone else. As the night neared its end, Zulfiqar realized that he would soon be left alone in the darkness with the ravenous wolves. He knew that whether he continued towards the forbidden area or returned to the village, he would inevitably confront the night. Being where he was at night meant signing his own death warrant, for hungry wolves and jackals roamed the hills, searching for prey to satisfy their hunger. Growing increasingly fearful, he raised his head once more and called out for the

Shaykh and the dervishes, desperately hoping for a miracle, a rescue from his torment. But hope dwindled, as there was no response from either of them.

Suddenly, the sound of a cricket broke the dead and painful silence, jolting him into action. Filled with fear, he instinctively moved his hand to defend himself, accidentally colliding with a rugged wall. A surge of pain shot through his hand, compelling him to withdraw it. He paused, lifting his head to the air, straining his ears to discern what was happening around him. The cricket's song echoed once more, and a wave of relief washed over him as he realized the sound originated from the insect. Extending his hand to steady himself and prevent a fall, he stumbled upon a protruding rock, causing him to feel bewildered, concerned, and surprised. Tentatively, he explored the rock with his hand, only to realize that it seemed to be part of a larger wall.

Carefully, he traced the wall, running his hand along its surface to examine it. It dawned on him that the wall consisted of a combination of rocks and mud, indicating its handmade construction. Pausing momentarily, he pondered the situation, then tested the wall once more, repeating the action several times to confirm his initial observation. Satisfied that the wall was indeed man-made, a glimmer of hope flickered within his heart. Proceeding cautiously, he followed the wall, meticulously feeling and assessing each individual rock that adorned its summit. Simultaneously, he remained vigilant, acutely aware of the persistent presence of an unknown creature pursuing him. Periodically, he rechecked the height of the wall to ease his mind.

As he ventured further, he noticed the wall growing taller, surpassing his own height. Raising his hand, he realized it no longer reached the top. Determining the height with the aid of his cane, he discovered it to be towering. Additionally, he observed another wall branching off from the left, connecting to the one he had been tracing. This discovery infused Zulfiqar with a renewed sense of hope, yet he remained perplexed and apprehensive. Continuing his exploration, his hands traversed the wall, until his knees abruptly encountered yet another wall directly ahead. Confident now that he was encountering a wall, one that seemed purposefully built and encircling a garden, he cautiously maneuvered around it, maintaining contact with its surface through his hands and cane.

Finally, the short wall encompassing the garden concluded, allowing his cane to enter an open space. Pausing for contemplation, he felt as though his senses were heightened, perceiving his surroundings more clearly. He surveyed the area around him, and then carefully tested the open space with his cane. As the cane connected with two raised platforms on either side of the entrance, he deduced that he was touching a platform situated in front of a house or room. A surge of hope surged within him, providing a semblance of comfort amidst the hardships and pain he had endured. With his head held high, he whispered cautiously and softly under his breath, "Hello? Is anyone here?"

He waited for a while, but received no response from anyone and heard no voices. As he called out for help, he began to sweep his cane around his surroundings, hoping to make contact with someone who might be alive. However, his attempts yielded no response; his cane only encountered the cold walls and the platform on both sides. The only sensation he felt was a gentle breeze caressing his face. He shivered, feeling both cold and a burning sensation on his hands and face. Raising his hand to his face, he realized that he was injured, and that blood was trickling down his cheek. Retrieving his handkerchief from his pocket, he wiped his face while surveying his surroundings, contemplating his next move.

Now, at least he had found shelter for the night, a place where he could seek refuge from the wolves. However, he suddenly remembered that he had not attempted to open the door and check if there was a roofed room inside. The thought struck him to investigate further. Using his cane, he cautiously tested the door and the walls of the room before stepping inside, meticulously examining every corner and confirming the presence of a ceiling.

As he pondered his options, he found himself at a loss for what to do. The discovery of the room made him briefly consider the possibility that Shepherd Ali had not deceived him this time. He speculated that since elves did not require rooms for themselves, it was likely inhabited by a human. But who could it be? For a fleeting moment, he completely forgot about the elves and the wolves, realizing he should return to the village as soon as possible and inform the townspeople that Shepherd Ali had indeed spoken the truth this time a human dwelled here.

However, his fleeting moment of clarity was soon replaced by a whirlwind of thoughts. He once again became lost in contemplation, uncertain of his next steps, who resided in the room, and whether he would be welcomed there. He desperately sought a safe place to spend the night, but no matter how hard he pondered, he couldn't find a definitive answer. In addition, the lingering concern that the place might belong to thieves and robbers haunted him, igniting fears of encountering them and facing potential harm. He became fearful and anxious once more, particularly as he heard the animal trailing him snort again.

Zulfiqar, who had been preoccupied with examining the walls and the room, had temporarily forgotten about the animal. However, with the resumption of the snoring sound this time louder and clearer his attention snapped back to it. He instinctively turned his head towards the source, his gaze fixated on the direction of the snoring. Gradually, he discerned that the noise likely came from a dog, though he couldn't be certain. Feeling the need to protect himself in case of an attack, he raised his cane as a defence.

"The crafty creature, pursuing me like a thief...could it be a dog?" he muttered, both questioning and wary of the animal's intentions.

Zulfiqar's instincts proved right. Unbeknownst to him, the dog that had been chasing him into the hills was actually protecting him. Now, it noticed a pack of wolves perched on a nearby hill, fixated on Zulfiqar and the room he had taken shelter in. The wolves locked their gaze on the dog and the room, sensing Zulfiqar's presence. As Zulfiqar appeared in the doorway, their snouts lowered to the ground, preparing for an imminent attack. The distant howling of the wolves sent such terror coursing through Zulfiqar that he nearly lost control of his bladder. He cautiously sat on the platform, raising his head to the air and sharpening his ears, which served as his keenest sense. Clutching his cane, his only means of defense, Zulfiqar could distinctly hear the dog's footsteps growing louder as it circled anxiously. Meanwhile, the wolves had begun sniffing the ground, closing in on Zulfiqar and the room. Although blind, Zulfiqar seemed to possess an eerie ability to anticipate their approach. The wolves' movements, drawing nearer to him, flooded his entire being with fear and panic. Descending from the platform, Zulfiqar positioned himself by the door, his cane held out protectively. He remained uncertain whether to stay put or retreat inside the room. Lost in his confusion, the sound of reed pipes suddenly filled the air. Zulfiqar recognized the familiar melody. He had always believed it was the music of the Elves. Before he could delve deeper into the source of the music and its player, he heard the shuffling of feet just outside the platform. It was as if someone or something was dancing and playing the reed pipes. His confusion only deepened, and he called out hesitantly, "Dervish?!" His voice trembled, carrying a mixture of concern and fear. Despite waiting anxiously for a response from the dervishes or anyone else, the silence remained unbroken, intensifying his pain. Zulfiqar now questioned the wisdom of venturing into this area and wondered why he had come in the first place. Suddenly, the sound of wood splintering shattered the oppressive silence, accompanied by the scent of smoke from a blazing fire. Zulfiqar pondered who could have started the fire, speculating that perhaps it was the Elf. He recalled the villagers' beliefs that the rising smoke from the forbidden area was a magical deception by the Elves, luring people to their doom. However, he knew the true source of this rumor was Mullah Mahmoud, who sought to deceive and frighten people, manipulating them into performing religious rituals for personal gain.

By recalling the rumor that the Elves used to start fires to deceive and prey on unsuspecting people, Zulfiqar became even more terrified and disoriented. He was so consumed by fear that he failed to hear the footsteps of the person who entered the room and stood before him, observing him. It took him a while to detect the scent of freshly brewed tea, which now permeated the air around him. Zulfiqar knew that someone was offering him a cup of tea, but he hesitated to reach out and accept it.

Eventually, a hand reached out and gently took hold of Zulfiqar's trembling hand, guiding it forward to grasp the tea saucer. The person made sure that Zulfiqar had a firm grip on the saucer. Now, Zulfiqar's hand shook with both fear and anticipation, akin to the delicate vibrations of a song resonating through a crystal glass.

"Dervish, is that you?" Zulfiqar called out; his voice barely audible due to his overwhelming fright. It took him some time to regain his composure and realize that he still held the tea saucer in his hand. With caution, he inspected the cup and confirmed its warmth, using his other hand to secure it. As Zulfiqar gradually regained his senses, he noticed that the tea had cooled, and the steam no longer wafted from the cup.

Summoning a trace of courage, he cautiously sat on the platform in front of the door and began to sip the tea, periodically surveying his surroundings with each gulp. Yet, despite his continued vigilance, an eerie silence pervaded the air, devoid of any movement or sound. After finishing the tea, Zulfiqar carefully placed the saucer beside him, then leaned out and peered into the room.

"Whoever you are, thank you very much," he expressed, waiting expectantly for a response that never came. Undeterred, he proceeded, "I apologize for intruding. I am blind and have lost my way in the morning. I shall depart without looking back, never to return.

Then, no matter how long he waited, there was only silence once again. Even the dog's snoring could no longer be heard. It didn't take Zulfiqar long to raise his head, his ears sharpened, listening intently to the sounds around him. He sensed that whoever had been in the room had now left. Zulfiqar's head moved in the air, following the direction of the footsteps he had heard. Soon, he detected the dog's footsteps, trailing whoever had exited the room. Zulfiqar continued to raise his head, straining to listen to every sound, determined not to miss anything. Through his acute hearing, he would gain a clear understanding of what was happening around him. His hearing served as his eyes at this moment.

Before long, he heard the sound of footsteps approaching him, accompanied by the dog following closely behind. The footstep sounds grew nearer to Zulfiqar, passed him, and entered the room. Zulfiqar fixated his gaze on the room door once again, attentively listening to the sounds emanating from within. His voice rose again as he spoke, "If there are no objections, I shall spend the night on this platform. I am a homeless beggar with no place of my own. I usually spend the night at the mosque... Please forgive me, I seem to have lost my way today. By sunrise, I will be gone, never to return. Unless, of course, I don't freeze to death in this bitter cold. I wouldn't survive the night out here; the wolves would surely tear me to pieces."

He waited again for a response, but once more, there was only pure silence. Suddenly, the dog grabbed hold of Zulfiqar's pant leg and began dragging him toward the room. Not knowing who was pulling him or why, fear surged through Zulfiqar's body, causing him to jump in fright. He believed that the Elves had attacked him, so he instinctively swung his cane in the air, defending himself. However, upon hearing the dog's snoring, he hesitated to strike the animal, gently patting it instead. He clung to the wall beside the platform, gathering his strength to resist. For a moment, he entertained the thought that the dog was actually an Elven creature attempting to lure him into the room to drain his blood and bring about his demise. He felt his heart racing, fearing he might suffer a heart attack. His voice barely audible, he cried out to God, the Prophet, and the Imam, seeking their help and protection. In his terrified state, he couldn't even comprehend his own words or whom he was invoking for assistance. Finally, as if growing frustrated by Zulfiqar's resistance, the dog momentarily released its grip on his pant leg and started barking furiously. The sound of the dog's barking jolted Zulfiqar, suddenly awakening his senses. With wide-open eyes, he fixated his gaze in the direction of the dog's voice and uttered, "Majnoon?!"

Zulfiqar recognized the sound of the dog, finding it eerily similar to the bark of Abbas's dog, named Majnoon, which meant "wanderer" or "lost in love." This connection prompted Zulfiqar to call out the dog's name. Whenever he heard the dog's bark, his mind would momentarily drift away from thoughts of Elves, thieves, and bandits, replaced instead by memories of Majnoon. However, a sudden recollection flashed through his mind – he had witnessed people attacking and killing Majnoon the dog. Fear gripped Zulfiqar even more intensely now. What if he had been mistaken, and this dog was not Majnoon but an Elf assuming his form? Moreover, it had been several decades since those events took place, and a dog's lifespan couldn't possibly extend that long. Nevertheless, the sound of this dog was an exact match to Majnoon's bark. Zulfiqar knew the dog well; each time he passed by the alley, Majnoon would greet him from the porch until he disappeared from sight. Zulfiqar's ruminations on whether the dog was truly Majnoon, or an Elf were abruptly interrupted by a man's voice that startled him in his tracks. "You can spend the night here and risk being attacked by wolves... or come inside and become the dog's roommate."

It took Zulfiqar a few minutes to regain his senses and realize that he had heard the familiar voice of a man inviting him into the room.

*****

Chapter 8
When the blind man becomes the eyes of the bright...

The scorching summer sun had risen from behind the foothills of the Village of Shourcheh, casting its radiant glow upon the village. It had been several weeks since Zulfiqar ventured into the forbidden area, and there was still no news of his whereabouts. Consequently, conversations in the village revolved around Zulfiqar and his mysterious disappearance. Imam Asghari found himself burdened by Zulfiqar's vanishing act, as people sought answers from their spiritual leader regarding his fate.

Imam Asghari's arrival had coincided with the cessation of the enchanting melodies produced by the reed-playing Elves, causing a commotion among the villagers. They attributed this sudden silence to the perceived miraculous intervention of their Imam, believing that he possessed the power to protect them from demons and Elves. As a result, they frequently sought his presence, clinging to the hope that he would once again demonstrate his extraordinary abilities and unveil the truth behind Zulfiqar's disappearance.

Despite his own trepidation and reluctance to even step out into his yard with towering walls, Imam Asghari managed to pacify the people with his assurances and claims of contemplation. He urged them not to fear venturing out at night, employing various tactics to divert their attention away from Zulfiqar. Some individuals gradually overcame their fear and ventured outside based on the Imam's words, but many others grew disillusioned with the absence of Zulfiqar, gradually accepting his fate as yet another victim of the forbidden area. As intended by Imam Asghari, Zulfiqar began to fade into obscurity.

Meanwhile, Mard Ali and Kal Akbar remained the only ones who steadfastly held onto the hope of Zulfiqar's return. Initially, Mard Ali spent his days above the cemetery, engaging in play and amusement while eagerly awaiting Zulfiqar's homecoming. However, as time wore on, frustration took hold, and he now perched himself on a stone slab above the cemetery, fixated on the desert hill. Anyone who approached him was met with his repeated exclamation, "The Elves devoured Zulfiqar... The Elves drank his blood," followed by fits of laughter.

Similarly, Kal Akbar positioned himself on the platform in front of his house every day, keeping a vigilant watch over the forbidden area in the hopes of glimpsing Zulfiqar's return. Fearful of the Elves, he continued to keep his shoes on at all times, never daring to remove them. Ghadam Baldy, recently enlisted as an informant and enforcer for Imam Asghari, earned his nickname due to his complete baldness. Ugly Ghadam carried out the Imam's commands unquestioningly, with a few other paid associates under his command. For several weeks, Ugly Ghadam and his men took turns stationed near the cemetery, anticipating Zulfiqar's possible return from the forbidden area. Their objective was to reach him first and deliver him to Imam Asghari before he had a chance to communicate with anyone else. However, as time passed, even their visits to the cemetery dwindled to one or two brief encounters.

But nothing could discourage Kal Akbar. He sat in the same spot from dawn till dusk, his gaze fixed on the hill, eagerly awaiting Zulfiqar's return. Even in these trying times, he wouldn't go inside to have his lunch. Instead, his daughter or son would bring it to him, right in front of the platform. Though he received his lunch begrudgingly, it seemed as if Kal Akbar's ears were deaf to any complaints. His focus remained solely on the forbidden area.

On a scorching summer afternoon, Kal Akbar sat as usual on the platform, staring at the hill, waiting for Zulfiqar. It was on this particular day that something extraordinary happened. In the midst of his vigil, his eyelids fluttered open, and there, in the distance, he caught sight of a shadowy figure slowly emerging from the forbidden area, making its way toward the village. He couldn't be sure if his eyes were playing tricks on him or if it was a genuine sighting. Fatigue from a sleepless night and weariness throughout the day clouded his vision, leaving him confused.

Leaning out from beneath the arch in front of his house, Kal Akbar fixed his gaze on the village, searching for his friend, Mard Ali. They would often exchange reports of what they had seen or heard. Seeking

Mard Ali's opinion on the apparition he had witnessed, Kal Akbar hoped to confirm whether he was mistaken or not. However, Mard Ali was nowhere to be seen that day. Silence enveloped the surroundings, and a nagging fear crept into Kal Akbar's mind that the approaching figure might be an Elf, and he would be the first to encounter it, perhaps being whisked away.

He pondered whether Mard Ali knew something and deliberately stayed away. Kal Akbar's gaze shifted between the desert and the advancing ghost, consumed by fear. His eyes grew heavy, and he struggled to keep them open. As the ghost drew nearer, Kal Akbar, now standing on the platform, wrestled with the decision of whether to retreat into his house or remain there to discover the identity of the ghost. He contemplated the possibility that the ghost could be Zulfiqar, and entering his house would cause him to miss the long-awaited reunion. Conversely, if the ghost turned out to be an Elf, it could easily pass through closed doors and walls, potentially harming him and everyone inside. This was a fate he wished to avoid, considering that being taken by the Elves would be preferable to them taking his entire family.

As Kal Akbar turned toward the hill, he stared at the ghost that was calmly approaching. Lost in thought, he pondered what to do. Suddenly, the sound of barking dogs startled him, causing him to jump in fear. Unbeknownst to him, he had even leapt off the platform like a startled chicken. His screams echoed throughout the village. Slowly, his pale face turned towards the source of the dog's voice. However, his terror and trembling from the plight of poor Kal Akbar took a few moments to subside before he realized it was Mard Ali playing a prank by mimicking a dog's noise.

Mard Ali was delighted by his own joke and started dancing around Kal Akbar, his laughter echoing for hundreds of meters. "Chicken... Kal Akbar is a chicken."

Without hesitation, Kal Akbar slapped Mard Ali on the back of his head. He chased after Mard Ali, punishing him by throwing rocks and anything within his reach. Mard Ali ran away, his laughter persisting. The playful banter between Mard Ali and Kal Akbar had entertained them so much that it seemed Kal Akbar had momentarily forgotten about the ghost drawing nearer from the hillside.

As the two played and fought, the sound of a dog barking resurfaced. Angered by Mard Ali's antics, Kal Akbar still believed he was responsible for the noise. "Cut it out, you crazy man!"

Suddenly, Mard Ali stopped abruptly, showing no concern for Kal Akbar catching up to him. He disregarded the anger and fury directed at him. Kal Akbar finally realized that Mard Ali's attention was fixated on something up the hill. Curiosity overcame him, and he halted to see what had captured Mard Ali's gaze. His eyes fell upon Zulfiqar, who stood a few hundred yards away, calmly observing them with his head held high and his eyes fixed above.

"Must be Kal Akbar and Mard Ali having fun?" Zulfiqar remarked.

However, Kal Akbar and Mard Ali were so bewildered and shocked that they seemed oblivious to Zulfiqar's words. They failed to notice Zulfiqar's dog standing beside him, barking as if greeting them, just as Zulfiqar did. It took nearly a minute for them to regain their senses and comprehend that it was indeed Zulfiqar standing before them—healthy and happier than ever. Moreover, Zulfiqar now had a dog, something he used to despise and wished ill upon. Yet, they questioned if they were truly witnessing the Zulfiqar they once knew or if the Elves had taken over his body, assuming his appearance. The fact that Zulfiqar, who detested dogs, now owned one added to their confusion. Eventually, Mard Ali's laughter erupted once again, growing louder. "Zulfiqar is possessed! Zulfiqar is a goblin! Zulfiqar is a goblin!"

As his laughter boomed loudly, Mard Ali dashed towards the village, shouting at the top of his lungs, "Zulfiqar has been possessed! He has transformed into a goblin, returned as a malevolent creature!"

With Mard Ali's departure towards the village, Kal Akbar's fear and trembling escalated. He cautiously retreated to his house, constantly keeping his eyes fixed on Zulfiqar in disbelief. Unsure whether he was witnessing the real Zulfiqar or the goblin that had taken over his body, Kal Akbar's voice trembled as he whispered, "Zulfiqar, can you confirm if it's truly you?"

However, Kal Akbar's voice barely reached Zulfiqar's ears. Lost in the confusion of observing Zulfiqar, Kal Akbar moved backward, edging closer to the entrance of his house where the goblin lurked beneath the platform. His stuttering voice whispered once again, "Zulfiqar, please, tell me the truth. Is this really you?"

Meanwhile, Mard Ali raced through the alleyways of the village, shouting at the top of his voice, capturing the attention of the startled residents. They were initially unsure of what to make of Mard Ali's words and whether to believe them. Zulfiqar's existence had long been forgotten by the people, making it challenging for them to accept his sudden return. Eventually, they began to acknowledge the truth as Mard Ali's persistent cries echoed through the village.

Mard Ali, still running, eventually arrived at the mosque. Bursting into the mosque's courtyard, he increased the volume of his voice, accompanied by an exhilarating dance. Unaware of the cultural significance, Mard Ali hurriedly entered the main mosque, oblivious to the fact that he was disrespectfully wearing his shoes, a taboo within the religious space. His voice now adopted the tone and fervor of a preacher, unintentionally imitating a religious performance and lamentation.

Upon Mard Ali's entry into the main mosque, Imam Asghari and a couple of others were engaged in a conversation. Startled by Mard Ali's words and actions, they were momentarily distracted from their discussion. Ugly Ghadam and a few others trailed Mard Ali, intending to restrain and remove him from the mosque premises. They deemed it important to prevent his continued dancing and chanting, given the news of Zulfiqar's return. However, Imam Asghari's composure was also shaken by the news, causing him to forget about his ongoing conversation with the other individuals. He abruptly rose from his seat and left the mosque, heading towards the mosque's courtyard ahead of Mard Ali and Ghadam Baldy, who were still engaged in their pursuit inside the mosque.

As Imam Asghari exited the main Mosque, Mard Ali followed him, still chanting his news, with Ugly Ghadam in tow. However, by the time Ghadam Ali and his gang had put on their shoes, Mard Ali had already vanished from the mosque's courtyard and made his way into the alley.

Ugly Ghadam attempted to pursue Mard Ali but was halted by the voice of Imam Asghar calling out to them. They saw their Imam fixated on the wheel atop the mosque's water well, deep in thought. It was evident that Imam Asghari believed it was crucial for Ugly Ghadam and his gang to quickly apprehend Zulfiqar before anyone else could question him or bring him before Imam Asghari.

"You must be ashamed that the man you are chasing, who seems crazy to you, possesses more courage and intelligence than all of you combined. Why are you running after this madman?" Imam Asghari questioned them. "The real news lies in the graveyard, where the jewel awaits. Yet, you are fixated on the jeweler. What are you waiting for? Hurry, make your way to the graveyard and ensure you find Zulfiqar. Bring him here before he has a chance to speak to anyone."

Mard Ali's spectacle continued through the alleys and backstreets of the village. The villagers were gradually becoming aware and accepting of the news of Zulfiqar's return from the forbidden area. Meanwhile, Ugly Ghadam and his gang took a shortcut through the fields, rushing towards the cemetery in a race to reach Zulfiqar before the approaching crowd. They sprinted through the fields, leaping over low walls and climbing over tall ones until they finally arrived at the alley leading to the cemetery, ahead of the others. Only Kal Akbar's house stood between them and their destination. From there, they could see the cemetery in the distance, as well as the hills leading to the forbidden area.

As word spread about Zulfiqar's return, more people started hurrying towards the cemetery to catch a glimpse of him with their own eyes. However, when Ugly Ghadam and his gang arrived, they searched high and low but could not find Zulfiqar. The absence of Zulfiqar instilled a sense of fear and panic in their hearts and minds. They were so disoriented that they hadn't even realized they had reached Kal Akbar's house. Finally, Ghadam Baldy's gaze fell upon Zulfiqar, seated under the arch on the platform in front of Kal Akbar's house, engaged in an animated conversation while enjoying a cup of tea with Kal Akbar. As their eyes met, Zulfiqar raised his head, uncertain whether Ugly Ghadam and his gang were allies or foes. The group stood in front of the platform; their confusion palpable. They noticed that Kal Akbar seemed completely engrossed in Zulfiqar's presence, oblivious to Ugly Ghadam and his gang's arrival.

Now, Ugly Ghadam and his gang stared at Zulfiqar and Kal Akbar with suspicion. They were doubtful and wondered if the goblin had possessed Zulfiqar or even Kal Akbar's body, waiting for them to approach so they could launch an attack. They particularly noticed that Kal Akbar showed no signs of blinking, which made them more uneasy. In contrast, back in the village where the controversy and Mard Ali's show continued, there was utter silence in front of Kal Akbar's house.

Just as Ugly Ghadam and his gang were stunned and confused, fixated on Zulfiqar and Kal Akbar, Zulfiqar's dog, who had been hiding behind the wall all along, suddenly barked. This startled Ugly Ghadam and his gang, causing some of them to jump back or even flee towards the village in fear. It took them a few seconds to realize that the dog, now standing between them and Zulfiqar, was staring at them. The dog then moved and jumped onto the platform, positioning itself between Zulfiqar and Kal Akbar. Surprisingly, Kal Akbar did not object to the dog's presence on the platform, despite the clergies considering dogs impure. However, people in the village overlooked this notion and had their own dogs. Sensing that Ugly Ghadam and his gang were about to attack the dog, Zulfiqar raised his voice and said, "Do not be afraid; he is my dog, Majnoon. He wouldn't harm you. He is very loyal, and he saved me from the goblin."

After joking with Ugly Ghadam and his gang about his dog saving him from goblins, Zulfiqar stood up, descended from the platform, and emerged from under the arch. He held his head high and his senses sharpened. The dog followed him and stood beside him, fixated on Ghadam Baldy. Meanwhile, the dog seemed aware that a large group of people was approaching from a distance. Zulfiqar stood a few steps away from Ugly Ghadam and then turned his head towards the hill, gazing at the desert for several seconds. Ghadam Baldy, still afraid, broke the silence with a stuttering voice, whispering, "Mr. Zulfiqar? Are... are you human?"

Zulfiqar turned and stared at him for a while. Though he was blind and unable to see them, he could sense that they were terrified. "No," he replied calmly, "I'm not human... both the dog and I have become goblins."

With that, Zulfiqar headed towards the village, with Majnoon, the dog, following closely behind. He had only taken a few steps when he stopped again, turning his head back towards Ugly Ghadam and his gang, who remained frozen in their positions after hearing Zulfiqar's revelation about himself and his dog. "Perhaps I have also become a dog... just like Majnoon."

Then Zulfiqar continued his walk toward the village with Majnoon following beside him. As they approached Ugly Ghadam and his gang, they cautiously moved to the side several yards away, making way for them. Surprisingly, this time no one dared to pick up a rock and attack Zulfiqar's dog. It was evident that there was still doubt among them whether Zulfiqar and the dog were human or goblin, and it seemed they had taken Zulfiqar's joke seriously. Zulfiqar and his dog had distanced themselves by several hundred yards from Ugly Ghadam and his gang. Finally, they began to question whether Zulfiqar had actually joked about the dog being a goblin, but they remained uncertain. Nevertheless, for reasons unknown to them, Ugly Ghadam and his entourage decided to follow Zulfiqar. Only Kal Akbar stayed behind in silence under the arch. No one knew what Zulfiqar had said to Kal Akbar that had astonished him so much.

Ugly Ghadam and his gang finally caught up to Zulfiqar in a hurry. However, upon seeing the dog, they slowed down and became unsure of what to do. The uncertainty lingered as to whether the dog or Zulfiqar was truly a dog or a human, or if a goblin had taken control of their souls. Consequently, they took a few steps further and continued to follow them. Ugly Ghadam knew that sooner or later he would have to confront Zulfiqar and determine if he was a goblin or a human. Zulfiqar and his dog entered another alley from the cemetery to the village. The crowd approached in groups, but as they neared Zulfiqar and his dog Majnoon, they hesitated to get closer. As Zulfiqar and his dog approached them, they instinctively moved away and cleared a path for them, trailing them from a safe distance. Some elderly individuals were perplexed when they saw the dog and were reminded of Kal Abbas's dog which had the exact same appearance. It brought back memories from their childhood. Ugly Ghadam was now somewhat convinced that Zulfiqar had not been possessed by a goblin, yet he remained cautious. As he gradually approached Zulfiqar, he made an effort not to provoke the dog, exhibiting a newfound bravery. He initiated a conversation with Mr. Zulfiqar. "Mr. Zulfiqar, you have returned. Welcome... but let us not forget that it was through the prayers and mediation of Imam Asghari that you returned safely. Imam is now waiting for you in the mosque, Mr. Zulfiqar."

Another member of Ghadam Baldy's gang interjected, "It is well-known that Shaykh Asghar's prayer was with him."

Before he could finish speaking, Ugly Ghadam struck him and pushed him so forcefully that he almost lost his balance. With a muffled voice, the gang member protested, "Shut up and bite your damn tongue... It's Imam, not Shaykh, Imam Asghari's prayer behind him."

"Well, I lack literacy, have I committed a sin by not understanding the difference between an Imam, a Shaykh, or a Mullah? First, he was a Mullah, then he became a Shaykh, and suddenly he claimed to be an Imam."

He attempted to rectify his statement, but it only worsened the situation. Another member of the Imam's group raised his voice, silencing him once again. "Well, if you don't comprehend, Mr. Zulfiqar does... Mr. Zulfiqar knows that if he doesn't visit the Imam first, he would disgrace himself. Imam Asghari would then expel him from prayer and Islam, and if he gets expelled, Mr. Zulfiqar will go straight to hell."

Another member of the group interjected. "Hell is nothing; he will be turned into a stone and won't be able to stay in the village anymore."

Ugly Ghadam addressed Zulfiqar, raising his voice. "Mr. Zulfiqar himself knows that he must visit the Imam first. He understands that the Imam must be informed of both good and bad news. He knows he will be well taken care of... He knows who the boss is here."

While Ugly Ghadam and his group continued to intimidate and talk to Zulfiqar, Mard Ali's voice could be heard from a distance. Shortly after,

Mard Ali was seen running amidst ten to fifteen children of various ages, leading them towards Zulfiqar. Among them, and riding a donkey, was a young boy. Before Mard Ali reached them, Ugly Ghadam realized he needed to regain control of the situation and called for prayer. "Allah Homma Saleh Alla Mohammad... Va Ale Mohammad."

The crowd responded to Hussein Ghadam Baldy's call, and the sound of people praying echoed for miles. Without hesitation, Ugly Ghadam assumed leadership, with his gang echoing his every word. They surrounded Zulfiqar, preventing anyone from getting close to him, while also urging the people to follow Ghadam Baldy's actions. "Pray louder in the name of the Imam's well-being and health."

Regardless of who initiated the prayer, the people obediently followed. Zulfiqar, confused, looked around for his dog, which had become lost in the crowd. Surprisingly, for the first time, nobody attacked the dog, making it momentarily untouchable. The previous notion propagated by the Mulla that dogs were unclean was not voiced this time. Soon, the dog was left behind as the crowd moved forward, barking persistently. However, the people's affection for the dog didn't last long. Initially fearful that Zulfiqar and his dog might be evil creatures, they felt relieved that their suspicions were unfounded. Consequently, they began pelting the dog with stones as before, driving it away from the masses. Despite the attacks, the dog paid no attention, running off to safety and then returning to follow the crowd, searching for Zulfiqar.

The crowd reached Mard Ali and the young boy who was sitting on his donkey, and they began to greet and bless them immediately. Mard Ali, caught up in the attention he was receiving, took the lead and started chanting. His wooden stick danced in the air, resembling the sword of the Imam, as if he were preparing for a battle against Islam's most well-known enemy.

Ugly Ghadam approached the young boy, who was riding on the donkey and waiting for the crowd to pass so he could continue on his way. He grabbed the boy from behind, pulled him down from his donkey, and signaled his gang to place Zulfiqar on the donkey. The shocked and unhappy boy shouted and fought to regain his donkey, but it was clear that his strength couldn't match that of the several greedy men who now held Zulfiqar up in the air and placed him on the donkey. Despite the boy's resistance and loud pleas, his donkey was not returned.

"Give back my donkey... If you don't believe in religion and faith, give back my donkey. I need to bring food home for my sick mother. Please give my donkey back; my mother is sick," the boy pleaded.

However, instead of listening to the poor boy, those who were about to hear him attacked him, labeling him as godless, atheist, and against Islam. It didn't take long for the boy's head and face to be covered in his own blood. Despite the brutality, the young boy refused to give up and continued to tear, beg, and fight to free himself from the clutches of Imam Asghari's men, all in an effort to retrieve his donkey. But it was no easy task; the force he faced was much stronger than his own. Through the arms and legs of his attackers, he could only catch glimpses of Zulfiqar riding his donkey while one of Imam Asghari's men held the donkey's leash, directing its path. The people following the pilgrims, who appeared to have returned from the house of God with greetings and blessings, continued on their way.

Meanwhile, Zulfiqar sat on the donkey, confused, with his head held high and his ears alert, trying to make sense of the situation unfolding around him. Suddenly, Zulfiqar's head turned towards a field beside him, separated from the road by a short wall. It was as if he sensed something. And he was not mistaken. Even though he was blind, it seemed as if he could see. Shaykh Ahmad, accompanied by Sattar and Asyeh, walked through the greenery and rows of fruit trees in the field beside the road Zulfiqar was traveling on, heading towards the village. They gazed at Zulfiqar with a gentle smile, but while Zulfiqar could see Shaykh Ahmad, Sattar, and Asyeh with his blind eyes, no one in the crowd could. Even the people rushing through the field, passing Shaykh Ahmad, Sattar, and Asyeh, as they approached to join Zulfiqar's entourage, remained unaware of their presence as if they were ghosts.

Upon seeing Shaykh Ahmad, Sattar, and Asyeh, Zulfiqar completely forgot where he was and that he was seated on a donkey, being taken like a king to the queen. Even as his entourage moved past the field and entered the housing area, where no field could be seen, Zulfiqar's head remained turned backward, searching for them.

It was at that moment when Mard Ali's wooden sword, twirling in the air, accidentally struck Zulfiqar's hand, snapping him out of Shaykh Ahmad's thoughts. Zulfiqar was so sharp-witted that even amidst the chaos, Mard Ali's voice could be heard, echoing, "They're fooling Mr. Zulfiqar, putting him on the donkey!"

As they progressed, a crowd gathered, with people pouring out of their homes to join the commotion. A fierce struggle ensued among both the young and the elderly to lay their hands on the donkey's leash that Zulfiqar was riding. Naturally, the stronger and more powerful individuals had a better chance of reaching the saddle and claiming the leash, making their pilgrimage successful.

Throughout this ordeal, the young boy, bleeding but determined, tirelessly pursued the crowd in an attempt to retrieve his donkey. Despite his desperate pleas and tears, explaining that his mother needed the medicine, mercy was scarce. Instead of listening to him, he was beaten and pushed back repeatedly by Imam Asghari's men, and even some of the onlookers. However, in his defense, the dog named Majnoon bravely attacked those who harmed the boy. Unfortunately, both the boy and the dog were pushed back and beaten. Nevertheless, they persisted, continuing their fight, and trailing the crowd, shouting, "Godless people, give my donkey back! My father will kill me if I don't return it... if any of you have any shred of religion or faith!"

Eventually, the crowd, led by Ugly Ghadam and his gang, arrived at the mosque. Mard Ali, with his wooden sword swinging through the air, fought the imaginary enemy while holding the donkey's bridle with his other hand, leading it forward. The atmosphere was electric, particularly with Mard Ali a few steps ahead of the crowd, firmly grasping the donkey's bridle. Consumed by rage and his fervor to fight Islam's imaginary enemy, he was oblivious to his actions and surroundings. Unknowingly, he entered the mosque courtyard, leading the donkey with Zulfiqar still struggling to maintain balance on its back, spinning his wooden sword in the air. His chants and boasting were the loudest.

Before the people inside the courtyard could react or those gathered for worship could comprehend the situation, Mard Ali, the donkey, and Zulfiqar entered the main area of the mosque. Mard Ali remained unaware that Zulfiqar, desperately trying to maintain balance, collided forcefully with the top of the mosque's entry door. As a result, he was thrown off the donkey and fell to the ground, incapacitated. Meanwhile, Mard Ali continued his frenzied chanting, searching for the enemy of Islam in front of Imam Asghari and a couple of others seated by the pulpit, waiting for Zulfiqar's arrival.

Imam Asghari stared in shock and confusion, while it took the people inside and those who had gathered outside a few agonizing seconds to grasp the gravity of Mard Ali's actions. Taking the donkey inside the mosque, where people came to worship, was a severe insult to their religious practices and to Imam Asghari himself. As people realized the situation, they erupted in curses, attacking Mard Ali in an attempt to punish him and remove the donkey from the mosque. Mard Ali released the donkey and continued to dart around the mosque, engaging in a battle with those who now genuinely believed themselves to be enemies of Islam. Amidst the chaos, the confused donkey cried out, adding to the pandemonium unfolding.

The atmosphere in the mosque was incredibly crowded. Upon entering the courtyard, they were startled to see a donkey seated at the foot of Imam Asghari, engrossed in his speech and prayer. This act was considered a grave insult to the sacred space. A wave of shock and surprise swept over the congregation, rendering them breathless. Inside the mosque, Imam Asghari remained seated at the pulpit, still trying to comprehend the unusual situation alongside a few bewildered individuals.

Imam Asghari's eyes darted back and forth, perplexed by the scene unfolding before him. His gaze shifted from Zulfiqar, lying on the mosque floor near the entrance, to Mard Ali, who recited religious verses while evading imaginary enemies of Islam in a fervent display. Meanwhile, the donkey ran around, confused and crying, while people attempted to drive it out of the mosque, resorting to physical force. It resembled a chaotic battlefield that Imam Asghari found himself observing.

When Mard Ali noticed the donkey's plight and its struggle against the crowd, he decided to join forces with it, incorporating its presence into his chanting. He exclaimed, "The donkey has ascended the pulpit! It has transformed into a mullah, a Clergyman! He has come to fight the enemies of Islam!"

Mard Ali's proclamation, declaring the donkey's newfound role and significance, effectively sealed his own fate. Within religious fanatical circles, particularly among Imam Asghari's followers, this was tantamount to signing his own death certificate. Unfazed, Mard Ali initiated his usual heated exchange with Imam Asghari's men. While pointing towards the donkey, he weaved through the crowd, willingly enduring the blows aimed at him, refusing to back down. "If I have said anything wrong, then hasn't the donkey graced the holy shrine as well? What sets us apart from the donkey? Nothing. In fact, the donkey may be wiser and superior to us. Isn't the donkey a human being too? And yet, he has come to the mosque, just like us."

Eventually, Mard Ali and the donkey departed from the mosque, heading back to the courtyard. As they left, the usual routine of prayers, greetings, and blessings resumed, as one or two individuals called for them. Finally, Mr. Zulfiqar, who had been helped up from the ground, was respectfully placed next to Imam Asghari.

Meanwhile, a young boy, bloodied and distraught, mustered all his strength as he entered the courtyard of the mosque in search of his donkey. However, his donkey was nowhere to be found. Not only had he lost his donkey, but he also found himself indebted to others. In his frustration, he was attacked and beaten once again, erupting in anger as he demanded the return of his donkey. He claimed that his donkey was a gift to Imam Asghari and that it would bring him blessings in heaven. Sitting by the flowing river outside the mosque, the boy, covered in blood, realized that his donkey had been forcefully taken as a religious offering for Imam Asghari, without his consent. Hopelessly, he pleaded to God for help, but it seemed as though even God had forgotten him. The only companion near him was Zulfiqar's dog, Majnoon, who had also lost his owner, Zulfiqar. Majnoon attempted to enter the mosque to find him, but he was beaten and chased away from the door. The boy, filled with despair, was comforted by Majnoon as the dog affectionately licked his wounds.

People entered and exited the mosque, oblivious to the weeping, bloodied boy. Due to the presence of the dog, they kept their distance, some even resorting to attacking the dog in an attempt to keep it away from the mosque.

Simultaneously, while Zulfiqar's dog was cleaning the boy's blood from his head and face, inside the mosque, Zulfiqar's head suddenly turned towards the back door leading to a field. He stopped sipping his hot tea, capturing the attention of Imam Asghari and others, who were puzzled by the situation. Despite Zulfiqar's blindness, he appeared to see a radiant light surrounding the back door as Shaykh Ahmad emerged from it, wearing a worn-out outfit and a familiar smile. "Shaykh... Shaykh."

Imam Asghari, unaware that Zulfiqar was whispering the name of Shaykh Ahmad, whom he had seen in a spiritual vision by the door, reached out and placed his hand on Zulfiqar's head.

"I am here, Zulfiqar. Do not worry."

However, what Imam Asghari didn't know was that after witnessing Shaykh Ahmad's spirit, Zulfiqar no longer perceived his surroundings, and all sounds became muted, leaving only Shaykh Ahmad's voice, which he recognized. "Do not worry, my friend. These events must unfold so that people can experience suffering and learn from it. Sadly, most of them will never comprehend the difference between right and wrong, even when the truth is presented before them. Only a few will accept it. As long as superstitions persist, the servants of God will endure torment."

With the words of Shaykh Ahmad, a profound serenity enveloped Zulfiqar's entire being, and a smile illuminated his lips and face. "So, Shaykh, are you suggesting that all of this was part of God's plan to help people understand the truth?" he inquired.

Upon hearing Zulfiqar's question, Imam Asghari, who had initially believed that Zulfiqar was participating in a staged performance arranged by his associates, approached him and exclaimed a prayer, 'Allahu Akbar.' The crowd joined him, creating a commotion within the mosque as they hurried to witness the scene. Ghadam Baldy, along with his gang and a few others, rose from their seats. Caught between the view of Zulfiqar and Shaykh Ahmad, they competed to kiss Imam Asghari's hand, while Ugly Ghadam raised his voice.

"People, you witnessed and heard with your own eyes and ears that Mr. Zulfiqar proclaimed that all of this was part of God's plan, which Imam Asghari has revealed to us," Ugly Ghadam declared. "It was Imam Asghari's request that sent him to the forbidden area, and he returned unharmed. No goblin could lay a hand on him... all of this is because of our Imam Asghari and his prayers. If it weren't for our Imam's supplication, Zulfiqar would have fallen victim to the goblins, who would have drained his blood. He wouldn't be here to convey this message to you. Come forward and receive the blessings by kissing the hand of your Imam."

Hearing Ghadam Baldy's persuasive words, the ignorant and superstitious masses rushed towards Imam Asghari once again, vying to kiss his hands and feet.

* * * * *

Chapter 9
After making some adjustments for clarity and coherence, here's the edited version...

A mysterious individual set fire to the village of Shourcheh. Upon Zulfiqar's return from the forbidden area, he remained unharmed. However, Ugly Ghadam and his gang were far from being idle. They intensified their efforts to promote their leader, Imam Asghari, resorting to deceitful tactics and demagoguery. They manipulated the people into believing that Imam Asghari's supposed miracle saved Zulfiqar from the goblins and ensured his survival. Consequently, the market for Imam Asghari and his followers grew even more crowded. People were willing to do anything to please their Imam, presenting him with gifts and even referring to him as the deputy Imam.

Curiously, Zulfiqar himself fell under this influence, gradually forgetting the events he had experienced in the forbidden area. He failed to disclose the truth to the people, and instead, entertained them with captivating stories. Each day, he spun new tales, mentioning Imam Asghari's assistance in his battles against the goblins. Zulfiqar understood that he had to follow the Imam's wishes and instructions to maintain his privileged position and financial rewards. Meanwhile, Imam Asghari's objective was to prevent people from realizing that the goblins in the forbidden area were merely a fabrication. He intended to devise a plan to feign their eradication, while the people continued to believe in their existence and Imam Asghari's role in combating them. This was the narrative that Imam Asghari and his allies successfully fed the people.

Unbeknownst to Imam Asghari, Zulfiqar possessed a cunning nature akin to that of a seasoned politician. While leveraging the Imam's influence to enrich himself, he withheld the complete truth about the forbidden area, including the presence of a silent beggar. Zulfiqar understood that revealing everything to Imam Asghari would jeopardize their alliance and potentially lead to the closure of his business. Thus, he skillfully kept Imam Asghari in the dark, making him believe that the goblins had befriended Zulfiqar and would no longer pose a threat to him. However, Zulfiqar did not want the people to discover the truth either, as their knowledge would likely disrupt the peace and tranquility enjoyed by the silent beggar. Moreover, Zulfiqar knew that Imam Asghari would rely on him for future visits to the forbidden area and updates, although these would be exclusively shared with the Imam and not disclosed to the people.

After a while, Zulfiqar noticed that the fever of his return and his storytelling had cooled off. People were no longer as interested as they once were, and even Imam Asghari paid little attention to him. This realization prompted Zulfiqar to leave the village of Shourcheh one early morning while everyone was asleep. He traveled to the neighboring village of Tikken, where he opened a new business and employed the same tactics as he did in Shourcheh. However, his business did not thrive there since the people of Tikken were not as superstitious as those in Shourcheh.

Nevertheless, Zulfiqar was determined to find success. He knew he had to adopt a new approach to captivate people's attention. With his superior skills in manipulation compared to Imam Asghari, Zulfiqar realized he needed to introduce a fresh narrative that would entice the crowd. Therefore, for the first time, he began speaking about the silent beggar he had encountered in the forbidden area. This new story quickly sparked interest and curiosity among the villagers, once again drawing them towards Zulfiqar.

People abandoned their work and daily lives, gathering around Zulfiqar to listen to his captivating tales about the silent beggar. Zulfiqar's charisma and storytelling abilities were truly remarkable, overshadowing even the Mulla, including Imam Asghari, who grew displeased with the attention Zulfiqar commanded. Interestingly, Zulfiqar didn't focus solely on the silent beggar. Instead, his stories incorporated various subplots, yet people eagerly embraced them. One particular story revolved around a tall man Zulfiqar had encountered in the forbidden area. According to him, this man appeared to be the silent beggar or possibly a goblin that had possessed the silent beggar's body. Zulfiqar vividly described the man's features, including a thick mustache, long white beard and hair, a gray robe reaching his ankles, and a gray collarless shirt. Strangely, nobody questioned how a blind man like Zulfiqar could perceive these details, including the color of the man's shirt. Perhaps, people were captivated by Zulfiqar's tales due to the previous accounts of the silent beggar's encounter with Karim Khan's gunmen from the village of Robat Karimi. Rumors had circulated about goblins attacking the gunmen, causing them to flee, while the silent beggar was allegedly taken away by these mythical creatures.

With Zulfiqar's latest news and storytelling, the legend of the goblins in the forbidden area and the mulberry tree spread like wildfire throughout the villages of Shourcheh and Tikken. It seemed like a competition arose between the two villages to host Zulfiqar and compare the intriguing and dramatic elements of his narratives. Zulfiqar's inconsistent descriptions of the dervish and the silent beggar further added to the confusion. Sometimes he likened the tall man to a dervish, while other times he connected him to the silent beggar known to the people. Consequently, the villagers grew increasingly perplexed, especially since the shepherd Ali, who had ventured into the forbidden area, never mentioned encountering any dervishes. The conflicting stories from Shepherd Ali and Zulfiqar transformed the forbidden area into a puzzling enigma, leaving the villagers uncertain about whom to believe: the dervish or the silent beggar.

Not long after, stories began to circulate among the people. Some even claimed to have secretly ventured into the forbidden area and encountered the enigmatic silent beggar, while others insisted, they had seen the dervish. People couldn't help but engage in conversations, speculating about the appearance of the forbidden area, the peculiar behavior witnessed, and the clothing worn there. Suddenly, everyone became a storyteller, reminiscent of the elderly men who would gather at the store corner under the sun. Even the mosque and public bathhouses were not exempt from the absence of stories, as they became venues for sharing and recounting tales and legends, especially popular among the children.

In these narratives, discussions revolved around the beggar's backpack, shovel, axe, sickle, water well, bucket, trowel, rope, and his faithful dog. The topic of his gun also emerged, with some claiming it had a single barrel while others insisted it had two. Furthermore, people discussed his tattered robe and how he traversed the rocky hills barefoot without any discomfort. Meanwhile, Imam Asghari refused to remain idle and capitalized on every minor incident to captivate and influence innocent, simple-hearted individuals. During his sermons from the pulpit, he skillfully intertwined words of lamentation and somehow linked the matter to religious figures such as the Imams, the Prophet, and the legends of Islam, such as Imam Ali and Imam Hussein.

Naturally, the rising legend of the silent beggar preoccupied Imam Asghari's thoughts. He saw the beggar as a problem, diverting attention away from himself. Additionally, Imam Asghari harbored a strong disdain for dervishes and their philosophy, despising their belief in the pure and genuine essence of religion while he focused solely on material gain. It was evident that the situation had become increasingly complex and distressing for Imam Asghari.

Imam Asghari's instincts were not misguided. Over time, news of Zulfiqar's journey to the forbidden area, the presence of strangers, silent beggars, dervishes, and goblins spread like wildfire. Some individuals believed that it was necessary to confront the goblins and resolve the issues once and for all. They also sought a solution regarding the dervishes and the stranger, whose presence Zulfiqar had disclosed in the forbidden area.

The situation became increasingly complex for Imam Asghari when people started approaching him daily, urging him to employ his demonstrated miracles and venture into the forbidden area to eradicate the evil presence of the goblins once and for all. However, this request posed a significant challenge for Imam Asghari, who was deeply afraid of entering the forbidden area. He dreaded the thought of being captured by the goblins, drained of his blood, and killed. Nevertheless, he couldn't confess his fear to the people, as he was the Imam and believed to be protected from harm by the goblins and evil forces. To shift the responsibility away from himself, he targeted Kadkhoda and Haji Ghazanfar, who had taken over the position of the former Haji Amir.

Imam Asghari assigned his men, Ghadam Baldy, and his gang, to deal with Kadkhoda and Haji Ghazanfar. Their duty involved regularly meeting with Kadkhoda, who represented the village in city matters and legal affairs, and Haji Ghazanfar, the wealthiest individual in the Village of Shourcheh. Haji Ghazanfar always extended his support and generosity to Kadkhoda, especially when it came to Imam Asghari. Consequently, Haji Ghazanfar's influence and authority reverberated throughout the village. Nothing occurred in the village without his knowledge.

From the very beginning, albeit secretly, a competition for power and influence between Imam Asghari and Haji Ghazanfar had been ongoing. However, this clandestine rivalry was concealed from the public eye, and they pretended to be the best of friends. Imam Asghari sought to burden Kadkhoda and Haji Ghazanfar with the responsibility of entering the forbidden area. Unfortunately, his attempts proved futile. Not only did people continue to visit Imam Asghari, but they also approached Kadkhoda and Haji Ghazanfar in search of assistance, albeit with some delay.

And finally, the problem reached a point where Imam Asghari, Haji Ghazanfar, and Kadkhoda had no choice but to respond to the demands of the people. Determined, they decided to venture into the forbidden area and confront the goblins, dervishes, the tulip beggar, and the forbidden territory once and for all. The long-awaited day had arrived. Kadkhoda, Imam Asghari, and Haji Ghazanfar mounted three mules, while one or two individuals took hold of each mule's reins. The crowd followed closely behind, with the entire village standing united, following their leaders.

Imam Asghari remained silent throughout the journey, his lips moving in whispered prayers that no one could hear. Ugly Ghadam led the procession, his men maintaining order among the crowd. At intervals, he called for prayers, which were echoed by the people. As they drew nearer to the cemetery, leading towards the forbidden area, the volume of prayers and shouts grew louder. Everyone wore visible prayers, hanging around their necks, as a display of faith to ward off the goblins. Some carried two or three prayers, covering both front and back, all inscribed by Imam Asghari himself. He had convinced the people that his written prayers would protect them from the goblins. Additionally, every person carried a small or large Quran, except for Mard Ali, who had neither a prayer nor a holy book. He danced and chanted at the forefront of the crowd, twirling his wooden sword in the air. He seemed oblivious to the actions and shouts of the crowd, treating them as enemies of Islam, against which he waged his personal battle.

As the crowd ascended the hill, entering the forbidden area, Ugly Ghadam rose and halted their progress. He announced that Imam Asghari was reciting a prayer to protect them from the goblins. A silence fell over the crowd, allowing the sound of the Imam's prayer to reach the forbidden area and the goblins. People's gaze shifted between the forbidden territory and Imam Asghari, who prayed silently, his words inaudible to others. A profound stillness settled over the hills leading to the forbidden area, as a war of thoughts raged within the minds of the people, within their realm of silence. After a while, the silence seemed to evoke memories of the goblins, causing the crowd's excitement to wane, replaced by fear and trembling that gripped their souls and entire beings. It was not only Imam Asghari's lips that trembled and whispered prayers, beseeching God, the prophet, and their Imam for help and deliverance from the goblins. It seemed as though all lips were sealed shut in unison.

Mard Ali, despite standing a few steps away from the congregation, continued to make jokes, laugh, and lament, even when everyone fell silent to recite prayers for the protection of Imam Asghari from the goblins. "Today, the goblins and fairies will devour the Imam," he exclaimed.

At this point, people's minds were so preoccupied with thoughts of goblins, dervishes, and the silent beggars that it seemed they either didn't hear Mard Ali's voice or chose to ignore it. Perhaps they didn't want to react or protest against him. The crowd remained silent as Imam Asghari moved forward, but everyone appeared to be speechless. Their lips were tightly sealed, trembling silently. It seemed that Mard Ali had grown impatient with people's hesitation and raised his voice, urging the frightened individuals to move. As Mard Ali shouted, the crowd snapped back to reality, their attention refocused on Imam Asghari, who would lead them forward. Unbeknownst to them, he was terrified and could lose composure due to fear. Nevertheless, with Kadkhoda and Hajji Ghazanfar each taking hold of one of Imam Asghari's hands, the three of them began walking, followed by the people.

After a while, they noticed a hut atop a hill surrounded by rocks, accompanied by a tall mulberry tree. The procession finally halted several yards away from the room, trembling with fear. Although they were stunned, their eyes darted around anxiously. The fear of goblins had gripped them so tightly that they failed to notice a small stream flowing from the top of the hill, passing by a mulberry tree, and merging into a large pond meant for cultivation. They were so consumed by fear that they couldn't sense or observe their surroundings. It was as if everyone had become deaf and mute, except for Mard Ali, who continued his distant chants while swinging his sword in the air, symbolizing the fight against the ancient enemy of Islam known as Shemar, with a colorful cloth wrapped around his head.

Imam Asghari, Kadkhoda, and Hajji Ghazanfar had dismounted from their mules. It was evident that they were no different from the people, equally afraid, or perhaps even more so. However, they had made an effort to conceal their fear, so as not to lose the respect of the crowd. Yet, it was clear to all three of them that their fear of goblins had led them to engage in a peculiar competition, each trying to show more respect to the others and encourage them to take the first step into the hut for inspection. Their exaggerated attempts to praise one another were apparent to the people accompanying them and seemed ridiculous. The crowd, familiar with the personalities of the three, understood that their compliments were born out of fear. As the congregation waited and observed, Haji Ghazanfar, Kadkhoda, and especially Imam Asghari continued to shower each other with compliments, vying for who should move forward first. This behavior was customary among the people, as the elder and most respected individual always walked ahead or entered a room first. However, this time, the people recognized that these compliments were not genuine signs of respect, but rather manifestations of fear. Their excessive flattery eventually irritated Mard Ali, and he raised his voice in protest, "Who among you is the coward? Haji, Kadkhoda, Imam Asghari, who is the coward?"

But this time, it seemed that Ugly Ghadam and his gang were the only ones who didn't care about Mard Ali insulting the three most influential men in the village. No one dared to confront or chase him, as fear of the goblins had consumed their souls and bodies. They believed that the goblins were hiding inside the hut, instilling terror in everyone. However, things took an unexpected turn when Mard Ali accidentally swung his woolen sword, a symbol of his fight against the enemies of Islam, and it landed forcefully on Ghadam Baldy's head. The impact was so intense that Ugly Ghadam retaliated by delivering a powerful punch, causing Mard Ali to cry out in pain, his agonized screams echoing through the hills.

This incident marked the beginning of a confrontation between Mard Ali and Ghadam Baldy's gang, with a few others joining the fray. The only notable difference was that this time Mard Ali's laughter carried a more pained and furious tone, but it didn't deter him from continuing the fight. He questioned why they were attacking him when he had merely mentioned infidelity, highlighting their own fear. He challenged them, pointing out that Imam Asghari was also afraid to enter the room, where they believed the goblins resided. He ridiculed Haji Ghazanfar and Kadkhoda, asserting that they were all cowards.

Mard Ali's provocative comments pushed Haji Ghazanfar, Kadkhoda, and Imam Asghari to protect their own reputations, reigniting the ongoing competition of who held more respect among them. They urged each other forward, attempting to enter the room. However, as they reached the entrance, they abruptly stopped, their faces pale with fear, resembling freshly fallen snow. They searched for excuses to avoid going inside but found none. An eerie silence filled the air, leaving them paralyzed and unable to take the next step. It was Mard Ali who broke the silence, taunting them as cowards and daring them to call forth the goblins to devour them.

Then, he turned towards the hut and yelled, "Goblins, fairies, dervishes, silent beggar, come out and take these cowards, suck their blood, and devour them!"

No response emanated from within the hut. Dread had gripped everyone, plunging them into an abyss of fear. Finally, Haji Ghazanfar mustered the courage to speak, addressing Kadkhoda and Imam Asghari. Despite his attempts to conceal his fear, his trembling voice betrayed him. "Kadkhoda, Imam, if there's anyone inside, they might have frozen to death. God would not approve if we did nothing... Kadkhoda, as a man of law, and Imam Asghari, as a man of God and the leader of the Muslims, it is our responsibility to step forward and investigate. We must go and see what has happened, once and for all."

But the same response was given to Hajji Ghazanfar by Kadkhoda, and Imam Asghari also shouted and echoed, instructing Hajji Ghazanfar to enter the room first since he was the eldest. Meanwhile, Mard Ali, who continued his chants and fought valiantly against the enemies of religion, grew weary once again. Despite this, he raised his voice and maintained his customary laughter, making jokes along the way. "Baba, is there anything to be afraid of? Didn't I say our Imam, Hajji, and Kadkhoda are all scared of goblins?"

Their dance resumed, but just before Ugly Ghadam and his gang had the chance to strike him on the head again, Mard Ali swiftly evaded them, laughing and chanting as he carried on with his fight, swinging his wooden sword through the air. He ran past Haji Ghazanfar, Imam Asghari, and Kadkhoda, eventually entering the room. Ghadam Ali and his gang abruptly halted a few steps away from the door, frozen in shock, much like the rest of the crowd. All eyes were fixed on the room's entrance, eagerly awaiting any sign or sound from Mard Ali. Silence engulfed the surroundings, making it difficult to breathe. Mard Ali remained inside the room without making a sound or indicating his departure.

Now, gripped with fear, the crowd unconsciously took a few steps back, their lips sealed, and their eyes fixed on the room's door. Once again, everyone's attention shifted to Haji Ghazanfar, Kadkhoda, and especially Imam Asghari, who instilled the most fear. The onlookers were expectant, anticipating their next move and hoping they would step forward to investigate Mard Ali's whereabouts. However, the three of them were overcome with even greater fear than the rest, hesitating and exchanging anxious glances, each waiting for the others to take the lead. Silence returned, consuming the atmosphere. People trembled at the mere sound of the wind.

Suddenly, Mard Ali burst out of the room, shouting loudly, right in front of Haji Ghazanfar, Imam Asghari, and Kadkhoda, who stood at the forefront of the crowd. Startled, they jumped back in fear. Imam Asghari lost his balance and fell to the ground, scrambling to get up and then fleeing along with the rest of the retreating crowd, consumed by fear. Mard Ali stood proudly in front of the open door, laughing at everyone as his voice reverberated once more. "You are crazy, frightened people! You're too late! He was scared just like you all are scared. He ran away like a chicken, just like you. The room is empty. Don't believe me? Come and see, Imam Asghari. The door is open."

Hearing the voice and seeing Mard Ali, it took a while for the crowd to come to their senses and realize that it was Mard Ali who had jumped out of the room, not the goblins, the silent beggar, or the older dervish holding a gun, as shepherd Ali had told them. The sight of Mard Ali restored the courage of Haji Ghazanfar, Kadkhoda, and Imam Asghari. Several people rushed to help and lifted Imam Asghari, who had fallen to the ground once again. Angry and filled with rage, Imam Asghari broke free from the crowd and stared at Mard Ali as if he wanted him dead right then and there. He then shifted his gaze towards Ghadam Baldy, and everyone understood what Imam Asghari's gaze meant.

In an instant, Ugly Ghadam and his gang started chasing Mard Ali once again, seemingly forgetting about the goblins. Chasing and harming Mard Ali became their primary focus. However, Mard Ali, while defending himself from their attacks as usual, did not back down and continued shouting, "Well, I was joking. I didn't commit a great sin, did I? No... Oh, what does this have to do with me? Your Imam is afraid of goblins."

Soon, Mard Ali was forgotten. Imam Asghari, seeing Hajji Ghazanfar and Kadkhoda cautiously approaching the room, rushed past them to ensure he wouldn't fall behind and that they wouldn't enter the room first. The fear of the goblins was no longer an issue, reigniting the rivalry between Imam Asghari, Haji Ghazanfar, and Kadkhoda. Each of them tried to outdo the others. Waiting for one another, showing respect, and offering compliments were now pointless. As usual, it was Imam Asghari who surpassed everyone, entering the room first, leaving Hajji Ghazanfar and Kadkhoda behind. Haji Ghazanfar and Kadkhoda followed Imam Asghari, engaging in a race to enter the room, but Ugly Ghadamand his gang blocked them. They even threw out a few people who managed to get in.

Now, the crowd competed to catch a glimpse of what was happening inside the room, peering through the doors and the small window. No one uttered a sound. The crowd was so absorbed that they didn't even notice Mard Ali slipping back into the room quietly and cautiously. He stood by the window, watching Imam Asghari and the others with his mocking smile. Pure silence enveloped the small, humble room. It seemed as if everyone was struck speechless, not knowing what to do or say. What could they say? The room was empty, devoid of the goblins and fairies that had filled their lives with fear and trembling for years. There were no cannons, tanks, guns, or bullets that people had expected to find. There was nothing but an old mat in the corner, two discarded plates and bowls, two spoons, two small pots, and an old jar that had slipped, along with two old teapots next to a pile of ashes.

Once again, it was Mard Ali who broke the silence with his voice. He kicked a pile of ashes as if he were shooing a soccer ball, and his usual laughter filled the room. "Imam, these are the ashes of their cannons and guns."

As Mard Ali struck the pile of ashes, attempting to display the remnants of the goblins' weaponry, the ashes scattered in the air, landing on the heads and shoulders of Imam Asghari, Kadkhoda, and Haji Ghazanfar, even entering their eyes. Mard Ali continued kicking the ashes, chanting as if engaged in a battle against Islam's enemies. The swirling ashes made it impossible for eyes to see one another. Ugly Ghadamand his gang hurried to the aid of Imam Asghari once again, pursuing Mard Ali. Despite the beating he endured, Mard Ali persisted in his chanting and fight against the enemies of Islam. "If I spoke of disbelief towards Islam, didn't the Imam mention the presence of goblins and fairies? So, where are they? Didn't they claim to possess cannons and guns? Well, I kicked the ashes of the goblins' cannons and guns."

Soon, Ugly Ghadam and his gang forgot about Mard Ali. His flattering voice resurfaced as he approached Imam Asghari, kissing his hands and feet. "Let us all offer a fervent prayer for the health of our esteemed Imam Asghari, the leader of the Muslims, who, through his miracle, saved us from the goblins."

Upon hearing Ghadam Baldy's call to prayer, the people's fear subsided, and they regained their courage. Their prayers echoed louder than ever as they rushed toward Imam Asghari to show their devotion. Now, everyone awaited their Imam's words, hoping for an explanation regarding the goblins, dervishes, and the silent beggar, and what had befallen them. However, before the Imam could utter a word, Kadkhoda spoke up. "There must have been something about him that prompted him to flee upon hearing and seeing us approaching."

Following Kadkhoda's statement, everyone began to share their opinions. "Perhaps he is a beggar who has gone begging and returned."

"Maybe he is a thief, seeking refuge here to avoid capture."

"What if he is a secret spy from the central government, sent to monitor our activities? Haji, Kadkhoda, Imam, we must remain vigilant."

"What if they are goblins and fairies? How can we be certain about their way of life? Imam Asghari, you must possess knowledge of their existence and habits, don't you?"

And once again, all eyes and ears were fixated on Imam Asghari as they eagerly awaited his words about goblins—how they live and what fate befell them. It was evident that Imam Asghari was lost in thought, seeking another means to manipulate the people once more. At last, his voice resonated through the air.

"I am certain and confident that this is yet another ploy orchestrated by the people of Tikken, who have been toying with us for many years. They seek to seize what rightfully belongs to the village of Shourcheh, to all of you, my fellow villagers."

Ugly Ghadam took the reins from his Imam. "Imam speaks the truth. Oh, the goblins and fairies, incapable of constructing a room or even starting a fire to cook their meals. Our Imam is absolutely correct; this is the handiwork of the Tikken people. Hajji Ghazanfar, surely you must concur. You are our revered elder and must speak the truth."

Hossein Ghadam Baldy, with his persuasive rhetoric and his invocation of Haji Ghazanfar as a man of God and village elder, placed numerous watermelons under Haji Ghazanfar, effectively manipulating him until he had no choice but to lend his seal of approval to Imam Asghari. Naturally, Haji Ghazanfar longed to address the people.

"Yes, I too concur with the Imam. This is the doing of our village's enemy, the godless people of Tikken, who seek to harm the village of Shourcheh."

With the affirmation of Imam Asghari's words by Haji Ghazanfar and Kadkhoda, it appeared that the matter of goblins, fairies, silent beggars, and dervishes had been resolved in the eyes of the people, thanks to their Imam. The blame for all these phenomena now fell squarely on the people of Tikken. Yet, unbeknownst to the people of Shourcheh, Imam Asghari had played yet another trick on them, initiating a new game to exploit them for his own benefit. A game that provided him with entertainment and advantage but would ultimately harm all the villagers of Shourcheh and Tikken.

Innocent and uneducated, the people began rushing to kiss Imam Asghari's hand, believing that he was the savior who had rescued them from the clutches of goblins. The hand-kissing, compliments, and exchanges between Imam Asghari, Haji Ghazanfar, and Ugly Ghadam were still underway when the howl of several wolves pierced the air, followed by Mard Ali's shouts, dance, fighting, and engagement with the enemy. The crowd was once again terrified.

"Oh my God, the people of Tikken have unleashed wolves upon us! They will attack and tear apart Haji and Imam Asghari! Run, run! The wolves are approaching, ready to devour you! Perhaps they are not wolves at all; they may well be goblins! Look! Do they not resemble goblins? They have come to drain your blood! Hurry, flee!"

It didn't take long for fear to grip the people once again as they spotted goblins perched on a small hill, overlooking the room, and preparing to attack. Mard Ali quickly informed them that those were not wolves but goblins, intensifying their fear. In an instant, panic spread, and the crowd scattered. Imam Asghari, Haji Ghazanfar, and Kadkhoda swiftly mounted their mules and rode into the midst of the crowd, ensuring that if the wolves attacked, the people would be the target, not them. Some lost their shoes while fleeing, but they didn't dare to stop and retrieve them, continuing to run barefoot. People trampled over each other, causing injuries, yet nobody halted to lend a hand. Even the most severely injured individuals promptly rose and continued their escape.

Overwhelmed by the threat of the wolves, the injured populace returned home, some with broken limbs and heads, unable to spare a moment to inspect the surroundings. Apart from a few individuals, nobody even noticed the water well on the other side of the mulberry tree or the graves at its base. Within a day or two, Imam Asghari's storytelling became once again consumed by tales of Ugly Ghadam and his gang. The story of the goblins, particularly the dervish and the silent beggar, dominated conversations. Some even claimed to have personally seen the silent beggar and the dervish wandering the village at night. They went further, linking a few thefts that had occurred in the village to these individuals. Unbeknownst to them, all these rumors and stories originated from Imam Asghari and were disseminated by his accomplices, Ugly Ghadam and his gang. In reality, the thefts were committed by Ugly Ghadam and his gang themselves, disguised as dervishes and silent beggars, who aimed to frighten and harm the people, causing chaos and damage to the village of Shourcheh. Blame was unjustly shifted onto the people of Tikken.

Imam Asghari knew that by inciting the people and turning them against the neighboring Tikken villagers, he could revive the longstanding animosity between the two villages, which had subsided for a while. This would serve to entertain the people by engaging them in a war-like conflict with the people of Tikken, providing Imam Asghari with more time and opportunities to exploit and manipulate them further. To instill even more fear, Ugly Ghadam and his gang staged nighttime attacks, wearing masks, and beating unsuspecting individuals. They also looted several houses, all of which were falsely attributed to the people of Tikken.

After a while, Ugly Ghadam and his gang's activities reached a point where, as night fell, all the doors in the village were sealed again for fear of an attack from the Tikken village. Visits between the villagers at night became shorter and mostly ceased. If they had to venture out, people moved in groups, carrying bright lights and cold weapons to defend themselves.

In the meantime, some courageous individuals occasionally dared to venture into the forbidden area in secret, hoping to catch a glimpse of the dervishes, the silent beggar, or perhaps even goblins. However, there was no trace of the dervish or the silent beggar. It was as if both had vanished into thin air. Of course, these individuals always kept their distance from the hut and the berry tree, scanning the area briefly before retreating. With each visit, they grew bolder, inching closer to the hut.

Meanwhile, Zulfiqar became increasingly scarce. No one knew where he spent his time or why he no longer interacted with the villagers or shared his stories. Whatever the reason, he remained silent, and his appearances became rare. Little did the people know that during this time, he was patiently waiting at the forbidden area, hoping for the silent beggar and his dog, Majnoon, to return. Zulfiqar wondered where the silent beggar had disappeared to and why. However, he was unaware that the silent beggar was none other than the famous Kal Abbas, who had chosen to remain mute to avoid being recognized by his voice.

* * * * *

And so, the silence persisted. Zulfiqar had no choice but to continue sitting on the platform in front of the hut, waiting for the silent beggar's return. The air grew colder, enveloping Zulfiqar's body and soul. Weariness consumed his thoughts, prompting him to engage in conversations with himself, hoping that the silent beggar might be nearby. "Who would have thought that in this dry year, where farming is failing all around, water springs forth in this desert as if it comes from the sea? You must be a man of God, or perhaps God loves you, silent beggar?" He waited for a response that never came.

* * * * *

Chapter 10
What can be done when a person leaves the world, but the people of the world do not leave him?!

The days came and went, as the cold, snowy winter replaced the vibrant autumn leaves. Spring blossoms, singing melodies of joy and happiness, gave way to the scorching days of summer. Time and place were in constant flux, but the silent beggar remained, patiently waiting to reach his destination. Seated before his humble abode, he gazed at the hills and rocks, awaiting his fate, accompanied only by his loyal dog who rested by his side.

Years had passed since the silent beggar last embarked on a journey. Having found solace in Sattar's company, he gradually settled in this place. Following Sattar's demise and subsequent burial next to Asyeh, the beggar took up Sattar's position. Despite his age, he diligently cultivated a small plot of land, yielding abundant and exceptional vegetables. In moments of respite, he would sit on the porch, observing the changing seasons—autumn, winter, spring, and summer—spending his days and nights awaiting the arrival of his destined moment.

Throughout this time, Zulfiqar grew increasingly attached to the silent beggar's presence. The beggar seldom uttered a word, yet Zulfiqar remained undeterred, engaging in conversations with him as if he were receiving responses. To coax the beggar into speaking, Zulfiqar resorted to conversing with himself, imagining the beggar's hypothetical replies. Occasionally, Majnoon, too, would partake in one-on-one exchanges with Zulfiqar.

As dawn broke, the sun's rays filtered through a small window corner, gently warming Zulfiqar's face as he lay sleeping on a worn-out carpet, draped in an equally worn sheet. The flies began buzzing around, landing on his hands and face, but Zulfiqar remained unperturbed, as though their presence was cause for celebration. A short distance away, the silent beggar reclined on another threadbare carpet, stretching his legs against the wall, and covering himself with a tattered sheet. Majnoon lay asleep near the door. Silence and stillness enveloped everything and everywhere.

Suddenly, the distant clamor outside jolted the silent beggar awake. His eyes opened, and darkness gave way to light. He listened attentively, wondering about the origin and cause of the commotion. Majnoon, too, perked up his head, his faint snoring momentarily suspended within the room's tranquility. The beggar rose, following Majnoon's lead, and stepped outside. Leaning against the window that faced the village, he peered into the distance, straining his ears. He was certain that the sounds emanated from the village of Shourcheh. Faint voices could be discerned, intermittently shouting names, summoning individuals—Haj Haidar's worker, the Kal Akbar family, the Ghafoori family—to come to Herang.

In ancient times, in the countryside, when there was a need to clear the streams that provided water to the fields for irrigation, the process involved removing weeds, debris, and excess soil that accumulated throughout the year. This accumulation hindered the smooth flow of water to the agricultural lands. A specific day was designated for this task, known as Herang Day. The term "Herang" originally referred to the dredging and clearing of large streams, allowing water to pass more easily.

On Herang Day, the elders of the village would announce the day in the mosque, and the Kadkhoda, accompanied by a few individuals, would walk through the village, calling out to the people, urging them to come and assist in cleaning the creeks. It was customary for one person from each family to participate in clearing the streams that supplied water to the farmland. They would remove grass and loamy soil, facilitating faster water flow. If someone couldn't attend, they were required to compensate by paying someone else who didn't own any land but could contribute their labor.

The silent beggar was well aware of these customs and knew that Herang was typically performed during late winter or early spring when farmers were less occupied with their own farms. Therefore, he found himself perplexed and contemplative, wondering about the reasons behind the call for Herang during the fall season. The silent beggar's attention shifted to Zulfiqar, who was engrossed in a battle with flies. The beggar hoped to ascertain whether Zulfiqar was awake or asleep, as if seeking his perspective and perhaps an answer. Zulfiqar was known for his ability to provide insight into various matters and possess knowledge of the events unfolding in the surrounding countryside.

As the sounds echoed through the village, Zulfiqar awoke, raising his head as he always did. His ears became more attuned to his surroundings. The silent beggar noticed Zulfiqar's surprise and realized that he, too, was unaware of what was happening in the village. Something must have occurred to summon the villagers to Herang at this time of year. Perhaps Imam Asghari was up to his usual tricks, cooking something up to deceive and exploit the people. Unable to bear the curiosity any longer, the silent beggar left his room and his gaze immediately fell upon his dog, also looking in the direction of the village from where the sounds emanated.

Filled with worry, the silent beggar ascended the hilltop, which provided a better view of the village. Majnoon faithfully followed, mirroring the silent beggar's every move. It was as if Majnoon sensed the beggar's concern and sought to share it. Majnoon knew that after Sattar's passing, the silent beggar sought solace in this peaceful place until death would relieve him from this world, reuniting him with Asyeh and Sattar on the other side.

The silent beggar understood that if people started flocking to this place, his tranquility would be disrupted. He worried more about his true identity being exposed—that he was none other than the renowned Kal Abbas, whose mansion had been forcefully taken over by Imam Asghari. Though unaware of the Imam's true identity as the killer of his older brother and their shepherd, the silent beggar knew that Imam Asghari posed a threat. This was not what the beggar had expected or desired.

The silent beggar no longer wandered or embarked on beggarly journeys; he sustained himself with the modest provisions he obtained from one or two plots of land and fruit trees in the vicinity, occasionally supplemented by what Zulfiqar brought. In his old age and with some physical limitations, he no longer evens visited the village cemetery, situated on the hill above the village, to pay tribute to his late parents with a mourning lament.

Lost in thought and filled with worry, he sat on a hill, his gaze fixed on the distant village. Beside him, Majnoon, his loyal dog, would occasionally lift his head and listen intently to the sounds emanating from the village, particularly when they grew louder. It was as if Majnoon, like the enigmatic beggar, sought to uncover Imam Asghari's hidden plans or the poisonous schemes he had concocted for the villagers.

The beggar, now aware that a crowd had gathered on the road above the village near the cemetery, pondered the significance of their presence. He wondered why the commotion centered around that area, as there was no creek or stream nearby. Typically, people gathered in front of the mosque or at the stream that needed dredging. Furthermore, he questioned the connection between someone's death and the necessity to venture towards Herang. The beggar found himself perplexed and lost in contemplation.

The howling of his faithful companion, Majnoon, snapped him back to reality. His attention was drawn to Zulfiqar at the bottom of the hill, making his way towards the village. It was evident that Zulfiqar's curiosity had gotten the better of him, compelling him to seek answers. Frustration etched on his face; Zulfiqar yearned to unravel the mysteries unfolding in the village. As he disappeared behind the hills, the beggar was left alone once more, accompanied only by the silence of the hills and his faithful companion, Majnoon.

Zulfiqar, who seemed to see everything, finally reached the hill overlooking the cemetery and the road, where a crowd had gathered. The crowd was so engrossed in the moment that they didn't even notice Zulfiqar as he made his way over the hill and sat down on a large stone slab, holding his head up in the air. With his ears sharpened, he listened intently to every sound, trying to figure out what was going on, while clutching his new, older flute that he had taken out of his pocket.

As Ghadam Baldy's voice rose, repeatedly calling for prayer, Zulfiqar knew that the arrival of Imam Asghari, Hajji Ghazanfar, or Kadkhoda was being announced. He didn't need to see them to know that, as usual, the three of them would be competing to reach the crowd first. On one hand, Haji Ghazanfar, the wealthiest man in the village, always used his money to influence people and generously paid khoums and zakat (religious taxes) to Imam Asghari. He believed he had a significant role in choosing the Kadkhoda and considered himself the lord and master of the village, believing he should have the final say.

On the other hand, Imam Asghari considered himself the religious leader of the people and the representative of the Guardian, Imam, and God. He believed his words held the utmost importance. Similarly, Kadkhoda, who saw himself as a representative of the law and the government, felt his authority should be respected, and he should have a say before the others. Kadkhoda often walked in the middle, sometimes aligning with Hajji Ghazanfar, and sometimes feeling obligated to be with Imam Asghari. By doing so, he kept both of them satisfied, as it seemed they both needed him on their side, resulting in them treating him well.

However, one thing was certain: all three of them would never let their secret competition be revealed to the people. They always showed respect for each other in public. Hence, the race to reach the people first was underway once again. Despite his overweight body and short stature, Imam Asghari managed to surpass Kadkhoda and Hajji Ghazanfar, reaching the people first, just ahead of Hajji Ghazanfar. Consequently, he was the first to address the crowd. Imam Asghari began his speech even before he reached the crowd, determined not to lose the spotlight to Hajji Ghazanfar, who was a step or two behind. As his voice resonated, the sounds of greetings and prayers subsided.

"The Muslim people of Shourcheh, who are more devout than those from other villages, it is religiously and traditionally obligatory for you to support this noble cause. I promise you that by doing so, all of you will undoubtedly go to heaven, and God will forgive all your sins."

Haji Ghazanfar climbed onto a towering rock, surpassing Imam Asghari in height, and began to interrupt him with increasingly loud speech. "Brave and faithful people of Shourcheh, Imam Asghari is right. We must heed the words of the representative of God, the Prophet, and the Imam. It is our duty to help build the road to the Shourcheh farm. If we neglect to construct this road and fail to claim the land that rightfully belongs to the people of Shourcheh, the godless people of Tikken will seize the opportunity and build their own road, taking over our farm."

As always, Mard Ali couldn't resist jumping into the conversation, squeezing himself between Imam Asghari and Haji Ghazanfar. "Yes, it is our obligation. Let's devour all the grass there... we're famished."

The game resumed for Ugly Ghadam and his gang, along with Mard Ali. Meanwhile, Kadkhoda seized the opportunity and quickly ascended to a higher ground than Imam Asghari and Haji Ghazanfar, taking over from Haji Ghazanfar and lending his seal of approval to Imam Asghari's and Haji Ghazanfar's words, so as not to fall behind the other two. Imam Asghari refused to remain silent and positioned himself on even higher ground than Kadkhoda, reciting and preaching to the people. He delivered a final speech and then, picking up a few small rocks, threw them aside to symbolize the commencement of road construction from the village of Shourcheh to the silent beggar's farm, invoking greetings and blessings. Inspired by their Imam's wishes, the people eagerly followed suit, wielding shovels, pickaxes, and sledgehammers, and the road construction began.

Ugly Ghadam and his gang refused to remain idle; they continued urging the people to pray, emphasizing that their efforts were in accordance with God's will. Now, the people worked while chanting prayers, their voices growing louder and louder as the work progressed. Some busied themselves by tossing dry weeds into the fire to produce smoke, while others circulated among the workers, serving them refreshing drinks.

Zulfiqar, still perplexed, wondered where the people were constructing the road and what they meant by Shourcheh's farm. Nonetheless, he had cleaned and prepared his old flute, which he had obtained from the silent beggar's place. In order to catch up with the caravan and announce his presence, he began to play. Its melodious tones soared through the air, delighting the listeners, and boosting their spirits, motivating them to work harder. The flute harmonized perfectly with the religious chants, creating an atmosphere akin to a concert or musical performance. However, Zulfiqar remained mentally puzzled.

Even the children enthusiastically lent a hand, carrying most of the materials and removing belts that didn't fit in the shovels, placing them aside by the roadside. The older women, too, were not idle; they refreshed the weary workers with their sweet syrup and jugs of cold water. Amidst the bustling activity of young and old, men and women, three men stood apart from the rest: Imam Asghari, Haji Ghazanfar, and Kadkhoda. They sat atop their mules, leisurely observing and engaging in conversation as if they were exempt from the village's toils, detached from its endeavors.

Before long, the loaded donkeys set in motion, and Zulfiqar, occasionally pausing to take a deep breath, turned his head towards the sky, his senses filled with the clamor of the people. Though still bewildered, he continued playing the flute. However, the resounding strikes of hammers, which had traveled to the very foundation of the rock upon which Zulfiqar perched, grew increasingly deafening. The pebbles, propelled by the force of the hammer blows, now found their way towards Zulfiqar's head, face, and feet. With no other option, he reluctantly moved away, and the melody of his flute was abruptly silenced. Seeking refuge from the unrelenting barrage of pebbles, he fled in search of respite, as if Zulfiqar existed neither within nor outside the people's minds, remaining invisible to their eyes. It was as if they, too, were blind, just like Zulfiqar.

Finally finding safety from the pelting stones, Zulfiqar managed to escape their assault. Yet, his thoughts still in disarray, he was taken aback as Ugly Ghadam approached him, embracing him tightly and planting several affectionate kisses on his face. "Mr. Zulfiqar, you are the eyes and light in Imam Asghari's heart. Without you, nobody would have known that the silent beggar had dug a well on his land, or that an aqueduct flowed there, brimming with water. Imam said that because of what you did, you are destined for heaven."

Zulfiqar, still bewildered by Ghadam Baldy's words, was startled as Mard Ali's voice replaced Ghadam Baldy's. Standing beside him and watching intently, Mard Ali's words reverberated in his ears. "Yes, Mr. Zulfiqar, precisely because you exposed and revealed the silent beggar's aqueduct and land, you will surely go to Hell."

Zulfiqar was deeply affected by what he had heard, feeling both overwhelmed and disoriented. He reached a point where he no longer wanted to hear the words of Ugly Ghadam or Mard Ali. Mard Ali's speech had made it clear what Ugly Ghadam meant, leaving him immensely sorrowful and devoid of the will to continue living. Self-hatred consumed him even more. Lost in his thoughts, he unknowingly walked away from them, unaware that he was heading towards a crowd. Before he knew it, he found himself in the midst of a chanting crowd fervently constructing a road. Summoning all his strength, he pushed through the crowd, freeing himself and creating distance between them. He wandered aimlessly, feeling bewildered and burdened, like a lost soul, his self-loathing intensifying.

It was at that moment that he recollected the years-long drought that plagued the region, particularly the villages of Shourcheh and Tikken, which suffered the most. He remembered a compassionate old woman who had brought him food one cold night when he was sleeping in the mosque. Grateful for her kindness, he began to pray for her well-being and blessings. In the midst of his prayer, he mentioned the ongoing drought.

"In this season of drought that afflicts everyone and everywhere, who would have imagined that just a few miles away, on the hill, there lies a field teeming with greenery and abundant water capable of irrigating the entire village of Shourcheh? It is all by the will of God. However, perhaps the people have committed sins, for if they cleanse their hearts and repent sincerely, the water from the aqueducts will flow abundantly, just like the forbidden water well that was drilled on a farm above the village."

What Zulfiqar remained oblivious to be the fact that within a week, all the villagers became aware of the existence of wells in the forbidden area. They flocked to Imam Asghari day and night, beseeching him to perform one of his miracles and bring an end to the drought. Realizing that the only way to address the villagers' demands was to assert the village of Shourcheh's ownership of the forbidden area promptly, Imam Asghari resolved to act swiftly before the neighboring village of Tikken learned about the water well and aqueducts on the destitute beggar's farm. It was imperative to claim ownership of the area on behalf of Shourcheh.

Therefore, he mobilized the people, urging them to build a road to the farm and secure their rights. They even christened it "Shourcheh's Farm."

Remembering what had transpired in the mosque, he realized that he was responsible for the unfolding events. Without hesitation, he hastened to the humble dwelling of the silent beggar. However, unbeknownst to him, a group of three individuals—Imam Asghari, Hajji Ghazanfar, and Kadkhoda—accompanied by Ugly Ghadam and his entourage, had set off for the silent beggar's farm long before his arrival. They presumed the place to be uninhabited, assuming that any visitors would come and go intermittently. Clutching his weathered cane, Zulfiqar embarked on his journey. Typically, when Zulfiqar was in a rush, it meant he carried firsthand information, and this occasion was no exception. The difference was that he earnestly wished not to bear the burden of such sorrowful tidings, for he himself was the cause.

Meanwhile, the silent beggar sat on a distant hill, puffing on his pipe and gazing thoughtfully towards the village. His loyal dog, Majnoon, sat beside him, while his snores expressed his displeasure at the unwelcome guests who approached the hill. They jokingly made their way towards the silent beggar's abode. Observing the gathering, the beggar realized that the commotion in the village must be connected to him and his dwelling. He had no doubt that their destination was his humble house. Overwhelmed with worry and despondency, he rose, walked, and entered his room.

Peering through a small window overlooking the hill, he watched as the uninvited guests drew nearer to his place. He settled against the wall beneath the window, deep in contemplation of his past and present. Memories of his life's journey flooded his mind. He pondered the choices he had made, reflecting on his actions, and discerning which were right and which were wrong. As he contemplated, he realized, after a lifetime, that he harbored regret for many of his past behaviors. He yearned to seek forgiveness from those he had wronged.

In his introspection, he came to understand the essence of life, likening it to the rhythm of day and night. The day brought forth beauty, warmth, light, happiness, and joy with the sunrise, but it faded all too swiftly, succumbing to the darkness of night. Sorrow, grief, and sadness followed, yet even the lifeless night eventually yielded to the return of light and vitality. Humans, too, traversed this cycle repeatedly.

The silent beggar grew weary of this ceaseless repetition. Isolated for a prolonged period, he spent countless nights and days immersed in deep contemplation, drawing invaluable lessons from life. Throughout his solitude, he pondered the duality of existence the good and the bad, the hardships and the comforts, the joys and sorrows, the friendships, and enmities. Ultimately, he realized that all would eventually cease, as if they had never existed, just like the cycle of day and night.

His ultimate realization led him to the conclusion that it would be better to forgive and forget the hardships inflicted upon him by others, particularly Sattar and Asyeh. He also hoped for forgiveness from those whom he may have wronged. He wished to convey to people that he had paid the price for his sins and now desired to spend the remainder of his fleeting life in peace and solitude, cherishing his privacy.

The silent beggar was deeply engrossed in his thoughts, causing him to take a moment to register the barking of his dog, Majnoon. As soon as he heard the dog's barks, he realized that uninvited guests must have arrived at his humble hut. Majnoon, in the meantime, had been pacing back and forth in front of the door, barking at the approaching intruders. Soon, the voices of Imam Asghari and one or two others grew louder.

"Get this filthy, unclean dog away from my sight! Where did it come from?" exclaimed Imam Asghari in a disdainful tone.

Ugly Ghadam and his gang joined in, shouting at the dog, and launching an attack by throwing rocks at Majnoon. Eventually, they managed to drive him away from the vicinity of the hut. However, Majnoon didn't give up. He retreated to the backyard, continuing to bark and express his protest against them. Unfortunately, as the attackers pursued him, his barks grew fainter and fainter.

The silent beggar wasn't pleased with the treatment his dog was receiving, but he remained absorbed in his thoughts, staring at the ground. Suddenly, Imam Asghari's voice emerged once again from outside. "Clearly, the presence of the dog indicates that someone must be inside the shed."

Imam Asghari then raised his voice, addressing the hut more forcefully. "You, the stranger inside! Don't you want an uninvited guest?"

Uncertain about what to do, the silent beggar found himself at a loss. At that moment, Haji Ghazanfar's voice joined the chorus of the uninvited guests. "Dervish, the guest is beloved of God. Are you inside or not?"

Kadkhoda interjected, "Haji, he may not be home, or perhaps something has happened to our neighbor. Wouldn't it be better for us to check on him?"

Imam Asghari took charge of the situation, stating, "Kadkhoda, Haji, we should not only offer our help but also apologize for our neglect towards our neighbor. We should extend our apologies, assist him, and make amends, especially considering he has no wife or children to support him."

However, Haji Ghazanfar interrupted Imam Asghari, adding, "There is no doubt that our intentions are good, not only to help our neighbor but also to seek his forgiveness for our past negligence. Besides, Imam and Kadkhoda, from what I have observed and heard, he appears to be a pious man, never causing harm or inconvenience to anyone, be it human or animal. Imam Asghari, we should have visited him sooner."

Upon hearing his name, Imam Asghari wasted no time and interrupted Haji Ghazanfar, speaking louder as he began to recite based on his religious beliefs. "Haji, Kadkhoda, according to our religious teachings, reaching out to your neighbor and checking on them is more important than praying for your entire life. It is considered more obligatory than prayer and fasting for Muslims. They also consider it more obligatory than assisting and supporting your own family, especially if the neighbor is a stranger and poses no harm. In such cases, it becomes even more mandatory. Imagine, Haji, if God forbid something terrible happened to our neighbor and we failed to help, it would be a grave sin."

All these speeches and discussions were an attempt to determine if someone was inside and would come out to greet them. However, no matter how long they waited, there was no response from within, except for Majnoon, who incessantly barked and attacked the crowd but was eventually driven away. Finally, Imam Asghari mustered some courage and cautiously opened the door, accompanied by a fervent prayer, followed by Haji Ghazanfar and Kadkhoda. The rest of the companions stood near the door and behind the windows, observing. As they entered, they all paused, their eyes falling upon the silent beggar squatting on an old mat beneath the window, staring at the ground as if he had just awakened or was seeking solace in God. The silent beggar didn't move his head and didn't know how to react or whether he should speak. For now, he chose to remain silent. He recognized them all, having dealt with them for many years, from the time when he was wealthy and powerful to his current state as the silent beggar who danced and

played for them, seemingly nobody. He remembered everything. He knew that the villagers hadn't come to see him with good intentions and a friendly heart, especially Haji Ghazanfar, Kadkhoda, and Imam Asghari, who he could already sense would stop at nothing to get rid of him and take his place. However, they were unaware of the silent beggar's true identity - he was none other than their blessing, Kal Abbas, though by now, no one even remembered who Kal Abbas was. Yet, he was well-acquainted with Haji Ghazanfar and Kadkhoda and knew where they came from. He knew they were the sons of those who had stolen his possessions when he was exposed as a thief, and now, he stood face to face with them. As he adjusted himself, the silent beggar's eyes briefly met Imam Asghari's, triggering a doubt within the imam that this beggar might not be who he claimed to be. The imam felt like he recognized him from somewhere, though he couldn't pinpoint the exact place. Of course, it was only Zulfiqar who had grown accustomed to the silent beggar's presence and spent most of his time with him, yet even he remained unaware of the beggar's true identity.

Still gazing at the floor in silence, the beggar observed the familiar faces of those who once claimed to be his friends and had once considered him their master. But when he needed their support, they turned into his worst enemies, driving him and his family out of their home and the village. Now, an individual who called himself an Imam had forcefully taken over his home under the guise of religion. Presently, they stood before him, preaching about friendship, honesty, neighborliness, brotherhood, equality, religion, faith, and camaraderie. However, the silent beggar, no longer the same Kal Abbas, had filled his existence with love, affection, peace, and friendship.

Without waiting for their blessings, the uninvited guests found the beggar silently rising to his feet and approaching the teapots to clean them. It seemed he intended to make tea for his guests, regardless of how he felt about them as friends. He did not utter a word or make eye contact with anyone. The uninvited guests respectfully stepped aside, relieved to see him move and realizing he intended to offer them tea.

As the beggar left the room, the guests surveyed the small space once more, only finding the same worn-out mat, a couple of old quilts and pillows, and a few pieces of dishes, teapots, and cups. Perplexed, they exchanged glances, unsure whether to sit outside on the platform in front of the room or inside. Eventually, Imam Asghari broke the silence.

"Haji, Kadkhoda, it is better to sit outside on the platform. The sun is pleasant, and we shouldn't hinder our neighbor from tending to his work. It appears he is making tea for his guests."

Everyone followed suit, leaving the room, and gathering on both sides of the platform in front of the door. Engaging in warm conversation, they eagerly awaited the hot tea. Meanwhile, the silent beggar remained inside the room, lost in contemplation, his gaze wandering aimlessly. Through a small window, he spotted his dog perched on a stone slab above the room, observing the gathering with evident displeasure. Mard Ali, chanting and defending the enemy of Islam, approached the dog. It seemed as though the dog and Mard Ali recognized each other, exchanging warm greetings and displaying friendly gestures as if they had been acquainted for ages. Majnoon, the dog, delighted to find someone other than the silent beggar and Zulfiqar who didn't consider him unclean or mistreat him, someone who seemed to enjoy playing with him, completely forgot about Imam Asghari and the others. However, the silent beggar wasn't entirely content. After years of solitude, he realized that the peace and tranquility of his life had been

disrupted. Furthermore, he pondered why they suddenly remembered him and his abode, seeking him out. What perplexed him, even more, was that he had heard their voice calling for Herang before their arrival. He knew their visit must be somehow connected to the call for Herang. Lost in thought, Imam Asghari's voice interrupted his musings once again.

"Neighbor, do you need any assistance?"

The silent beggar turned to notice Imam Asghari's head appearing in front of the door, his gaze evaluating him. Their eyes met briefly, but it was enough to shake the silent beggar and dispel the negative energy that had engulfed him. He disliked the way the Imam looked at him, causing him to regain his composure. He picked up the brazier, exited through the back door into the backyard, and began setting it on fire to make tea.

In the backyard, Majnoon leaped over the wall and approached the silent beggar. Mard Ali, who had lost his playmate, frowned, and climbed up to sit on the wall, observing the interaction between the beggar and the dog. For some unknown reason, he found himself lost in thought, pondering over someone and something he couldn't quite identify.

The silent beggar was no different from Mard Ali; his mind wandered aimlessly. He wasn't even aware that Majnoon stood next to him or that Mard Ali had joined the group of onlookers, watching his every move. Lost in contemplation, he stared into the burning flame, contemplating his next course of action. Suddenly, he remembered that he needed to fetch the teapot. Upon entering the room to retrieve it, he was taken aback to find the platform empty, devoid of any occupants. He gazed at the vacant platform in astonishment, making sure he wasn't mistaken. He wasn't. Surprised, he scanned the area through a small window overlooking the mulberry tree, hoping to locate his uninvited guests. To his surprise, they had gathered near the water well and the opening of the small aqueduct, where water was springing out. He also noticed a couple of individuals standing by Asyeh and Sattar's graves, inspecting them. Realizing that this situation could spell trouble, he worried about potential questions regarding the graves' occupants. Anxiety consumed his thoughts as he pondered whether Zulfiqar had discovered Asyeh and Sattar's resting place and informed others. He also wondered if Zulfiqar had learned his true identity and shared it with the crowd. His mind raced, contemplating the best course of action amidst the chaos, neglecting to acknowledge Imam Asghari's raised voice shouting towards him.

"Neighbor, I am blessing the water wells and praying for their sustenance," Imam Asghari's voice echoed loudly. "Water is a blessing in these times of drought, which has caused suffering and misery everywhere. You must be a devoted servant of God, and your strong faith has earned you this special blessing. I pray that it never dries up like the other aqueducts around us."

After hearing Imam Asghari's unsettling comments, the silent beggar found them unpleasant and bothersome. However, they served as a wake-up call, reminding him of the reason they were all there in the first place the scarcity of water. The encounter shed light on this crucial issue. Despite his reluctance to engage in a face-to-face conversation with Imam Asghari, the silent beggar quietly took the jug of water, filled the teapots, and carried them with him as he left the window. He headed towards the backyard to make tea over the fire, which had now subdued its intense flames.

Placing the teapots beside the fire, the silent beggar stood there, lost in contemplation. He pondered the idea of resuming his travels, but his aging body lacked the strength required. His intention was to remain there until his time came to cross over to the other side, where he hoped to find freedom at last. As he was lost in his thoughts, the barking of his dog brought him back to reality. He turned and noticed a few individuals peering into the backyard from outside, behind a relatively short wall. The silent beggar fixed his gaze upon them, and his piercing stare unnerved each of them.

Despite their attempts to show respect, the individuals received no response from the silent beggar. Instead, they began repairing the wall. The silent beggar tried hard to recall if he knew any of them but failed to recognize any familiar faces. Majnoon, his dog, continued to bark at them, but they were too intimidated to approach him. Concerned by the sudden appearance of these people and their unexpected assistance in fixing his wall, the silent beggar pondered their identity. He knew everyone in the village of Shourcheh but couldn't place any of these individuals. Their presence left him puzzled. He wondered where they had come from but found no answers, only further confusion.

Suddenly, Mard Ali's voice interrupted his thoughts. "More thieves have come to steal your land. They are from the village of Tikken, hurrying to keep up with the people of Shourcheh... hello, master."

Upon hearing Mard Ali's voice, the silent beggar turned his gaze and saw Mard Ali sitting on the short wall, wearing his usual smile. Mard Ali held up a piece of debris from the wall that was being repaired. "Look at them. They have come to steal your water. They are water thieves."

Hearing Mard Ali's voice and catching sight of him, Majnoon rushed over to him. The dog bounded towards Mard Ali once again, diverting his attention from the silent beggar, and they started playing together. However, the silent beggar couldn't help but ponder on whether Mard Ali recognized him or not. Even though he greeted him as before, saying "Hello Master," he still wasn't certain. Ultimately, he picked up the brazier and carried it into the room, placing it in its usual spot.

Imam Asghar, Kadkhoda, Haji Ghazanfar, and a few others returned, settling down on the platform in front of the door. They were engrossed in lighthearted banter and had no inkling that the people of Tikken had also arrived at the farm. These newcomers were busy repairing the walls, claiming the land as their own. The silent beggar prepared two cups of tea, placing them on a plain plate outside the door. Then he realized he had forgotten the sugar cubes. He retraced his steps and grabbed a small ball filled with sugar cubes, placing it beside the tea. As he returned to the window, his gaze fell upon more villagers from Tikken, with more approaching. The dog and Mard Ali remained engrossed in their play, seemingly detached from the world around them. Suddenly, the silent beggar's attention was drawn to Zulfiqar, who had his head held high. He hurried towards the room, sensing that Zulfiqar had an urgent and significant report to share. The silent beggar's intuition proved correct, for even before he reached the platform, Zulfiqar's voice rang out, brimming with excitement. "Come out, Mr. Silent beggar! Come out, I have hot news for you, where are you, dervish?"

As Zulfiqar's voice echoed through the air, the crowd before the podium fell into a hushed silence. No one uttered a word or made a move; all eyes were fixed on him, eagerly anticipating his breaking news. Zulfiqar's cane swung dangerously close to Imam Asghari's foot, dangling precariously from the platform's edge. Yet, with a swift maneuver, Imam Asghari deftly withdrew his foot, narrowly avoiding the cane's impact as it struck the platform instead.

Leaning against the garden wall adjacent to the platform, which extended from beneath the arch at the same height, Zulfiqar sought support. Despite the arrival of autumn, the sunflowers stood tall in the two gardens flanking the platforms, their vibrant petals reaching toward the rooftop. Bees buzzed busily from petal to petal, indulging in the flowers' nectar before taking flight, their triumph evident as they disappeared into the vast expanse of the sky.

Setting his cane against the platform's wall, Zulfiqar sensed a disquieting presence nearby, as if he were being observed. The congregation remained eerily silent, their gaze fixated upon Zulfiqar, observing his every move, awaiting his next pronouncement. Removing his hat, he retrieved a handkerchief from his pocket and began to dab the sweat from his forehead. Once satisfied that all was well, Zulfiqar donned his hat once more, his voice rising once again.

"Step forth, Mr. Silent Beggar, and witness the deeds of these rootless, godless individuals. See how they have forgotten about their own aqueduct, its once abundant flow diminishing day by day, while they busy themselves constructing a riad to connect you to the village... Where are you, Mr. Silent Beggar? I could almost taste the freshness of your tea on the breeze."

Then, with his head held high, he picked up his cane and walked under the arch, positioning himself between the two platforms. At that moment, he felt a flicker of uncertainty, unsure if anyone was watching. He scanned his surroundings, his gaze darting from person to person. Imam Asghari, Kadkhoda, Haji Ghazanfar, and the others remained silent, so still that not a breath could be heard, lest Zulfiqar detect it. What had started as a playful game had transformed into something serious. Everyone presents now pondered their next move, their eyes fixed on Zulfiqar, their smiles filled with mockery and silence.

Unbeknownst to Zulfiqar, elders such as Imam Asghari, Kadkhoda, Haji Asghar, and other influential individuals from the village of Shourcheh had gathered on both sides of the platform, seated in anticipation in front of the room. They initiated a conversation with the quiet beggar who remained inside, speaking to him directly. "Mr. Silent beggar, come out and witness the transformation of these people. Until yesterday, they evicted you from your home and chased you out of the village. But today, they are constructing a road for you, extending their friendship and camaraderie. Mr. Silent beggar, come and see the sumptuous meal they have prepared for you. Come and take a seat, witness the culinary skills of Imam Asghari and Haji Ghazanfar. Come on, Mr. Silent beggar, come and observe how your water wells have made you the most favored person in this village. Come out and witness how you can outwit them and rise above. Where are you?"

A moment passed without a sound, and Zulfiqar regained his senses momentarily. He once again raised his head, surveying the surroundings. Kadkhoda, Haji Ghazanfar, and Imam Asghari's rage reached a boiling point. They were bewildered and at a loss, their confusion so profound that even if stabbed with a sharp knife, their blood would refuse to flow. Their enraged gaze remained fixed on Zulfiqar as they contemplated what to do next. They understood that the silent beggar likely held Zulfiqar in high regard, and harming him might upset the beggar. They had no desire to incur the beggar's displeasure. Still doubtful, Zulfiqar raised his voice once more. "Come out, and I will reveal to you the true nature of this impostor, Imam Asghari. He will concoct yet another false verse from the holy book Quran and declare that your farm and water aqueduct are subject to khoums and zakat (religious taxes) based on religious law. He will make it permissible to seize everything you possess, and soon they will cast you out into the desert... to perish."

Standing right in front of Imam Asghari, Zulfiqar's speech was not over yet, that cautiously and skeptically he decided to sit on the podium. Not knowing he was sitting on Imam Asghari's lap, he had not yet fully touched Imam Asghari when Imam's hands rose and hit Zulfiqar hard on the head and pushed him forward so much that Mr. Zulfiqar was thrown and crashed onto the people on the opposite platform inside Haji Ghazanfar's lap. Now it was Haji Ghazanfar's turn to pour his heart and soul on Zulfiqar, and he did not hesitate, his attack begun with the help of others sitting beside him, within a blink of eyes, Zulfiqar was pushed away from Haji Ghazanfar and crashed onto the ground between the two platforms right in front of Imam Asghari. It had not yet dawned on him that the army of Islam led by Imam Asghari and the ration-eaters of Imam, had fallen to Zulfiqar. With Imam Asghari who was enraged and out of control was landing the most blow, even Haji Ghazanfar and Kadkhoda did not sit idle and begun to kick poor Zulfiqar. Now the fists and kicks of Imam Asghari and his gang were falling on the defenseless Zulfiqar. It seemed there was no concern if he was an old man and defenseless. Zulfiqar was trying to get away from underneath the people's arms and legs of the soldiers of Imam and entered the room as he began shouting out asking for the silent beggar's help. Just as Zulfiqar's hand reach the door, they come across the silent beggar's foot who appeared in the doorway holding on to a plate with a few hot teas inside of it, and grabbed it tightly. Struggle between Zulfiqar and the people as he is trying to scape his attacker through the silent beggar's foot, causes the tea tray was released from The Silent Beggar's hand and the cups and saucers from the tray full of hot tea spilled and poured on the head, neck, and face of Zulfiqar continued his effort paddling to escape beating and perhaps death. But again, Imam Asghari, Kadkhoda and Haji Ghazanfar continue their beating and did not intend to consent, as if they had gone to war of blind war. All of them trampled on Zulfiqar's back and head and face with their thick leather boots.

Just as the silent beggar came to Zulfiqar's aid, trying to pull him inside the room to save him, the sound of a dog barking was heard from the front of the platform, followed by the shouting voice of Mard Ali who began to shout out at the Imam Asghari and others who were busy to punish Zolfqar. "Oh, if you are not a Muslim why do you hit the unfortunate helpless blind? If you are man enough and you feel so strong, then go and fight those people from Tikken who are here. You are godless. Let go of that poor helpless blind man."

At that moment, Mard Ali was consumed by rage, completely disoriented and unaware of his surroundings. He was fervently trying to protect Zulfiqar, shouting at the top of his lungs. However, he was not immune to the punches and kicks intended for Zulfiqar. Despite his best efforts to fend off the attackers and guide Zulfiqar to safety, the blows kept coming. Eventually, Zulfiqar managed to drag himself through the motionless beggars and into the room.

The crowd, led by Imam Asghari, showed no signs of relenting. They were on the verge of barging into the room when they unexpectedly encountered the silent beggar. Their eyes locked with Imam Asghari's furious and bloodshot eyes, and they engaged in an intense and challenging stare-down. Haji Ghazanfar, Kadkhoda, and the others retreated, but Imam Asghari refused to back down. He continued to lock eyes with the silent beggar, seething with anger, expecting the beggar to move aside so he could resume his assault on Zulfiqar.

However, the silent beggar remained unfazed, neither blinking nor budging. It was at this moment that Haji Ghazanfar spoke up. "Shaykh, Imam, let him go... He made a mistake. Imam, let him go and sit down. He is a blind and shameless man, blind without eyes and shameless. Don't bother, Imam. Come and sit. We can deal with him later."

Mard Ali interjected, raising his wooden sword in the air, and shouted, "Well, Haji is right... Let him go. Haji says the blind man feels no shame. If you, who have sight, possess any sense of shame, how can you expect the poor blind man to have any? Where is your shame? Show it, if you have any. Why do you all target the defenseless, helpless blind man? Are you afraid of the people from Tikken? If you truly consider yourselves brave, then go fight those Tikken people who are stealing your water right under your noses!"

Imam Asghari could only hear fragments of Mard Ali's protest amidst the chaos, particularly his questioning of whether people with sight had any shame. Angrily, he shouted at Ghadam Baldy, "For God's sake, get rid of this crazy man for a few minutes!"

Following Imam Asghari's order, Ugly Ghadam and his gang swiftly moved to remove Mard Ali from the scene, as they had done before. However, Mard Ali refused to back down, and their chase ensued. "I am not uttering blasphemy. Why must you confront only a pitiful, impoverished blind man? If you are truly courageous, then go face the Tikken people who have come to steal the silent beggar's water. You can see that they are one step ahead of you, repairing the walls."

None of the people gathered in front of the platform could comprehend Mard Ali's intentions. Their anger towards Zulfiqar had blinded them, preventing them from seeing anything beyond their own rage. Even the workers repairing the wall behind the platform were unnoticed. Imam Asghari, with the intervention of Haji Ghazanfar and Kadkhoda, finally sat down on the platform facing Haji Ghazanfar. However, his gaze remained fixed on the silent beggar, as if he had gleaned something from the beggar's eyes that others had missed. The atmosphere was suffused with silence, occasionally interrupted by Mard Ali's grumbles and the barks of dogs. The silent beggar diligently collected the shattered cups and saucers strewn between the two platforms and carried them to a nearby room.

Imam Asghari, still simmering with anger, broke the silence and began to speak passionately about the earth, time, and various other subjects. The rest of the congregation joined him, engaging in short conversations with one another. Amidst this exchange, Ugly Ghadam raised his voice. "Imam, it has been said that the blind has no shame and will not feel remorse. If you order, I am prepared to spill his blood in the name of religion."

Imam Asghari's voice, filled with hatred and anger, cut him off. "Haji, we have had our fair share of encounters with these ignorant and godless individuals who reject our holy messengers and Imams. They now seek to deceive us in broad daylight, insulting our religion and faith."

Kadkhoda interjected, "If only we had silenced them from the beginning, cutting their tongues and putting them in their rightful place. We wouldn't have to deal with them here and now."

Imam Asghari's gaze briefly fell upon Zulfiqar inside the room before locking onto the furious eyes of the silent beggar. At that moment, the melodious call to prayer emanated from behind the silent beggar's dwelling, reaching their ears from miles away. Only Majnoon, the dog, responded with his incessant barking. The audience, sitting on the platform, was taken aback, unable to fathom how quickly the road to the silent beggar's house had been constructed, stretching several hundred yards from the humble hut. Forgotten were the silent beggar, Zulfiqar, and Mard Ali as everyone stared in astonishment towards the source of the enchanting sound.

Their eyes landed on Mard Ali, now more impassioned than ever, twirling his wooden sword in the air once again, his wailing recommencing. He was prepared to wage war against Islam's greatest enemy. "People, why are you still seated? Are you blind, deaf, or simply afraid of the thugs from Tikken? They have come to steal the silent beggar's water right before your eyes, and yet you sit there like cowards. Stand up! The thugs have claimed the house too!"

Everyone remained perplexed, their minds unable to comprehend Mard Ali's words until Ugly Ghadam finally spoke up. "Imam, Haji Agha, Kadkhoda, why are we sitting here while the people of Tikken have deceived us and built their road here before us? Look, they have already reached this place and are busy repairing the house and farm while we're stuck here, fighting among ourselves and with a blind, deranged man."

For a brief moment, the crowd failed to grasp Ghadam Baldy's message. Confusion filled the air as everyone abruptly rose from their seats and ventured outside the arch. To their surprise, they discovered that those chanting about the legendary mystic warrior were actually from the village of Tikken, not their own village of Shourcheh. Furthermore, they observed that many of them were repairing the road leading from Tikken to the silent beggar's residence and farmland. A collective astonishment gripped the crowd as they exchanged bewildered glances, rendered speechless.

Meanwhile, inside the room, the silent beggar peered out through a small window, observing the commotion in the crowd. Simultaneously, he handed Zulfiqar a handkerchief to clean himself. Zulfiqar, filled with a mixture of suspicion, fear, and embarrassment, composed himself, raised his head, and attentively listened to the voices outside. It seemed that understanding the events unfolding beyond the room held greater significance for him than his own well-being. The silent beggar poured a cup of tea into a small bowl, added some sugar, and offered it to Zulfiqar before taking a seat beside him. In an instant, Zulfiqar eagerly gulped down the tea in two or three sips. The silent beggar proceeded to prepare and light his pipe, seemingly unaffected by the turmoil outside. He inhaled the smoke a few times before passing the pipe to Zulfiqar. Without hesitation, Zulfiqar ignited the tobacco, astonishing the silent beggar with the intensity of his inhalations and exhalations. Soon, the room was filled with Zulfiqar's smoke, enveloping the surroundings. Leaning his head against the wall, the silent beggar drifted into deep contemplation, closing his eyes. It was as though he deliberately sought to avoid witnessing or contemplating the unfolding conflict between the people of Shourcheh and Tikken.

The smoke from the pipe slipped out of the window, disappearing into the air. Outside the room, there was no sign of controversy or commotion. The sight of the silent beggar saddened his heart deeply. He realized that he could no longer be alone and spend his days with his secrets and needs. This intrusion into his privacy was a first, and he knew it wouldn't stop from now on. Aware of the troublemakers from the village of Shourcheh, he knew their presence was not without reason. They wouldn't inadvertently show kinship, equality, kindness, or brotherhood. It was all part of a game, a plan to never leave him alone.

He also knew that everyone was gathering around his aqueduct. Now he understood why the villagers, who didn't want to see his shadow in the village, suddenly regarded him as their best, favorite, and most respected man. They were interested in his farm and aqueducts, not him. They even named the farm "Shourcheh's Farm." He knew his farm was situated between the villages of Tikken and Shourcheh, making it a disputed property. The Tikkenians defeated the village of Shourcheh and constructed a road to his farm from Tikken. Both villages sought to claim ownership of the silent beggar's property, which he had inherited from Sattar. The water from his farm was vital to both communities.

Now people from Tikken were also present, and they referred to the silent beggar's farm as "Tikken Farm." His farm had two names, and people from both villages claimed ownership, while the silent beggar, the actual owner, seemed to have no say or existence. Curiously, no title or deed had been issued for the property, and until a few months ago, no one dared to venture there. The truth was that no one knew about Sattar, the one who built it, being present. Now everyone considered the silent beggar as the customary and legal owner of the farm, and both villages knew they had no right to claim it.

In fact, some believed that the claim of ownership over the silent beggar's farm was, in fact, a favor to him by the villages of Shourcheh and Tikken. Otherwise, someone like Imam Asghari would sneak up, bribe their way into ownership, and the silent beggar would be easily thrown out. The silent beggar could also perceive that both villages, Tikken and Shourcheh, had gathered on his property to stake their claims. It was only a matter of time before they turned on each other, leading the authorities to intervene. If someone recognized him, the Law Men would take him away, which was not what he desired in his old age when he was around 90 years old, awaiting his time to pass and join Asyeh and Sattar on the other side.

However, it was certain that Imam Asghari would not step back so easily and allow the farm to be taken over by the Village of Tikken, giving them ownership of its water. The silent beggar could now hear the voices of Imam Asghari, Kadkhoda, and Haji Ghazanfar from outside. They were shouting at the people of Tikken who were busy repairing the silent beggar's house and the road in front of it. No matter how loudly they shouted, the repairs continued. Majnoon, the silent beggar's dog, refused to give up and kept barking, trying to enter the room to be with his owner. However, he was repeatedly attacked and chased away. Mard Ali also continued to boast and chant, coming to the dog's defense. In the midst of all this, Imam Asghari occasionally cursed at Majnoon, wanting to suffocate him, but the dog persisted.

Inside, the silent beggar and Zulfiqar sat in silence, lost in thought about what might be happening outside. The commotion caused by the dog made them realize that a fight between the two villages, Tikken and Shourcheh, was imminent, and it would likely be a bloody conflict. Their suspicions were not unfounded. Imam Asghari was a cunning man who would seize any opportunity to create conflict between the two villages, as it would only benefit him. He would involve the people in the conflict and then sit back, laugh, and take advantage of the situation. Imam Asghari, being smart enough not to initiate a fight at that moment, knew that the people of Tikken outnumbered them significantly. With their larger numbers, the people of Tikken could inflict severe damage upon them. Moreover, Imam Asghari had no credibility with the people of Tikken; he was considered a thief and a swindler, so they might come after him first.

Recognizing the need to retreat strategically, Imam Asghari approached Haji Ghazanfar and Kadkhoda, taking them aside and whispering in their ears. He instructed them to seek help from the village immediately. Kadkhoda wasted no time and sent Ugly Ghadam to the Village of Shourcheh for assistance. While Ghadam was on his way, Imam Asghari and his entourage decided to pull back and wait for help to arrive. At Imam Asghari's request, they didn't wait idly. Instead, they quietly and carefully began repairing the area around the water well. Imam Asghari's attention was fixated on the people of Tikken, concerned that they might protest or claim ownership of the well. He was prepared to retreat without conflict if necessary.

Imam Asghari also frequently recited and spoke about Imam Hussein, the Islamic legend who went to war and sacrificed his life to bring water to his people. He compared their actions to Imam Hussein's, emphasizing the significance of water. He then took Haji Ghazanfar and Kadkhoda to the side and whispered to them, "Haji, Kadkhoda, the main asset of this farm is this water well and its aqueduct, which we are taking. However, this fight will likely end up in the hands of the police and the court. That's where we claim that whoever has taken any section owns it, while we hold control over the water well and its aqueduct. Then we turn off the water supply, leaving them with everything else. When they have no water, everything will dry up, and eventually, they will leave... and we will take it all."

As usual, Mard Ali echoed Imam Asghari's words and continued his chanting and fighting.

Inside the room, the silent beggar remained seated next to Zulfiqar, enjoying his privacy while smoking his pipe. He pondered over the ongoing events and contemplated what would unfold. Peering through the windows on all four sides of the room, he heard the commotion outside—people trespassing and dividing his property—as if he, the silent beggar, didn't exist or had no rightful claim to the land. Despite witnessing the same individuals discussing friendship, kindness, and God just minutes ago, it all seemed to dissolve within moments, as if water evaporating. He observed how they were now consumed with seizing what belonged to him, oblivious to his existence.

Soon, people from both sides gathered, their shouts accompanied by shovels, sticks, clubs, rocks, and anything else they could find. The violent struggle to forcibly claim someone else's property had begun. Imam Asghari didn't stop there; he rallied his followers, proclaiming that their fight was for the righteousness of their religion and promising guaranteed entry into heaven, especially for those who died in the process. Now, no one could distinguish friend from foe. Majnoon, out of fear, had sought refuge atop a hill and barked incessantly. Mard Ali, riding a wooden horse, recited religious verses while synchronizing his performance with the dog's barks, as if he were part of the play. Wolves appeared on the hillside, seemingly perplexed by the scene before them, but eventually wandered off, becoming mere spectators.

Inside the room, the silent beggar remained seated, lost in contemplation, puffing on his pipe. Zulfiqar, positioned beside him, held his head up in the air, attentively listening. Fearing that the violence might spill inside, the silent beggar promptly rose and secured all the doors and windows, leaving behind whatever he could find to reinforce them further. However, he himself remained unmoved, calmly smoking his pipe, awaiting the revelation of his destiny's next chapter. Zulfiqar stood behind one of the windows, raising his head to observe the surroundings before eventually sitting down. The expression on Zulfiqar's face seemed to suggest that he could witness the brutalities unfolding outside seeing who was striking whom and whose heads and faces were being injured. It was as though he could discern whose blood was trickling down.

Outside, Imam Asghari, who sought to avoid getting involved in the fight and being harmed, hurried away from the escalating violence. He found refuge on a large rock overlooking the scene, where he began reciting ancient Islamic legends that stirred people's emotions, making them willing to sacrifice their lives for their beliefs. However, the fighting eventually reached his location, rendering it futile and unsafe to stay. He urgently made his way towards a nearby room, but to his dismay, he discovered that the door had been shot and his attempts to gain entry were in vain. Witnessing the bloodshed that ensued, Imam Asghari grew fearful and sought higher ground, eventually climbing a wall with his characteristic agility, and reaching the rooftop where he stood tall. From there, he passionately shouted out verses and stories, invoking the memory of Imam Hussein, who led the renowned religious battle known as the Battle of Ashura. He exhorted the people to fight, assuring them that even in death, they would be considered fortunate and would ascend to heaven alongside Imam Hussein. Assuming a leadership role from his elevated position, he encouraged the people to engage in combat, even at the risk of injury or death, all in the name of faith.

Meanwhile, Haji Ghazanfar went out of his way to issue orders, purposefully avoiding the fray. Occasionally, he glanced at Imam Asghari on the rooftop, harboring envy and resentment towards his nimbleness and intelligence. Inwardly, he seethed with jealousy. Kadkhoda, seizing an opportunity amidst the chaos, hurriedly approached Haji Ghazanfar, whispering in his ear that it would be wise for him to leave the scene and head to the police station to file a complaint against the people of Tikken before they did the same. Kadkhoda asserted that the first party to file a complaint would gain the upper hand. Furthermore, he claimed to have connections among the law enforcement officers, including the Sergeant, suggesting that Haji Ghazanfar should immediately approach the Sergeant and bribe him before the villagers from Tikken did so, ensuring that the

Sergeant would favor their side. Acting upon Kadkhoda's advice, Haji Ghazanfar swiftly departed, making his way downhill and disappearing behind the hills to find safety. Meanwhile, the unfortunate people continued to be battered and torn apart, their heads, limbs, and faces bloodied, staining the cold earth around the abandoned beggar's house. The cacophony of shouts and insults drowned out even the barking of dogs. Everyone was now consumed by malice and violence, their eyes and hearts obscured by blood. No one remained in control, and the competition to inflict harm on one another grew increasingly savage. Attempts at mediation only resulted in more beatings and bloodshed, with neutral parties quickly becoming participants in the brawl. Normally, disputes would be settled through mediation by impartial individuals, leading to a resolution. However, in this situation, any semblance of mediation was impossible. No one could discern who they were fighting against anymore. Even Imam Asghari and Haji Ghazanfar, as well as the leaders and elders of the village of Tikken, such as Rostam Khan and his advisors, could only watch the battle from a distance, powerless to quell the chaos. The violence had spiraled beyond anyone's control. Even if these leaders attempted to intervene, their voices would go unheard, and their orders would be disregarded. Bloodlust had blinded the combatants, rendering them deaf to reason.

During that entire duration, the silent beggar remained seated in the corner of his room, maintaining a serene composure. It was now the third occasion that he had refilled his pipe with tobacco, and as he lit it, wisps of smoke once again billowed upward. Zulfiqar's gaze remained fixed skyward, anxiously attuned to the sounds around him as if he could visually perceive the events unfolding. As he looked up towards the ceiling, the resonant voice of Imam Asghari pierced the air, emanating from the rooftop with thunderous intensity, commanding his soldiers to fight relentlessly. "They are godless foreigners, and their blood is permissible to be spilled. This is the day of jihad... the day of judgment. Slay the infidels, and your place in heaven shall be secured."

Simultaneously, amidst the chaos of battle, a piercing scream erupted, originating from the heart of the conflict. The cry reverberated with urgency. "You godless creature! You've taken the life of an innocent boy... cease this madness! The police will arrive, and all of you will be taken to jail... you have extinguished a young life... he is now lifeless. We bear the stain of blood on our hands... they will seize our home and our land. You have slain the youth."

Amidst the tumultuous crowd, an old man's anguished cries pierced through, alerting the people that a young boy had been slain. Gradually, their attention turned to the distressing sight of the boy lying on the ground, his chest soaked in blood. He appeared to be around fifteen years old, desperately clinging to his fragile existence. Stirred by the old man's frantic screams, a silent beggar finally stirred from his humble abode. He emerged, passing through the onlookers who had ceased their brawls, save for a few, their bodies drenched in crimson, fixated on the wounded boy. Reaching the boy, who lay near the aqueduct, his body barely recognizable under the bloodstains, the silent beggar extended a hand and seated himself beside him. Tenderly placing his palm on the boy's bloodied forehead, he sought signs of life. Discovering a flicker of vitality, he promptly resolved to do whatever he could to save the boy's precious existence.

Meanwhile, the old man, his hand entwined with the boy's, continued his impassioned lamentation, cursing everything and everyone that crossed his mind – the earth, time, and more. The sight of the young boy and the blood-soaked figures surrounding him bewildered the onlookers. Gradually, their bewilderment gave way to fear, permeating every fiber of their beings. They questioned their actions and their motives, gripped by a profound sense of dread. One by one, gripped by panic, they fled, disappearing behind the distant hills like water spilling onto the ground.

Without hesitation, Imam Asghari descended into the courtyard with the same nimbleness and expertise with which he had ascended the roof. Evading the few individuals who remained to assist the wounded boy, he hastened towards Haji Ghazanfar, who too was fleeing. Together, they vanished into the anonymity of the hills. They walked briskly, outpacing even Mard Ali, who, overwhelmed by the horrors he had witnessed, sought his own escape. It was as though the unfortunate young boy, slowly succumbing to his wounds, was no longer regarded as a fellow human deserving of aid. Only the old man, the silent beggar, and Zulfiqar remained, their presence a haunting testament to the boy's tragic fate. The young boy clung tightly to the old man and the silent beggar's hands, beseeching them for help in his battle between life and death. All they could offer was their prayers, tears streaming down their faces, as they watched him perish in cold blood.

Zulfiqar emerged from the room, standing over them. True to form, he raised his head, fixating on the sky, his voice growing more intense with each passing minute, questioning, "Has the destitute soul departed? Is he gone?"

The silent beggar's dog stood by their side, fixated on the young boy who fought desperately to cling to life. The dog's muted cries echoed in the air as it circled the boy, a poignant display of shared grief. It seemed as though the dog sensed and understood the boy's plea for help, conveyed through his tight grip on the silent beggar's hand and the unwavering gaze into his eyes. The silent beggar, no longer able to contain his emotions, wept. Tears streamed down his weathered cheeks, his sobs joining the profound silence that enveloped everyone's hearts.

The old man, Zulfiqar, and the dog could scarcely bear to witness the boy's final breaths. The silent beggar's tears fell onto the boy's blood-soaked chest, mingling with the crimson pool, as if the drops pierced the very essence of the blood and surrendered to its fate, mirroring the boy's own demise. Eventually, the boy's hand relaxed its grip on the silent beggar's hand, and the silent beggar knew that he had passed away. With a sense of helplessness, he gently closed the boy's eyes, feeling the coldness of death in his own hand, chilled by the gentle breeze. The icy sensation coursed through his entire body, leaving him trembling.

Amidst the deafening silence, broken only by the old man's sobs, Zulfiqar's voice shattered the stillness once more. "The poor soul has departed...?" he uttered. The dog lay on the ground, holding its face in its paws, fixated on the lifeless form of the boy. It emitted a soft, mournful howl as if shedding tears. Occasionally, it would rub its paws against its face and eyes, as if wiping away the imaginary tears.

It was a moment of profound sorrow, rendering the silent beggar speechless. Tears welled up in his eyes, blinding his vision, as he grappled with the misfortune that had befallen him once again, unsure of what to do. He now had a small flock of sheep; more milk than he needed, with Zulfiqar seemingly enjoying it even more than he did. Over the years, during his free time, Sattar had planted a variety of fruit trees around their dwelling, which had flourished and bore abundant harvests, from walnuts and almonds to apricots and apples, even cherries. Sattar's efforts had provided them with a means of sustenance. Yet, the silent beggar knew that his solitude had been shattered. Aware that the authorities would swiftly descend upon his farm due to the murder that had taken place there, he anticipated the chaos that would follow, with officials swarming like locusts over the neighboring villages. Despite having no involvement in the fight that led to the boy's killing, and even losing his only ewe amidst the turmoil, he would still be subjected to questioning and scrutiny. He pondered how he could explain his identity, his origins, and most crucially, the identities of those buried in the graves—Asyeh and Sattar. He dreaded being labeled a murderer, an accusation he desperately wanted to avoid. Perhaps he should flee and wander once more, but age had worn him down, and he lacked the strength to embark on such a journey.

The silent beggar's intuition proved correct. The sun had yet to set when the Law Men descended upon his farm, led by the head Sergeant, and simultaneously infiltrated the neighboring villages. The lifeless body of the unfortunate young boy still lay in front of the silent beggar's humble abode, and out of concern for his own well-being, he refrained from touching it to avoid any potential trouble. Instead, he respectfully covered the boy with cloth, wood, and tree branches, securing them with heavy stones to ward off scavengers and predators. Additionally, he made sure to conceal Sattar and Asyeh's graves with similar makeshift structures, hoping to divert the attention of the Law Men.

The compassionate elder who had announced the boy's demise remained by the silent beggar's side, refusing to leave him alone in his time of distress. As soon as the Law Men made their appearance, he wasted no time in assuring them that the silent beggar had no involvement in the murder. He emphasized that the beggar had been inside his room the entire time, unaware of the conflict erupting between the villagers that eventually led to the tragic incident. The elder further disclosed his own participation in the altercation until he discovered the lifeless body of the young boy. Nevertheless, despite the elder's testimony, the silent beggar was not exempt from interrogation.

* * * * *

Chapter 11
When politics force friends to be seen as enemies and enemies to be considered friends...

A month had passed since the tragic murder of the young boy. Law Men continued to commute to the village of Shourcheh, diligently visiting the silent beggar's chamber in their quest for answers. As was customary, both villagers spared no effort in offering lavish meals, including kababs and other delicacies, to the Law Men. This competition between villages aimed to win their favor and influence them to take their respective sides. Consequently, life had become unbearable for the villagers, particularly individuals like Haji Ghazanfar.

Meanwhile, the grieving old woman from Tikken, who had lost her own son, remained unwilling to accept the situation. No one could definitively determine the cause of the young man's death. All they knew was that during the midst of the altercation, he was stabbed in the heart and fell, succumbing to his wounds. Although a few villagers from Shourcheh had witnessed Ugly Ghadam using his knife to deliver the fatal blow, fear held their tongues in check.

Moreover, in addition to the tragedy of the young boy's demise, tensions escalated over the silent beggar's house and farm. Each village claimed ownership, intensifying the Law Men's predicament. This further complicated matters for the silent beggar, who was now compelled to disclose his origin, real name, and the purpose behind his prolonged presence as a beggar. It was no easy task for him to undertake daily journeys either to meet the Law Men or visit the city's police station. The distance from his house to the station required several hours of arduous walking, a daunting feat for an elderly man with diminishing strength.

During this period, Zulfiqar faithfully remained by the silent beggar's side, assuming the roles of his attorney, guardian, and spokesperson. Majnoon, the loyal dog, refused to abandon the silent beggar. He accompanied them on their journeys, waiting patiently outside the police station while they conducted their business. Often, the poor dog faced mistreatment and abuse from people, causing him to flee, yet he would always return, faithfully waiting for their return from the station.

Throughout these trials, the silent beggar chose to maintain his silence and composure. He believed that being a beggar and mute since childhood, his purpose was to traverse life, detached from the constraints of place and time. He possessed no birth certificate, and his parents had passed away many years ago when he was a young child. Now, in his old age and feebleness, he had resolved to live there until his last breath.

Nonetheless, the head of the Law Men remained perplexed about the silent beggar's reasons for settling in this particular area, a place that had long been considered forbidden and believed to be inhabited by goblins. Furthermore, the silent beggar himself was unaware of his own name, having forgotten both his first and last names. In a lighthearted tone, the head of the Law Men jestingly addressed the silent beggar, saying, "Surely your name must be 'Competent'?"

Zulfiqar spoke at length. "Saleh, surely the Sergeant will devour him more than anyone. I bear witness, Sergeant, that if someone claims to be a prophet today, I believe and follow him. I bear witness that I have never heard him utter a word... I am the one who speaks for both of us incessantly. God is my witness; even after all these years, I have never heard his voice because he never speaks. Sometimes, I think I hear a broken voice, like 'SALEH,' but I cannot determine if it is his voice, or perhaps the murmurs of goblins, fairies, or even God... It calls his name, Sergeant, as if he is conversing with God in a secret code. And sometimes, unknown people come from all around to see him, hoping for healing. Sergeant, I witnessed him leading them. If I'm lying, I pray that God should strike me down this very moment and make me suffer."

Sergeant turned to another Law Men who was preparing a written statement and jokingly said, "Well, his name is Saleh, so according to this blind man's account, his family must also be prophetic, and his farm should be called Saleh Prophet Farm?"

Upon hearing the Sergeant's remark, Zulfiqar blushed, lifted his head high in the air, and gazed into space as he spoke, "Sergeant, God is my witness, forgive me. I consider him an Imam. Sergeant, though I lack sight, on some nights when he would go beneath the berry tree and pray, it felt as if light radiated all around, even visible to my blind eyes... Well, I should say I sensed the presence of light everywhere. Perhaps that is why water is flowing from the wells during this drought."

The Sergeant grinned once again and turned to the other policemen, continuing his jest, "Well, surely when the silent beggar dies, they'll bury him there, and his haunt will become a shrine. They'll call it Saleh Payghambar (The Honest Messenger)!"

At the mention of the silent beggar's potential shrine, Imam Asghari's ears suddenly perked up, his eyes grew wild as if struck by lightning. Kadkhoda and Haji Ghazanfar were seated beside Imam Asghari, while Rostam Khan and his entourage from the village of Tikken occupied the other side of the room, all eagerly awaiting their turn to speak. Now, Imam Asghari, who had remained silent until this moment, could no longer contain his anticipation of being questioned. He appeared lost in thought, smiled with his enigmatic face, and whispered to himself, "His name is Saleh, his family name is Payghambar (messenger), so his full name is 'Saleh Payghambar.' The Honest Messenger of God!"

Imam Asghari wasted no time and took charge of the discussion, determined to shape the outcome. "Sergeant, we have also heard numerous accounts of strange occurrences regarding the lighting in that area. Sometimes, we ourselves have witnessed peculiar lights from our rooftop. I personally saw it with my own eyes, and Haji Ghazanfar and Kadkhoda can confirm that one night, while we were smoking hookah on the porch, the hill suddenly lit up for a few moments. It happened right where the silent beggar's haunt is located. At the time, we didn't think much of it, fearing people would dismiss it as superstition. However, I believe it was God's will, a means to reveal the truth and teach us about the realities of life. Sergeant, such happenings, like lightning, occur for a reason. There must be a purpose behind it, a noble one. Perhaps, the wisdom behind this is to dedicate the silent beggar's house and property as religious tax (khoums) for the Imam. People could then gather there for prayer and worship, bridging the divide between the villages of Shourcheh and

Tikken. This would put an end to the curses, quarrels, fights, and bloodshed between the two communities. By bestowing the property to the Imam, it would become inviolable. Sergeant, fighting on the Imam's property would be akin to fighting against the Prophet, against the will of God."

A profound silence enveloped the gathering as everyone pondered Imam Asghari's proposal. Rostam Khan and his entourage also fell into deep thought. Throughout this time, the silent beggar remained seated, gazing at the floor as if he were not present. Haji Ghazanfar, Kadkhoda, the representatives from Tikken and the security personnel contemplated the matter as well. Breaking the silence, Imam Asghari turned to the Sergeant, addressing Zulfiqar and the silent beggar, seeking to win their support. "Who could be more suitable than Mr. Zulfiqar to look after the silent beggar until his passing? And afterward, he could continue to care for the place. Zulfiqar has no place to call his own, especially considering his old age and blindness. This arrangement would be in the best interest of both Zulfiqar and the silent beggar. The silent beggar knows that Zulfiqar is his devoted and faithful friend, who will stand by his side until he reaches heaven and joins God. I believe he would be content with this resolution."

Sergeant twirled his long and twisted mustache, his gaze fixed on Zulfiqar, whose face lit up with joy upon hearing Imam Asghari's words. Observing the reactions of everyone in the room, Sergeant pondered the possibility that Imam Asghari might have suggested a viable solution. He was grappling with the challenge of dealing with two conflicting villages and an unidentified beggar with no known background. Whichever side he chose, the other would disagree, and the conflict would persist. However, Sergeant believed that invoking the name of God and involving the Imam and religious factors would instill fear in people, preventing them from acting foolishly and risking divine punishment.

Finally, he raised his voice and spoke, "Imam's suggestion may not be a bad idea, provided two conditions are met. Firstly, we must obtain the consent of the deceased's relatives, and secondly, compensation must be paid."

Then, turning to the silent beggar, Sergeant continued, "The second condition is that we cannot donate someone else's property to anyone, even if it is for the sake of God. In this case, we have no way of determining if the beggar is lying about his identity. Therefore, the silent beggar must agree to donate his property to God willingly, for the sake of God's will and religious purposes. Alternatively, he can choose to make Zulfiqar the representative and custodian of his property, if he wishes."

All eyes in the room now focused on the silent beggar, who remained seated, silently staring at the floor. Silence enveloped the space once more. Finally, the beggar's gaze shifted to Zulfiqar. Zulfiqar raised his head, eagerly awaiting the beggar's decision. Ultimately, the beggar shook his head, signifying his agreement to dedicate his property to God and appointing Zulfiqar as its representative and custodian. He also requested a place to live on the property for as long as he was alive.

"Well, congratulations, Mr. Zulfiqar," Sergeant declared.

Imam Asghari, not waiting for Sergeant to speak, announced the silent beggar's agreement, eliminating any doubts. Zulfiqar's heart swelled with joy upon hearing Imam Asghari's voice, as if sugar had melted within him. He was ready to dance under the moon. Through Sergeant's mediation, both villages of Shourcheh and Tikken paid damages to the deceased's mother, obtaining her consent, and finally resolving the case.

The silent beggar's entire farm was declared an endowment for religious purposes, under the control of Imam Asghari, the current Imam. Zulfiqar became the trustee and custodian, while the silent beggar found himself without a place to call his own. He could be evicted at any time by Imam Asghari, with no recourse available to him.

Finally, the turmoil of cursing, fighting, and litigation over the silent beggar's property came to an end, bringing a temporary sense of tranquility. However, unbeknownst to Sergeant and the others, Imam Asghari had no intention of remaining silent and allowing the silent beggar to live peacefully until his demise. Right from the start, Imam Asghari harbored ulterior motives and skillfully manipulated everyone, especially the villagers of Tikken.

To begin with, Imam Asghari claimed ownership of the farm, declaring it as his own property. By entrusting Zulfiqar, he had created a sense of indebtedness within him towards both Imam Asghari and the village of Shourcheh. Consequently, Zulfiqar aligned himself with Imam Asghari and the village of Shourcheh, supporting their cause. Imam Asghari expected Zulfiqar to provide water to the village of Shourcheh while denying any access to the village of Tikken.

In the event that Zulfiqar refused to comply with Imam Asghari's demands or deviated from his will, Imam Asghari had ample time and political prowess to remove Zulfiqar from his position and replace him with someone who would fulfill all his desires. In either scenario, the farm and its aqueduct water would fall under the control and authority of the village of Shourcheh, with Imam Asghari at the helm.

Little did anyone know that Imam Asghari had more tricks and manipulations up his sleeve. With time, he planned to execute these maneuvers, sever ties with the silent beggar and possibly Zulfiqar, and seize complete control of the entire farm. This was particularly facilitated by Rostam Khan, who lacked the shrewdness and tactics of his influential father, Assad Khan, making him an easy target for Imam Asghari's deceit.

Following that incident, Zulfiqar garnered a special level of respect from the villagers in both Shourcheh and Tikken. Being a servant of God, he took great pride in his newfound status, sometimes even losing sight of his own identity amidst the glory it brought him.

But what Imam Asghari failed to realize or consider was that while he believed everything was settled in his eyes, nothing had been resolved or settled in the eyes of the people of Tikken. Soon, they awakened to the fact that Imam Asghari had manipulated them, and they were merely pawns in his game. Determined not to give up the silent beggar's farm, the people of Tikken remained vigilant and watchful, observing every move like hawks.

The manipulation and competition between the two villages persisted, particularly for control over the silent beggar's farm and his aqueduct. Each village sought to win over Zulfiqar and, more importantly, the silent beggar's favor. Suddenly, both the silent beggar and Zulfiqar became highly esteemed figures in the eyes of both villages. As a result, people from both communities showered them with an abundance of gifts.

Under Imam Asghari's guidance, Haji Ghazanfar sent a sheep to the silent beggar. In less than a day, the people of Tikken brought him two cows, which they tied up in front of the silent beggar's humble dwelling. The villagers of Shourcheh presented him with a donkey, while the people of Tikken brought a horse. This cycle of competition and gift-giving continued endlessly. One village would offer bread, while the other brought honey and raisins. Amidst this ongoing rivalry, Zulfiqar skillfully orchestrated meetings, ensuring that both villages remained oblivious to his true intentions. Zulfiqar understood that the more competition he fostered between the villages, the greater control he would wield and the more his own interests would be served.

Within a few months, the people of Tikken constructed a small stable next to the silent beggar's abode, housing a multitude of donated animals. Upon hearing this news, the inhabitants of Village Shourcheh promptly built a structure adjacent to the stable and filled it with hay for the animals.

Meanwhile, despite all the attention and gifts bestowed upon him, the silent beggar remained unimpressed. He became increasingly withdrawn, engrossed in his thoughts, secrets, and desires. Consequently, his reactions perplexed everyone, leaving them unsure of how to proceed. He knew well that their actions stemmed not from genuine kindness or respect but from relentless greed to seize his property. Nevertheless, their efforts persisted.

Each village embarked on a mission to plant trees around the farm. Soon, a row of trees stretched from the farm, connecting both villages along the road they had constructed to reach the silent beggar's property. The more the villagers pushed, the more the silent beggar distanced himself from both communities. He refused to align himself with either Shourcheh or Tikken. In fact, he rejected both villages and desired no involvement with either of them.

The villagers' displeasing behavior not only failed to bring happiness to the silent beggar but also left him increasingly despondent and isolated. Now, he spent most of his time in solitude, yearning to join Asyeh and Sattar on the other side. Although burdened with sorrow, he contemplated revealing the truth to Rostam Khan about his brother Sattar and how he had lawfully and mystically constructed the house and farm, implying that it rightfully belonged to Rostam Khan. However, he feared that doing so would expose his true identity as none other than Kal Abbas. Such a revelation would unleash a volatile situation, akin to opening a can of gasoline that could ignite a flame he might not be able to control or withstand, potentially consuming him entirely.

Meanwhile, Imam Asghari grew increasingly annoyed with the silent beggar and devised a plan involving Ugly Ghadam and his gang. They would frequently visit the silent beggar's farm, disrupting his peace in an attempt to persuade him to allow the construction of additional wells above the existing one. Their intention was to claim ownership of the aqueduct and divert the water to irrigate their own lands in the village of Shourcheh.

At the same time, the silent beggar faced a similar predicament with the people of Tikken, with Shaykh Gonabadi acting as the connection between them. Unlike Imam Asghari, Shaykh Gonabadi was a kind-hearted and honest man, indifferent to material possessions. Despite being the religious representative of Tikken, he didn't succumb to the pressure of his villagers and privately advised the silent beggar to distribute the water equally between the two villages. He emphasized that the final decision should rest with the silent beggar, as it was his property. Shaykh Gonabadi harbored mistrust towards Zulfiqar, who was absent during their conversation. It was during this conversation that the silent beggar confided in Shaykh Gonabadi, sharing the truth about Sattar, Asyeh, and his own identity. Unknown to them, Zulfiqar, who was mediating between Shourcheh and Tikken, overheard everything without revealing his knowledge to them.

Zulfiqar, being more skilled than Imam Asghari in manipulation, saw an opportunity to exploit the revelations about Asyeh, Sattar, and Kala Abbas. As the mediator between the two villages, he could now play them against each other, ultimately achieving his own goals.

The game between the cat and the mouse played out between the two villages, and the silent beggars continued, but it remained fruitless despite repeated attempts. Meanwhile, Imam Asghari's patience had worn thin, especially upon learning that the silent beggar held a special respect for Shaykh Gonabadi. This revelation infuriated him and filled him with fear that the silent beggar might yield to Shaykh Gonabadi's influence, following his advice and relinquishing the farm and aqueduct to Tikken village, causing Shourcheh village to lose everything.

Furthermore, Imam Asghari realized that he would be the first to suffer if such a scenario unfolded. People would start doubting his claim as the Imam and his supposed possession of miraculous powers, which were associated with each Imam. Inevitably, Imam Asghari's influence and the respect he had cunningly acquired through lies, manipulation, and deceit would be undermined.

Driven by these concerns, Imam Asghari swiftly took action, determined to eliminate the silent beggar once and for all before any of these potential threats jeopardized his position. However, he knew that disposing of the silent beggar would not be an easy task. Additionally, he anticipated that the people of Tikken would not remain idle but would continue their efforts to acquire the silent beggar's farm.

On the other hand, Imam Asghari feared that killing or beheading the silent beggar would raise suspicion among the people of Tikken. They would undoubtedly launch an investigation into the incident, and his true identity would be revealed. It would be unveiled that he was not the genuine Imam of the Muslims, but rather Moharram, a wanted criminal who had assumed the name Asghar to deceive the people.

With these considerations in mind, Imam Asghari decided to pursue an alternative strategy to deceive the silent beggar. Luckily, fate seemed to favor him when he heard from Ugly Ghadam that two graves had been spotted near the mulberry tree. He was bewildered as to why no one had taken any action regarding these graves. Seizing this opportunity, Imam Asghari instructed Ugly Ghadam to visit the silent beggar's place and verify the existence of the graves. Ugly Ghadam promptly carried out his task and headed to the silent beggar's farm, bringing along some treats for Zulfiqar, the silent beggar's companion.

While Ugly Ghadam and his group engaged in lively conversations and conducted their inspection, the silent beggar remained huddled beneath a tattered blanket, deliberately avoiding any interaction. He simply desired to be left alone. Ugly Ghadam carefully examined the area surrounding the mulberry tree and confirmed the presence of two graves. Satisfied with his findings, he swiftly returned to report the news to his master, Imam Asghari.

Imam Asghari, who had discovered a means to confront the silent beggar, took immediate action. He enlisted the aid of Ugly Ghadam and his gang, who were secretly well-paid by him. The gang, led by Ghadam Baldy, embarked on a mission to spread a rumor throughout the village. They alleged that the silent beggar was not only a thief but also a murderer who had forcibly taken over a farm after killing its rightful owner. They claimed to have discovered the graves of the true owner, whom the silent beggar had supposedly slain. The origin of the rumor remained unknown as it spread.

In response, the silent beggar urged the villagers to approach Kadkhoda, requesting an investigation into the matter. He encouraged them to file a complaint with the authorities and seek justice. The villagers, unknowingly fulfilling Imam Asghari's wishes, rallied behind the cause and promptly lodged a complaint. Kadkhoda, upon receiving the complaint, reported the fabricated news orchestrated by Imam Asghari to the authorities.

It didn't take long for word to spread that the silent beggar was accused of being a thief and murderer. The news became a topic of conversation, giving people a reason to gather and share their own interpretations of the events.

* * * * *

Chapter 12
When a single event shatters the foundations of humanity and the world...

The winter was bitterly cold. The chamber, the field, and the surrounding trees, including the majestic mulberry tree, were adorned with a beautiful blanket of snow, appearing even more majestic than the earth and the passing of time. Two massive branches of the mulberry tree extended east and west, casting their white umbrellas over Asyeh and Sattar's graves and the humble hut, concealing them beneath nature's frozen artistry. Despite the snow covering them, the graves still peeked through, adorned with scattered debris, both small and large.

Silent and still, the smoke from the beggar's pipe gracefully swirled in the air, dancing beneath the archway before vanishing into the wintry atmosphere. The beggar, with his head and face hidden by long, unkempt white hair, clearly untouched by scissors or razor for years, sat in profound silence. The whiteness of winter encompassed everything as far as the eye could see, and the air was so frigid it seemed to crack the very rocks. The beggar pondered the peculiar beauty that snow bestowed upon the lifeless winter landscape, despite its chilling nature. Snow had the unique ability to envelop the ground, the trees, the walls, the ruins, and the settlements, adorning them all uniformly with its pristine white, transforming even the most dilapidated ruins into a captivating vista. He emptied his pipe in the garden beside him, the ashes gracefully mingling with the snow, and filled it again with fresh tobacco. The smoke from his pipe ascended once more, gracefully swirling in the air, disappearing beyond the walls and ceiling of the room, while his gaze remained fixed upon the mountains in silent contemplation.

As he took his first or second puff from the newly filled pipe, he noticed several dark specks emerging in the distance, slowly advancing from the foot of the hills towards him. The specks grew larger and larger. Gradually, he discerned that they were riders, but their identities and intentions remained unknown. Particularly in such harsh winter conditions, with snow blanketing the ground, it was unusual for anyone to traverse these hills. The possibility of them being torn apart by hungry wolves loomed ominously. Zulfiqar had left for the village, and due to the heavy snowfall, he hadn't been able to return. Thus, the silent beggar found himself alone, and it seemed that the riders were searching for him as they descended the hill. As they drew nearer, a sense of unease gripped him. He was so preoccupied that he unknowingly refilled his pipe with fresh tobacco, oblivious to the fact that he had just done so. The dark specks had now transformed into a discernible group of horsemen, unmistakably the police. His shifting emotions revealed his discontent upon recognizing them. He surmised that the troublemakers or ruffians must have lodged another complaint, prompting the police to appear amidst such treacherous snowfall. This realization only amplified his concern and disappointment at their arrival. Old and weary, he struggled to leave the room, but Imam Asghari had denied him the tranquility and peace he yearned for in his final years. Each day, he longed for the moment of departure to the other side, to be liberated from this world and its inhabitants, hoping it would finally come and release him from his worldly burdens. At last, the riders arrived near the humble hut, their bodies fully cloaked in snow, their hats serving as the sole indicator of their identities.

The snow continued to fall relentlessly. The Law Men positioned themselves a short distance away from the hut, their gaze fixed upon the silent beggar and their surroundings. Ignoring their presence, the beggar remained motionless, as though unaware of their existence. His eyes were locked on the snow, lost in contemplation. Eventually, Sergeant Timur Khan, the leader of the Law Men and seemingly of the same age as the beggar, rode his horse closer and halted a few meters away. He scrutinized the beggar intently, studying him. The beggar, seated on the platform beneath the arch, remained unmoving, his gaze still fixed on the snow before him, seemingly oblivious to Sergeant Timur Khan's presence. Slowly, Sergeant Timur Khan unholstered his rifle and advanced cautiously towards the beggar, as if he were preparing to aim at both the beggar and his dwelling. Observing this, the other Law Men surrounding him followed suit, raising their rifles. However, the silent beggar remained unfazed by the commotion unfolding around him. He maintained his gaze upon the snow, puffing on his pipe, the smoke swirling in the frigid air, traversing from beneath the arch and vanishing into the sky. Silence and stillness enveloped the scene.

At last, the resounding blast of Sergeant Timur Khan's rifle shattered the tranquility, its echoes resonating through the hills. Just as the silent beggar had a chance to react, a white wolf tumbled from the rooftop, landing in the snow before the platform. With the gunshot and the fallen wolf, the silent beggar turned his head and fixed his gaze upon the wounded and bloodied creature struggling for life on the snowy ground. The sound of Sergeant Timur Khan reloading his rifle seemed to jolt the beggar, alerting him. In an instant, he sprang to his feet and positioned himself between the wolf and Sergeant Timur Khan, shielding the wounded animal. It was as if he understood Sergeant Timur Khan's intention to fire additional shots, to end the wolf's suffering. By placing himself in front of the defenseless creature, the beggar implored Sergeant Timur Khan to spare his life. Their eyes met and locked in an extended moment, until Sergeant Timur Khan finally relented, lowering his gun. The beggar then averted his gaze from Sergeant Timur Khan, turning to sit beside the injured wolf, offering it comfort and solace.

For a while, the injured wolf lay in agony, its blood staining the pristine white snow in front of the arch a testament to its fierce struggle against death. The silent beggar remained there, a steadfast sentinel, observing the wounded wolf as it painstakingly dragged itself towards the hill, leaving a crimson trail behind in the snow. Once assured that no one would disturb the injured creature, the beggar returned to the platform, resuming his seat. He continued to gaze at the blood-soaked path, resembling a narrow road leading the wolf away. Sergeant Timur Khan dismounted his horse and positioned himself in front of the beggar, between the two platforms. His gaze shifted back and forth between the ailing wolf and the beggar, contemplating their connection. After a few contemplative moments, his focus settled mostly on the silent beggar, as if he had a notion of the beggar's true identity. However, he sought confirmation before drawing any conclusions.

Sergeant Timur Khan pushed open the room door with his rifle and carefully inspected the interior before entering. Meanwhile, the other Law Men stood ready with rifles, meticulously scouring the surroundings. Upon noticing Sergeant Timur Khan, the silent beggar became lost in his own thoughts, deeply affected by the sight of the Law Men. As he observed them, his worry grew. Smoke from his pipe once again spiraled into the snowy air, disappearing over the roof. Inside the room, Sergeant Timur Khan poured himself a hot tea and remained vigilant, never taking his eyes off the silent beggar, studying his behavior from within. The warmth of the tea seemed to offer solace in the cold snowy day. He poured a second cup and, while drinking it, stepped out onto the platform beside the silent beggar, continuing to observe him. Eventually, he sat on the opposite platform, directly facing the silent beggar, intensifying his scrutiny. It appeared as though he intended to coax the silent beggar into speaking. However, his efforts were in vain, as the silent beggar continued to smoke his pipe, fixated on a wolf desperately trying to evade death. It was as if Sergeant Timur Khan and the other Law Men weren't present, observing his every move.

Unbeknownst to the silent beggar, Imam Asghari had spread a rumor suggesting that the beggar had murdered the original owner and buried them at that very location. This gossip had become a topic of discussion everywhere, even in the tea houses nearby. One rainy day, while Sergeant Timur Khan was enjoying his tea at a shop, he overheard a conversation among a few individuals seated nearby. They were discussing the silent beggars and the forbidden area when, amidst their chatter, one of them suddenly mentioned the name "Kal Abbas." The individual claimed, "I swear this silent beggar must be none other than Kal Abbas, the notorious bandit who has evaded the law and hidden himself there all these years."

Upon hearing the name Kal Abbas, Sergeant Timur Khan abandoned his half-finished tea and hurriedly made his way to the police station. Although Sergeant Timur Khan only worked sporadically, this time he felt compelled to personally investigate the identity of the silent beggar.

Accompanied by several fellow Law Men, he set off toward the beggar's location. Now, he stared at him as if he knew exactly who he was. "Old man, can you speak or not? I refuse to believe you are mute. Are you truly unable to speak? Or is this all an act? Perhaps you've broken the law and are hiding here to avoid exposure... What is your name? Surely, you must have a name?"

Sergeant Timur Khan finally broke the silence, but the silent beggar seemed oblivious to his voice, his gaze fixed on the bloodstained wolf. Despite its injuries, the wolf summoned its remaining strength and crawled a few hundred meters into the snow, staining it with its own blood. The silent beggar yearned to rise and assist the wounded creature, but his frailty held him back.

Sergeant Timur Khan's attention momentarily shifted to the other Law Men, who had thoroughly inspected the entire area but found nothing suspicious. Now, all the Law Men had gathered in front of the platform, fixated on the silent beggar. With a gesture, Sergeant Timur Khan handed an empty cup to one of his colleagues and invited them to join him for tea. The cup was accepted, and one of the policemen entered the room to pour tea.

Returning his gaze to the silent beggar, Sergeant Timur Khan couldn't shake the feeling of familiarity, though still uncertain if he was indeed Kal Abbas or someone else entirely. Regardless, he was certain that this individual must be familiar with him, and he yearned to meet the beggar's gaze once more, to uncover his true identity. Moments passed, filled with an engulfing silence, accompanied only by the sound of the Law Men sipping tea from the limited number of cups.

Sergeant Timur Khan's gaze remained fixed on the silent beggar, who in turn kept his attention on the wounded wolf in the distance. Strands of hair obscured his eyes, making it difficult to discern their true expression. Eventually, it was Sergeant Timur Khan's voice that shattered the silence once more. "Old man... There are rumors circulating that you murdered the unfortunate owner of this property, intending to claim it as your own and evade the law. I am here to uncover the truth, and I won't rest until I do. Even if it means digging graves, I am prepared to do what is necessary. I will not leave this hill until I uncover the truth. Do you understand?"

It was then that the silent beggar discovered why Sergeant Timur Khan was there. He was there to find out if the rumor was true or not. Interestingly, no one knew the original owner of the farm, its name, or its origin, except the silent beggar. Observing some changes in the silent beggar's expression, Sergeant Timur Khan grew more curious about his identity. He continued talking to the silent beggar, but the beggar remained fixated on the wounded wolf, refusing to utter a word. Only a brief accidental glance was exchanged between the silent beggar and Sergeant Timur Khan before his attention returned to the fading wolf in front of him.

That single glance changed everything; the silent beggar seemed to recognize Sergeant Timur Khan as his old royal best friend. It appeared that he had been waiting for Sergeant Timur Khan's arrival all along, but he desired to be alone with his friend, not surrounded by many lawmen. He wished to grieve with his friend at the end of his life, before his imminent death. However, lost in his thoughts, the silent beggar hesitated to speak in the presence of the other lawmen. Sergeant Timur Khan noticed that the silent beggar's gaze briefly shifted from each lawman until it settled on him. At that moment, Sergeant Timur Khan understood the true identity of the silent beggar and the unspoken message he was trying to convey.

Realizing that the silent beggar yearned for solitude with his old friend, Sergeant Timur Khan turned to the rest of the lawmen. "You guys go ahead and head down the hill to Kadkhoda's house. I will join you there later. Go now and refrain from discussing anything about this place or my presence. If you speak, countless rumors will circulate in the coming days. Stay there until I arrive, regardless of how long it takes."

Although the lawmen were somewhat puzzled by Sergeant Timur Khan's request to leave and his decision to stay behind, they obeyed their boss and mounted their horses, riding towards the village. It didn't take long for Sergeant Timur Khan to see them vanish behind the hills, leaving only their horse tracks on the white snow. As the lawmen departed,

Sergeant Timur Khan turned his attention back to the silent beggar, who remained fixated on the dying wolf, struggling to escape death. Each passing moment seemed to draw the beggar closer to the wolf, evoking memories of his past life.

Sergeant Timur Khan poured two cups of tea and placed one in front of the silent beggar. He then took a seat on the opposite side and, while sipping his own tea, spoke once more. "It's time to open your heart. I haven't waited all this time just to miss the opportunity to learn my friend's story. I am here now, and when I descend this mountain, I will retire."

Now there were only two old friends amidst the white snow and the encompassing silence. Timur Khan eagerly awaited the moment when the taciturn beggar would part his lips and open his heart to his dear friend, Timur Khan. Finally, Sergeant Teymur Khan fulfilled his duty by revealing his true identity. He disclosed to his friend that he had recognized him as none other than Kal Abbas, his long-lost companion, and triggered a flood of memories from their past encounters, both joyful and painful. Timur Khan took a deep puff from his pipe, allowing the smoke to swirl inside him before gracefully escaping his mouth and nostrils, dancing freely in the air. It carried with it the beggar's thoughts, mind, and heart, transporting them into the realm of the past, where they were inundated with cherished recollections. In a moment of catharsis, the once-silent beggar found his voice and began to speak, recounting his final farewell to his friend and unveiling the trials and tribulations that had befallen him. It was as if the silent beggar had once again transformed into Kal Abbas, his former self.

Fifteen years ago...

A gentle breeze rustled the branches and leaves of the mulberry tree, causing them to sway in a graceful dance. Seated on the platform, the silent beggar indulged in his pipe, the wisps of smoke intertwining with the pleasant gusts, meandering towards an unknown destination. His eyes fixated on a tattered gray fabric resting at the base of a mulberry tree, adjacent to a grave adorned with rubble, setting it apart from the rest. This time, he knew all too well who lay beneath it. However, he struggled to fathom how Sattar, so advanced in years, could remain immobile for hours, engrossed in secret conversations and hidden yearnings with Asyeh. The silent beggar pondered the impossibility of enduring such prolonged moments on the platform, simply smoking his pipe. Sattar's loyal dog, Majnoon, positioned himself between them, his watchful eyes fixated on the worn-out cloth and Sattar concealed beneath it. With each sound and movement, Majnoon attentively redirected his gaze, ensuring the safety of Sattar, his guardian, from any potential harm.

It had been over a month since the Silent Beggar had found Sattar. He now knew that Sattar Kew, the Silent Beggar, was actually Kal Abbas, his childhood friend who had always stood up for them against the villagers when they needed him. Despite being just fourteen years old at the time, Kal Abbas had shown incredible courage. However, from the moment they reunited, Kal Abbas had been eager to know what had happened to Sattar during all those years.

He was desperate to learn about Sattar's life in the villages of Shourcheh and Tikken, where he had managed to remain hidden all these years without anyone suspecting his presence, not even Kal Abbas himself when he held a position of power. Kal Abbas was known for his exceptional awareness of even the slightest occurrence in the village. However, he had no inkling that the mischievous goblin who used to terrorize the villagers and play the flute was none other than Sattar.

This revelation had initially shocked Kal Abbas, and he had spent hours observing Sattar in his house. He was amazed to see how calm and at peace Sattar seemed to be. In fact, Kal Abbas was so astonished that he wanted to make sure it was truly Sattar sitting in front of him after more than fifty years. Sattar, on the other hand, did not greet him in the customary manner of their childhood; he simply behaved with composure and wore a contented smile, clearly happy to see Kal Abbas.

Over the course of several weeks, Sattar gradually explained to the Silent Beggar the events that had unfolded after his escape from the army. On a snowy day, he had encountered Mashhadi Hassan Gorken, who was digging a grave. Initially confused about why the grave was being dug in that particular location instead of the village graveyard, Sattar, out of compassion and without asking questions, decided to assist Gorken in the task.

Little did he know that he was digging the grave of his beloved wife, Asyeh, with his own hands. It was later revealed to him how brutally she had been killed by unknown assailants. Consequently, Sattar chose to remain by her side, refusing to leave her alone in death, as he shared his deepest secrets and needs with her. To ensure he wouldn't lose the grave, Sattar had planted a small seedling that had now grown into a large berry tree, serving as a poignant symbol of their eternal connection.

The snoring sound of the dog abruptly interrupted the beggar's silent contemplation, shattering his thoughts and daydreams about the enigmatic encounters and shared experiences with Sattar. As his gaze shifted towards the slumbering canine, he recollected Sattar's revelation that the dog had once saved his life. When the other beggars had mercilessly beaten him, this loyal creature had barked incessantly, alerting others and preventing further harm. Sattar had confided that his soul had witnessed the entire incident, lurking in the shadows. Through dedicated meditation and practice, Sattar had acquired the ability to separate his soul from his physical body. While his body remained present, his soul traversed to the villages of Shourcheh and Tikken, visiting his long-lost parents. These memories of Sattar animated and, simultaneously, faded within the beggar's mind and soul. The dog's snoring served as a poignant reminder of the night it had trailed Mashhadi Hassan Gorkan, faithfully remaining by his side ever since. However, what captivated the silent beggar, even more, was the enigmatic fate of Mashhadi Hassan himself.

Mashhadi Hassan Gorkan, the gravedigger, had orchestrated a ploy to dissuade Zulfiqar from venturing into the area where Asyeh had been buried, intending to frighten him away. Yet, it was Sattar's ethereal presence that intervened, aiding him by manipulating shovels in front of Mashhadi Hassan Gorkan. While simultaneously whispering haunting words into Zulfiqar's and others' ears, Sattar's spirit instilled bone-chilling fear. Mashhadi Hassan Gorkan had intuited that it must have been Sattar's or Shaykh Ahmad's soul coming to his rescue. At first, witnessing his shovel levitating inexplicably, Mashhadi Hassan Gorkan had been petrified, teetering on the verge of a stroke. Yet, Sattar's soul whispered soothing reassurances into his ear, assuring him of its benevolence. Gradually, he acclimated to the supernatural occurrences, placing his trust in what he was told. Thus, he became an active participant in this eerie game, successfully frightening Zulfiqar and the others, compelling them to flee in terror of the perceived goblins. Subsequently, Mashhadi Hassan Gorkan sought refuge at Sattar's abode, finding solace in its welcoming embrace, never to return to the village.

Mashhadi Hassan Gorkan's steadfast refusal to return to the village stemmed from his awareness that he would be compelled to explain the mysterious presence and his unscathed return. The villagers, no longer gripped by fear of the supposed Elves lurking in that vicinity, would inevitably venture forth, unearthing Asyeh's grave. Furthermore, they would discover that Sattar was the orchestrator behind the unsettling and distressing game they had experienced. Thus, his choice to remain by Sattar's side was driven by a sense of contentment, for it shielded him from the probing inquiries and the potential unveiling of uncomfortable truths.

Then he decided to assist Sattar in constructing the room and digging a well. Together, they built aqueducts and developed farmland, meticulously planning the placement of trees. He also contributed to the excavation of several other water wells and constructed a small aqueduct exclusively for their own use. Initially, they would collect the water in a small pond, and upon its filling, they would open a small gate, allowing a substantial flow of water to irrigate their agricultural lands and the trees they had planted. However, prior to possessing their own farmland and fruit trees, they resorted to covertly gathering necessary provisions from the nearby villages of Shourcheh and Tikken. In such instances, if they encountered anyone, they would swiftly conceal themselves in the darkness, creating eerie sounds to scare away intruders who would mistake them for goblins. Consequently, the residents would hastily retreat into their homes, securing doors and windows promptly. Subsequently, they would commence praying fervently to God, the Prophet, and the Imam, seeking protection from the mythical Elves. Regrettably, despite forty or fifty years of unwavering devotion, neither God, the Prophet, nor the Imam responded to their pleas, leaving them without assistance. Nonetheless, they persevered, continuing their prayers and pleas for help."

Back to the present.

The snow still lay untouched in its pristine whiteness, casting a cold and cloudy atmosphere. Timur Khan puffed on his pipe, watching the smoke rise and dissipate into the misty air before reaching the platform atop the arch. The silent beggar remained seated, motionless, lost in a world of memories. He, too, smoked a pipe, but his tobacco and fire had long since expired. Unaware of this, he continued to gaze at the blood trail left by the wolf, etching a narrow path through the snow. It was as if he sought to utter a final word to his comrade, Timur Khan. With a somber tone, he spoke, "My grave will be on the other side of Asyeh's. I have started digging it, but it remains unfinished. I must complete it soon if the snow allows me."

Believing he had finished speaking, the silent beggar kept his eyes fixed on the wounded wolf, even though its form was barely discernible. It seemed that he shared a profound connection with the dying creature, either grappling with his own mortality or simply yearning for release from this existence. Timur Khan patiently awaited his friend's next words, anticipating the continuation of his life story. He briefly glanced at the wolf, which had now moved far away, leaving no trace of its blood on the snow. The wolf vanished into the wintry haze, but the silent beggar could still perceive its shadow, almost two hundred meters away from the room. The bloodstains left by the wolf had visibly weakened the silent beggar, draining his strength. Despite the blustery conditions and obscured vision, the silent beggar remained perceptive, observing everything alongside the wolf. It was as though he saw and felt with his heart, transcending the limitations of his physical sight. The wolf lay on the snow, staring directly into the silent beggar's eyes as if engaged in silent conversation. As the wolf's life force waned, the silent beggar felt its breaths slipping away, mirroring his own fleeting existence. The wolf's head came to rest on the cold snow, its eyes fixed and unblinking, peering into the depths of the silent beggar's soul. It was as if the wolf recognized their shared kinship, acknowledging the silent beggar's similarity to itself. The wolf's spirit stood before the platform, communing with the silent beggar, their connection woven solely through their spiritual essence. It appeared as though the wolf anticipated the silent beggar's spirit joining its own, completely disregarding Sergeant Timur Khan. Timur Khan remained unaware of the wolf's spiritual presence, unable to see or feel what unfolded before him. Breaking the silence, he finally spoke, his voice tinged with urgency, "Alright, Kal, what do you want to do now? Shall we stay here?"

Timur Khan waited expectantly for a response, but it seemed the silent beggar was entranced by the wolf spirit, impervious to Timur Khan's words reaching his ears. Raising his voice, Timur Khan called out louder, "Kal? Kal?"

Timur Khan anxiously awaited, extending the duration of his wait in hopes of hearing the voice of the silent beggar. However, his expectations were in vain. Growing increasingly concerned that his friend may have passed away, Timur Khan rose from the platform and descended towards the location of the silent beggar. Unbeknownst to him, he unknowingly traversed the path that led him between the two platforms, where the spirit of the wolf lingered. Timur Khan arrived at the spot and shook the silent beggar, only to realize that his longtime companion had departed from this world, leaving him forever.

Overwhelmed by what he had witnessed, Timur Khan found himself in a state of confusion, unsure of his purpose or what actions to take next. Lost in his thoughts and the weight of the moment, he inadvertently failed to notice that the spirits of the silent beggar and the wolf stood together between the platforms, observing him. They then gradually faded into the snow and the passage of time. Now, there remained only a deadly silence and Sergeant Timur Khan.

Unaware of his own actions, Sergeant Timur Khan absentmindedly took the silent beggar's pipe, placed it between his lips, and began to smoke, oblivious to the fact that the fire had extinguished. The last words spoken by his departed friend, the silent beggar, echoed in his ears. "My grave will be on the other side of Asyeh's... I have already started digging it, but it remains unfinished. I must complete it soon, if the snow permits me."

* * * * *

The snow-covered hills above the Village of Shourcheh basked in the gentle caress of the sun. Zulfiqar's weathered cane sank into the snow and emerged; a few days having passed since he last heard from the silent beggar. Unbeknownst to Zulfiqar, the Law Men and Sergeant Timur Khan had visited the beggar at his farm. As the sun rose, Zulfiqar contemplated taking the opportunity to return to the beggar's dwelling where he resided now. Silence enveloped the surroundings, with no figures, images, or voices in sight or earshot. Only silence prevailed, accompanied by the white expanse of snow and the rhythmic sound of Zulfiqar's cane piercing the air.

It didn't take long for Mr. Zulfiqar to reach the beggar's humble abode. Standing before the platform, he raised his head to the sky, his ears attuned to every sound. Upon reaching the hut, a sense of unease washed over him. He didn't need sight to perceive that something was amiss; he could sense it. Addressing the silent beggar, Zulfiqar called out, "Hello Kal? Are you inside or outside?"

Recently, the beggar had requested Zulfiqar to call him Kala. As he received no response or indication of any presence, Zulfiqar continued, "The snow was relentless for the past few days, making it difficult to come here... but as the snow ceased and the sun emerged, I made my way... I don't know why I was worried about you."

With no answer forthcoming from the silent beggar, Zulfiqar's concern grew. His head tilted towards the sky once again, his ears finely attuned in the hopes of catching even the faintest sound. Standing between the two platforms and in front of the door, it appeared that no one was in the vicinity, and silence prevailed. Zulfiqar turned his head to the air, further honing his hearing. "Kala?!"

As he received no response, Zulfiqar's cane began to explore the platform, checking if Kala was seated there. Inadvertently, the cane struck a person sitting on the platform. Zulfiqar experienced a fleeting relief as he resumed his one-sided conversation, moving to sit on the opposing platform. "Thank goodness, you're still alive and unharmed. I was worried about you amidst the heavy snow... Is your tea ready, Kala?"

Yet, no reply was heard from anyone. A renewed sense of worry gripped Zulfiqar, prompting him to call for the dog. "Majnoon?"

The dog remained silent, offering no response. It was then that Zulfiqar caught a sound emanating from behind the hut. His head instinctively turned towards the source, his ears sharpening to capture every nuance. Before he could fully adjust his sitting position, several Law Men appeared, standing before the platform. Perplexed, Zulfiqar wondered who stood in front of him, sensing their presence as horsemen. "Are you Law Men?"

But there was no answer once again. Zulfiqar was unaware that Sergeant Timur Khan's men were standing beside him. When they noticed their chief, Sergeant Timur Khan, sitting at the corner of the platform near the door, wrapped in a blanket, they were so startled that they couldn't even hear Zulfiqar trying to talk to them. Sergeant Timur Khan was not wearing his uniform. His hands, feet, boots, shirt, and pants were covered in mud. Even his horse was inside the room. It turned out he hadn't slept all night. After several days of Sergeant Timur Khan's absence from the village, they grew worried and came looking for him. A few Law Men's gazes fell upon the base of a mulberry tree, where they noticed a mixture of snow and mud. It was evident that someone had dug a hole there and concealed it with mud and snow. They searched for the Silent beggar but found no trace of him. One of them, confused, turned towards Sergeant Timur Khan, and asked, "Sergeant, are you okay? What happened here? Where is the old man?"

Upon hearing the policeman's voice, Zulfiqar suddenly became alert and confused, realizing that the person whose cane he had encountered was Sergeant Timur Khan, not Kala. Zulfiqar's ears became more attuned, and he kept his gaze fixed on the arch's edge.

The Law Men dismounted their horses. One of them entered the room and took out the horse, while another approached Sergeant Timur Khan. "Sergeant, how are you? What happened here?"

Finally, Sergeant Timur Khan stood up, and his deep, calm voice was finally audible. "Nothing happened, everything is fine."

"What about the old man? What happened to him?"

"Nothing. He wandered off, gone forever... he won't come back again. He made our job easier."

Sergeant Timur Khan then mounted his horse, unaware that he wasn't wearing his jacket. One of the Law Men picked up his jacket from the podium and handed it to him. "Sergeant, it's still cold outside. Put on your jacket, or you'll catch a cold."

Sergeant Timur Khan took his jacket, clutching it tightly, and gazed towards the mulberry tree where the mud and snow were mixed. A moment of silence ensued, with everyone looking at each other, trying to decipher what had truly transpired. Finally, one of them spoke up. "Sergeant, did Kala mention when he would return?"

Zulfiqar's voice rose as his head remained raised and his ears perked up. It was then that Sergeant Timur Khan turned towards him, only now noticing him, and stared as Zulfiqar expressed his concern once again. "I apologize for my impudence, Sergeant, but I wanted to ask... you see, we had become accustomed to each other's company recently... that's why I inquired about his return."

"Never. He has left forever," Sergeant Timur Khan replied.

After hearing Sergeant Timur Khan's words, Zulfiqar was in shock and in a state of introspection. The Law Men rode off, while Sergeant Timur Khan remained standing beneath the mulberry tree, gazing at the graves covered in snow and mud. The number of graves had now increased to three, yet the other Law Men were unaware that Sergeant Timur Khan was bidding farewell to his friend Kala Abbas, who had been laid to rest next to Asyeh.

"Sergeant, if Kala never returns and is presumed dead... what will happen to this place, Sergeant?" Zulfiqar shouted from under the platform, ensuring his voice reached Sergeant Timur Khan. His attention shifted from the grave and his departed friend, Kal Abbas, as he turned towards Zulfiqar, observing him intently before responding, "He said everything belongs to you... he knew you had no place, and he believed you would be a worthy custodian for it."

"A custodian? But if this place becomes a shrine, who will be its trustee?" Zulfiqar whispered.

"You never know. Perhaps one day it will indeed become a shrine," Sergeant Timur Khan replied.

With that, Sergeant Timur Khan departed, joining the other Law Men who had been patiently waiting. They rode away, soon disappearing into the distance. Now, only Zulfiqar remained, along with the hut, the silence, and the memories of Sattar, Asyeh, Kal Abbas, and their faithful dog, Majnoon. Two months later, Sergeant Timur Khan also succumbed to a stroke in his sleep and passed away.

* * * * *

Chapter 13
When superstitions supplant authentic religious convictions, and religion itself morphs into a platform exploited by deceitful individuals and unscrupulous groups...

One or two months had passed since the silent beggar's death and burial. The snow had melted, losing its white purity, yet the eternal tranquility and gentle breeze of the hills remained unchanged. Zulfiqar sat on the platform; his gaze fixed upon the hills. During this period, he had ample time for introspection, secluded in the once Forbidden area, once home to the Elves, untouched by human presence for over fifty years.

However, everything had now changed. The Elves were no more, and the forbidden designation was lifted. The memories of Sergeant Timur Khan had resurfaced and then faded away in Zulfiqar's mind, soul, and spirit over the past months. He had begun to believe that he had finally found a place to spend his remaining years peacefully until his demise. But he was well aware that as soon as the people of Village Shourcheh and Tikken learned of the silent beggar's passing, they would swiftly rush to the farm, competing to claim ownership of the land and the aqueduct.

Zulfiqar anticipated that his serenity would be shattered, his days filled with chaos and darkness. For years, both villages had suffered from drought, and with the abundance of water present, he did no doubt that a fierce struggle would ensue between them to seize control. It mattered little what the silent beggar had conveyed to Sergeant Timur Khan. Firstly, the sergeant was no longer alive to testify; he had long departed from this world. Even if he were alive, who would the farm belong to? Who would take up the responsibility? Who would care? No one.

Zulfiqar also acknowledged that he couldn't engage in a battle with both villages. He knew he had no choice but to align himself with either Shourcheh or Tikken and stand against the other. That's why he remained alone, refraining from visiting either village, giving himself time to contemplate his options in the wake of the silent beggar's absence.

After weeks of contemplation and careful consideration, he concluded that partnering with the village of Shourcheh would prove more advantageous. Imam Asghari seemed to have made peace with Zulfiqar, having already expressed at the police station that Zulfiqar should be entrusted with the farm. Zulfiqar was well aware of Imam Asghari's cunning nature, realizing that their relationship would be laced with venomous intent. However, despite this knowledge, Imam Asghari remained his best choice. Hence, before the people of Tikken became aware of the silent beggar's demise, Zulfiqar decided it was crucial to visit Imam Asghari first and establish a friendly bond with him.

It was dusk when Zulfiqar embarked on his journey to the village of Shourcheh. He knew that after every religious ceremony, the leaders such as Haji Ghazanfar, Kadkhoda, and the other pilgrims would gather at the confiscated mansion of Imam Asghari. They would celebrate their supposed victory, discuss the events that transpired, and indulge in extravagant gourmet meals, shielded from the prying eyes of the impoverished majority, whose dreams of such luxury remained distant. Determined, Zulfiqar made his way directly to Imam Asghari's mansion.

By the time Zulfiqar reached Imam Asghari's house, night had fallen. Without invitation, he knocked on the door, only to be stopped by a few guards. Zulfiqar explained that he had an important message to share with the Imam, and after some deliberation, the guards reluctantly granted him entry. Inside, the elders had congregated in the opulent room previously belonging to the wealthy Kal Abbas. Tea, hookah, fruits, and sweets adorned the space. It was customary for some to spend time in a smaller room to smoke and perhaps even drink before returning to the main gathering. However, Zulfiqar was not among those privileged few who enjoyed such luxuries. He was merely part of a small group of servants tasked with providing these extravagances.

Zulfiqar's sudden arrival, coupled with the recent incident involving the silent beggar during the road construction, remained fresh in everyone's minds, particularly in the thoughts of Imam Asghari, Haji

Ghazanfar, and Kadkhoda. Due to this, he had been barred from attending the mosque or participating in any of Imam Asghari's gatherings. In fact, Zulfiqar rarely made appearances in the village of Shourcheh anymore. If he did visit, it was done secretly, far away from prying eyes. Thus, it came as a shock to everyone in the room when Zulfiqar appeared at Imam Asghari's house, especially in the company of such influential individuals. They wondered how he had dared to show his face there.

As Zulfiqar entered, dressed entirely in black, it was evident from his teary eyes that something terrible had transpired. He began sobbing, attempting to force a few tears to trickle down his face for all to witness. His performance continued as he constantly wiped away the tears, perpetuating the facade of sorrow. It was all an act, designed to manipulate their emotions and sell his fabricated anguish. Zulfiqar played his game so convincingly that even the blind, deaf, and mute would have perceived his tears and pain. Prior to his arrival that day, he had purposefully inflicted wounds upon himself and meticulously orchestrated his portrayal of misery, leaving no room for doubt or sympathy.

And now, with the silent beggar's passing, he knew he had to deliver his most captivating performance to secure his place in the silent beggar’s house. His plan was to settle down there until his own demise. However, achieving his goal required the assistance and support of Imam Asghari. For weeks, Zulfiqar had been contemplating, strategizing, and practicing diligently. Aware of the consequences, he understood that revealing Sattar's story and his ownership of the farm would result in Rostam Khan, Sattar's older brother, inheriting the land, depriving the villages of Tikken and Shourcheh of their rightful access to water. In the event that Imam Asghari showed hostility towards him, Zulfiqar resolved to align himself with Rostam Khan, showcasing Sattar's grave and winning Rostam Khan's favor. Nonetheless, he was unsure if Rostam Khan would allow him to reside on the land and maintain control until his death. Hence, his best strategy was to play both sides and keep them at bay.

However, Zulfiqar's pitiful state and audacity to appear in Imam Asghari's home indicated to everyone present that he must have important news to share. Just then, Ugly Ghadam entered the scene and, upon seeing

Zulfiqar, raised his voice and moved to throw him out. Imam Asghari intervened, stating, "Ghadam? Mr. Zulfiqar is our guest, and a guest is a gift from God."

Imam Asghari's voice, perceptive and astute, captured something that others failed to notice about Zulfiqar, causing Ugly Ghadam to halt and retreat. From that moment, Zulfiqar became the most significant guest in Imam Asghari's eyes. True to the nature of many Mulla members, Imam Asghari swiftly changed his stance and perceived Zulfiqar as a divine gift, altering his words, direction, and character to benefit himself, even if it meant harming others or straying from religious principles. Recognizing the potential advantage of befriending Zulfiqar, Imam Asghari saw him as a key figure to assume control of a farm above the village and its aqueduct. As a smile graced Imam Asghari's face, the other attendees also grew calm, forgiving and forgetting Zulfiqar's past. Suddenly, he became their most trusted friend and a gift from God. They treated Zulfiqar with honor, seating him between Imam Asghari and Haji Ghazanfar. Tea and sweets were promptly offered by Imam Asghari and Haji Ghazanfar, while Ugly Ghadamplaced a freshly prepared hookah before Zulfiqar. At that moment, Zulfiqar felt esteemed and respected, akin to a king among kings who had entered the gathering. Overwhelmed by the attention and respect bestowed upon him, Zulfiqar couldn't help but cry uncontrollably. Through tears, he began to share his account while simultaneously sipping cup after cup of hot tea and puffing on the hookah.

"Imam Asghari, the esteemed one, and Haji Ghazanfar, and Kadkhoda, I swear by God that I am afraid to visit the silent beggar's house. You won't believe what occurred there—suddenly, lightning struck in every direction. The lightning was so magnificent and vibrant that even my blind eyes could perceive it. Both Shaykh Ahmad and Shaykh Gonabadi were struck to the ground, utterly dumbfounded."

Imam Asghari's voice grew louder upon hearing the names of Shaykh Ahmad and Shaykh Gonabadi, abruptly interrupting Zulfiqar's speech. He took the cup of tea and handed it to Zulfiqar, saying, "Drink your tea first to feel better, Mr. Zulfiqar."

Then, he leaned in and whispered shrewdly behind Zulfiqar's ear, "Do not mention Shaykh Ahmad and Shaykh Gonabadi here."

Zulfiqar refreshed his throat with a sip of tea and continued, "Now that Imam Asghari has permitted me to reveal the whole truth, in the midst of this radiant scene, I suddenly witnessed the form and presence of Imam Asghari standing amidst the light. He had a smile on his face, bestowing his benevolence upon a humble beggar who sought forgiveness from the Imam with his meek eyes. Without hesitation, Imam Asghari extended his hand to the beggar, granting him forgiveness. The beggar then revealed that he had dedicated the farm as a religious tax to Imam Asghari and that I should serve as its guardian and the Imam's representative. Suddenly, an angel appeared beside the Imam, and the brilliance intensified to the point where barely any eyes could see. Remarkably, despite my blindness, I could clearly see and comprehend. The beggar closed his eyes in contentment and vanished into the light as if he had never been there. Subsequently, Imam Asghari took my hand and said, 'Zulfiqar, fasten your belt. You shall oversee this place for the remainder of your life.' Overwhelmed with fear, I fainted. When I regained consciousness, neither the Imam nor the beggar were present, and the beggar remained untraceable for the past two weeks as if he had disappeared like water absorbed by the earth. That is why I have come to kiss the hand of the Imam."

To conclude his act, Zulfiqar reached out to grasp Imam Asghari's hand and kissed it several times. Following him, Ugly Ghadam hurried towards the Imam and also kissed his hand. In the blink of an eye, everyone present joined in, vying to reach and kiss the hand of their revered Imam. With humility, Imam Asghari silenced Mr. Zulfiqar and continued with his deceitful and manipulative speech. "Mr. Zulfiqar, let us not speak of our miracles any longer. Some miracles should remain untold. You have become a man of God, Mr. Zulfiqar. Drink your tea."

Observing that he had successfully gained the Imam's approval and solidified his position, Zulfiqar suddenly ceased his weeping and his face flushed. He began to eat and drink. However, he knew he mustn't stop now. He understood that he had ignited the fire and needed to bake more bread before it cooled down. While eating and drinking, he resumed his performance, and his speech flourished once again. "Imam, you had once or twice mentioned that you saw wisdom in that farm. You personally witnessed the light there on a few occasions. You advised against discussing it openly for now, mentioning that there was a message that must first reach you. Initially, I didn't believe it, feeling like a foolish and misguided idiot. But Imam, you had known all along. In your soul, you stated that the farm must be dedicated to the Imam's will and transformed into a shrine. You even named it."

Then he turned to Haji Ghazanfar and Kadkhoda and continued, "Haji Kadkhoda, even now you should be able to see the light from here... Look! You guys are men of God as well, and if you do not see it, then what is the difference between you, who are men of God, and just regular people? Go ahead and look... If you do not see the light there, that means you are not men of God... Look."

Zulfiqar got up and went to the porch overlooking the hill where the farm was located. On his way, he invited Hajji Ghazanfar, Kadkhoda, and everyone else. As the Imam rose, the rest didn't hesitate and accompanied him and Zulfiqar. It didn't take more than a minute for everyone to gather around the Imam and Zulfiqar outside on the large porch. Normally, Majnoon, Kal Abbas' dog, would be on guard there to watch Asyeh, but this time there was no sign of the dog, Asyeh, Kal Abbas, or Sattar. Love, honesty, and humanity were absent. Now there were only people and their lies and manipulations, and all their eyes were fixed on the farm above the village. Zulfiqar continued his show, knowing that now was the best opportunity to involve Hajji Ghazanfar and Kadkhoda in his play and somehow force them to acknowledge that they also saw the light up there. He understood that he needed to convince them to join his side. So, he turned to them again and said, "Hajji, Kadkhoda, look! Didn't I say there is still light there in this dark night? You can still see the farm. The effect of the lights still remains and hasn't disappeared. If no one else can see the light, Hajji, Kadkhoda, you two, as men of God, must be able to see it. Otherwise, how could you claim to be men of God and not see the light when Imam Asghari and I can see it, even though I am blind?"

It was dark everywhere, and everyone was staring toward the farm, trying their best to see the light up there. Everything and everywhere was silent. It seemed as if everyone was waiting for someone else to speak up and confirm whether they saw the light or not. However, as Zulfiqar waited, no one uttered a word. Luck did not favor him this time. Even Imam Asghari remained silent. Zulfiqar knew he couldn't give up just yet, so he turned to Imam Asghari and said, "Imam, it is as clear to me as day and night. If no one else can see the light, you, as the Imam and a man of God, must see it before I do. You witnessed it yourself, Imam. By remaining silent, it might go against God's will, and perhaps God wouldn't approve. You once told me that only people with pure faith and those close to God can see the light. My Imam, you cannot stay silent any longer. Haji Ghazanfar, Kadkhoda, both of you are men of God, and you cannot remain silent either. You must tell the people that as men of God, you see the light. You must speak the truth. Staying silent against God's will is nothing but a sin and implies that you are not men of God. Do you remember, Imam, when you said that a Muslim without faith cannot see the light?"

Now all eyes were on Imam Asghari, waiting to see his response. They were eager to know if their respected Imam also witnessed the divine light, just like Zulfiqar. Zulfiqar's actions had put Haji Ghazanfar, Kadkhoda, and especially Imam Asghari in a precarious position. If they admitted to not seeing the light, it would imply that they were not the men of God they claimed to be. On the other hand, if they claimed to see the light, they would be lying. Furthermore, if other people confirmed that they couldn't see the light at the farm, it would complicate matters even further. The situation was particularly challenging for Imam Asghari, as he was not only expected to see everything as the Imam but had also previously agreed with Zulfiqar that he had witnessed the light.

Imam Asghari, who had been contemplating whether to align with Zulfiqar or not, found himself unable to remain silent any longer. He had a responsibility to fulfill his duties as the Imam and provide an answer to the people. Zulfiqar, intentionally or not, had made it easier for him to lie. At that moment, as Haji Ghazanfar's skeptical comment reached Imam Asghari's ears, he promptly interrupted him to prevent Haji Ghazanfar from claiming to have seen the light before him. Imam Asghari, raising his voice, began speaking as if reciting a prayer at the mosque.

"O God... Forgive us for the sins we were unaware of... I bear witness to Your miracles. What a beautiful lightning, as if it descended directly from the sky, illuminating the mulberry tree and shimmering on the wells and aqueducts... God, forgive us. Of course, I see the light."

Then, turning to Zulfiqar, he continued, "However, Mr. Zulfiqar, as we have mentioned, not everyone can perceive the divine light. Individuals must attain a certain level of religiosity and draw closer to God before they can witness such brilliance."

Now, Haji Ghazanfar was not pleased that Imam Asghari had cut him off, seizing the opportunity to present himself as more religious and spiritually connected than Haji Ghazanfar. Haji Ghazanfar had initially intended to deny seeing the lightning, but now he too was confused. Like the others, they were caught in a dilemma, unsure of what to do or say. The more they searched for the light, the more disappointed they became when they found none. However, they were reluctant to speak the truth, fearing they would be labeled as impious or non-Muslim. Before Haji Ghazanfar could make a decision, Haji Mohammad, an elderly man, spoke up and attempted to make a jest.

"Seems our eyes must be blind, for they cannot perceive the lightning."

Imam Asghari swiftly interrupted Haji Mohammad, shouting, "Even if your eyes were blind, as a true Muslim who believes in God, you would still behold as much light as Mr. Zulfiqar."

Then, Imam Asghari turned to Haji Ghazanfar and inquired, "Hajji, as a pilgrim, a man of God, and a true Muslim, are you capable of perceiving the lightning?"

Haji Ghazanfar gazed at the desert in silence for a moment, before finally whispering, "Haji Mohammad, look again with your heart. Even Zulfiqar could see with his blind eyes, yet you couldn't see it? Can't you see what color is this clear green?"

"Hajj, it is well known that your heart is with God. It's true that all your prayers have been accepted by Him, unlike those who cannot perceive the light. They lack enlightenment and fail to see the divine illumination. They cannot truly be called Muslims, for they reject religion and faith, making them infidels. Now it is clear who among us are Muslims and who are non-Muslims."

Imam Asghari affirmed that Haji Ghazanfar was a devoted pilgrim and a true Muslim based on his false confession of seeing the lightning. He declared that those who couldn't witness the lightning were either non-Muslims or individuals distant from God's grace. After Haji Ghazanfar's confirmation, Kadkhoda also claimed to see the lightning. Gradually, one by one, others too began to see the light emanating from the sky, illuminating, and blessing the farm above the village. Suddenly, they all became devout Muslims and theologians. Their hearts were cleansed, and the entire desert sparkled before their eyes. However, Haji Mohammad remained the exception, insisting that he couldn't see any light. He was branded as someone disconnected from God.

In less than an hour, news of the lightning and the silent beggar's farm around the aqueduct spread throughout the village, arousing everyone's curiosity. All eyes turned to the hill in anticipation of witnessing the phenomenon. Under Imam Asghari's guidance, led by Ghadam Baldy, they set out towards the hill seeking blessings and forgiveness for their sins. The entire cemetery and hill were illuminated as if by the sun, as people carried oil lanterns to light their way. Strangely enough, no one questioned the need for lanterns if the lightning was already illuminating the desert. Moreover, everyone claimed to see the lightning, fearing the label of non-Muslim and the wrath of God if they admitted otherwise.

It didn't take long for the crowd to reach the humble dwelling of the silent beggar, showering it with greetings and blessings. The mulberry tree and the water well were adorned with colorful fabrics, and people gathered to make vows. Imam Asghari ascended the pulpit and recited the few subjects he had memorized, including the shrine of Imam Hussein and the triumphant Battle of the Euphrates River. The women wept with such intensity that their tears could have filled the well for a month. They prayed in groups, sobbing inconsolably.

As the morning approached, the weary yet blessed people returned to their homes after acquiring the highest paradise for themselves. Each of them carried a secret, a desire to be blessed by God like Imam Asghari and Zulfiqar, to witness the divine lightning and gain the same power. They yearned to be true Muslims without resorting to falsehood and sin, avoiding the path that would lead them to hell.

However, it appeared that the truth about their deception, pretending to have seen the lightning, remained buried in the graves of all except a few. They feared damaging their reputation among their peers and neighbors, not wanting anyone to believe that their inability to witness the lightening meant they were not genuine followers of Islam.

* * * * *

Chapter 14
When superstitions take precedence over religion and replace it...

The day was well underway, with the scorching sun casting its rays upon the village of Shourcheh. Once again, a gathering had formed around Imam Asghari, Haji Ghazanfar, and Kadkhoda near the cemetery on a small hill by the road that led to the quiet beggar's farm. People were flocking from every corner to join the assembly. A few yards away, a group of individuals diligently dug two holes under the guidance of Ghadam Baldy, who called for prayers. The voices of peace and blessings grew louder with each shovel piercing the earth, resonating through the air. In close proximity to the pits, a couple of sheep stood, prepared to be sacrificed.

The pleas and struggles of the helpless sheep went unnoticed amidst the chorus of greetings and prayers. Their innocent eyes locked onto the sharpened knives wielded by merciless butchers, aware of their impending fate. They silently begged for mercy, their gaze fixated upon their executioners, as they awaited their release from this world.

Zulfiqar arrived, joining the crowd, and found himself positioned alongside Imam Asghari, Haji Ghazanfar, and Kadkhoda at the head of the cemetery. However, confusion marred Zulfiqar's thoughts as he pondered why the people had once again congregated near the cemetery and the road leading to the hill and the farm. No one had informed him of the proceedings beforehand, and he couldn't help but feel unsettled. Mard Ali, as usual, brandished his wooden sword, and upon Zulfiqar's arrival, he took a seat beside him, raising his voice as he always did. "It's a wedding, Zulfiqar. They're bringing a bride."

Zulfiqar grew even more bewildered upon hearing Mard Ali's proclamation that it was a wedding, and a bride was being brought forth. The crowd continued to swell, with mourners, bearers, and wailers multiplying in number. The butchers honed their knives with increasing intensity, preparing for the impending slaughter. A dispute arose between one sheep and its burly executioner, debating whether the sheep should have a final drink of water before their blood was shed. It was customary to offer water to the sheep before their demise, but in the eyes of the sheep, it seemed akin to taking a fatal poison. However, the resilient creatures staunchly refused to drink, showing no intention of surrender.

All eyes, including those of the butchers and the rest of the crowd, fixated upon the top of the road leading to the city as if anticipating the arrival of a significant figure. And at long last, when the heads of a few donkeys and a group of people emerged from behind a hill along the road, the crowd erupted with sudden excitement. The joyous clamor of the people ascended to the heavens, accompanied by Mard Ali's enthusiastic proclamation. "The bride has arrived... they've brought the bride."

Seeing the men and the donkey approaching from the top of the road, Mard Ali dismounted, his sword dancing in the air as he pursued those rushing towards the donkey carrying a mysterious, heavily covered load. Halfway there, Mard Ali and his companions reached the donkey, each vying to grab and hold its reins. The group accompanying the donkey refused to let anyone else take control, sparking a struggle among the newly arrived pilgrims. It was a spectacle to behold as they competed to touch the concealed load or even the donkey itself. They were undeterred by kicks, punches, or beatings with wooden sticks—nothing mattered except the chance to touch the load as if it held the divine touch of the Messenger of God. They believed that one touch would fulfill their needs and secure the highest place in God's paradise.

Mard Ali's wooden sword continued to whirl through the air, engaging in a battle against the perceived enemies of Islam. He beat back the newly arrived pilgrims, who, despite the beatings, refused to yield. At times, Mard Ali positioned his sword between his legs, assuming a horse-like stance as he rode around the mass of people, fighting the invisible enemy of Islam.

As the donkey neared the crowd, a competition among the butchers ensued. Each sheep was hoisted into the air and forcefully brought down to the ground as if the butchers aimed to demonstrate their strength by delivering the most powerful blows. Some people rushed to hold the sheep's limbs while others sat on their bellies, applying tremendous pressure to prevent any movement. The sheep's snorts were held by the skilled butchers, who positioned the sharp edges of their knives against the animals' snouts. The executioners' eyes remained fixed on the donkey and its impending arrival.

Finally, the donkey and its load arrived, triggering a flood of people storming towards them with thunderous greetings and salutations, desperate to touch either the load or the donkey itself. Ugly Ghadamand his gang attempted to beat people away from the load, but their efforts were futile. The scent of burning Especial dry weeds filled the air, emanating from an open brass container, momentarily blinding everyone. Some individuals sprinkled rose water, including the donkey's load, trying to counteract the overpowering aroma. The combined fragrance of Especial dry beads and rose water intoxicated the surroundings, affecting even the most stoic among them.

As the donkey reached the edge of the pits, the butchers engaged in a fierce competition to swiftly sever the sheep's snorts. Their goal seemed to be to demonstrate who could behead their sheep first, letting its blood flow and proving themselves as the most skilled executioner. They aspired to receive the reward from their Imam and secure a place in God's paradise. The sheep were beheaded, and while they still struggled with death, their throats were brought to the edge of the pit, allowing their blood to flow into the cavity that now housed the two bases of the large sign carried by the donkey. The people's prayers remained incessant, their voices resounding throughout the scene. Motionless, the corpses of the unfortunate sheep lay scattered on the ground. Amidst the chaos, superstitious individuals fought to kiss and touch their Imam Asghari, and some even sought to congratulate Haji Ghazanfar and Kadkhoda. "May your new Shrine be blessed," they exclaimed, with faith in their hearts.

Now, Zulfiqar stood apart from the crowd, lost in thought. It was then that he realized what was happening. Imam Asghari had ordered the installation of a colorful sign along the road leading to the silent beggar's farm. They had even chosen a name for it - "the Noor Shrine of

Shourcheh". The sign had been placed on top of the hill, overlooking the road that passed above the village and the farm. In doing so, they had deceived the village of Tikken, claiming the farm as belonging to the village of Shourcheh.

Imam Asghari had intentionally kept Zulfiqar unaware of the sign until it was erected, fearing that Zulfiqar might inform the village of Tikken and claim a reward before they could do the same.

By stealing the Shrine's sign, Imam Asghari, Haji Ghazanfar, and Kadkhoda felt as though they had cemented the ownership of the silent beggar's farm for the village of Shourcheh, naming it after the Noor Shrine of Shourcheh. They believed that anyone passing through the road would see the sign above the village of Shourcheh and assume that the road originated from there. They also spread the rumor that the village of Shourcheh had witnessed a divine sign in the form of lightning, suggesting that the farm rightfully belonged to Shourcheh, not Tikken. They purposely named the Shrine 'Noor' and added 'Shourcheh' to emphasize the connection.

However, Zulfiqar had already informed Imam Asghari about the truth regarding Asyeh, Sattar, and the silent beggar. He revealed that Asyeh was Sattar's wife and that Sattar had created the farm, leaving it in the care of the silent beggar, where all three of them were now buried. Upon hearing Asyeh's name, Imam Asghari recalled how he himself had killed her before changing his name from Moharram to Asghar. He felt no remorse for his actions, but he warned Zulfiqar not to mention Sattar's name or his connection to the farm. Instead, Imam Asghari instructed Zulfiqar to mention only Kal Abbas and Asyeh's relationship, stating that Kal Abbas was Asyeh's husband, and they had sought refuge on the farm to evade the law. Since both Kal Abbas and Asyeh hailed from the Village of Shourcheh, Imam Asghari argued that legally the farm should belong to Shourcheh.

Taking it a step further, Imam Asghari swiftly issued a fatwa, proclaiming Asyeh as a brave defender of Islam. Suddenly, Asyeh, who had been cast out of the village and labeled a whore, was now portrayed as an oppressed, virtuous woman, comparable to the revered Zahra, the

Prophet's wife. The rumors spread quickly, fueled by the sighting of the light, connecting it to the gallows and the Imam's lineage. It was claimed that the Imams and the Prophet himself had manifested there to purify Asyeh and Kal Abbas through the divine light, referred to as 'Noor' in Farsi. Thus, they were relieved that the farm now belonged to the Village of Shourcheh.

Imam Asghari contemplated future plans, envisioning the calming of the situation. Once things settled down, they intended to create a small stream from the farm, channeling water to irrigate their fields in the Village of Shourcheh.

But the happiness of Imam Asghari, Haji Ghazanfar, and the rest of the people of Shourcheh did not last more than one night. The next day, news arrived that the people of Village Tikken had erected an even bigger sign than the one in Shourcheh on the road to the Silent Begging farm. They named it 'The Shrine of Saleh Payghambar', meaning 'The Shrine of the Prophet.' They removed all the colorful clothes that Imam Asghari had asked people to hang on the mulberry tree and replaced them with their own vibrant fabrics. Additionally, they installed a sign facing the village of Tikken on the mulberry tree. Unbeknownst to Imam Asghari, the village of Tikken had spies in Shourcheh who promptly reported any happenings, big or small, to Rostam Khan in Tikken.

Upon learning about the rival sign and the use of the term 'Shrine,' Rostam Khan wasted no time and took immediate action. Within a day, they set up their own sign right in front of the village of Shourcheh. However, Rostam Khan carried out these actions discreetly, without making much noise and with greater political correctness. This is why they chose the name previously suggested by Sergeant Timur Khan. Rostam Khan knew very well that these controversies would likely involve law enforcement, so using the same name proposed by the Head of Law Enforcement, Sergeant Timur Khan, increased their chances of gaining support from law enforcement authorities.

Rostam Khan did not stop there. Under the cover of darkness, they ordered the placement of their shrine sign on the mulberry tree and adorned it with colorful clothes. They even added three tombstones on the graves of the silent beggar, Sattar, and Asyeh, inscribed with the endowment and gift of Tikken to its people. All of this was done to create the illusion that the silent beggar and the other two deceased individuals were from the Village of Tikken, thus asserting their claim that the silent beggar farm legally belonged to Tikken. There was no mention of Asyeh and Kal Abbas, who were from the Village of Shourcheh. Furthermore, Rostam Khan had no knowledge of Sattar, who was the original creator of the farm. Only Zulfiqar, Sergeant Timur Khan, and Imam Asghari were aware of the truth.

News of the schemes orchestrated by the Village of Tikken spread throughout Shourcheh like wildfire. It was clear that these actions did not sit well with the villagers and only fueled their anger. The battle over the shrine, it's naming, and the ownership of the farm escalated to a level far worse than before. In the blink of an eye, both villages began plotting how to defeat and kill their adversaries. Hatred, animosity, and the desire to claim ownership of the silent beggar's farm consumed both sides. Aqueducts were hastily constructed from each village, aiming to connect with the aqueduct at the farm and divert water to their respective villages. Not stopping there, both villages started removing each other's colorful clothes hanging from the mulberry tree and replacing them with their own.

The act of breaking each other's tombstones and replacing them with their own persisted continuously. However, this destructive behavior only benefitted the makers of the tombstones. Whenever they encountered one another, they would engage in violent fights, attempting to inflict as much harm as possible. Consequently, anyone venturing into that area always traveled in groups, ensuring they carried cold weapons for self-defense or offense.

The situation deteriorated to the point where Law Enforcement had to intervene, resulting in the presence of authorities in both villages. Naturally, they did not spend their time there without cause. As per custom, the villagers were obligated to provide food, which came at a considerable cost. Every time they served lavish dishes like kababs and various other delicacies, there was competition between the two villages to impress the Law Men in hopes of garnering favor. In such cases, leaders such as Imam Asghari and Haji Ghazanfar would approach and request financial aid from the impoverished and unfortunate, claiming it was their duty to contribute to the expenses of the Law Men and the court. They labeled it as the share of the Imam, a charitable act for the sake of God and the Prophet, promising eternal paradise to those who participated. However, Imam Asghari, in particular, was notorious for his collection of donations from the poor, and it was evident that most of the money went directly into his own pockets, with only a small portion actually benefiting the Law Men.

Not only did the Law Men revel in their time there, but people like Imam Asghari derived even greater pleasure from the situation. The more he could deceive the people, the happier he became. Consequently, he had no intention of resolving the conflict and would discreetly employ his paid men like Ugly Ghadam to instigate further confrontations whenever it seemed that a resolution was within reach. Unfortunately, all of this occurred under the guise of religion, with Imam Asghari manipulating the situation to convince the people that fighting the enemies of Islam was their religious duty. The suffering and hardship endured by the innocent and impoverished mattered little to him; in fact, he relished it. Ultimately, it was the poor people who were the primary victims, while Imam Asghari and those like him lived lives of luxury, indulging in drinking, eating, and even secret opium consumption, resembling kings. Everything they preached as beneficial to the people was, in fact, only advantageous to themselves.

That was why the quarrel and enmity between the two villages, led by rioters and thugs, continued unabated. Once again, it reached a point where both villages believed that only through force could they seize control of the silent beggar's farm and its aqueduct, thereby resolving their long-standing problem. To this end, Imam Asghari made the decision to issue a 'fatwa' and implement a jihadi ruling, as bestowed by a recognized religious authority like himself, in order to fight the perceived enemy of Islam. Such a cause was considered the highest honor for any Muslim, promising eternal bliss in heaven, especially for those who sacrificed their lives. And so, with this mission in mind, a mass of individuals set forth, armed with wooden sticks, clubs, and knives, under the leadership of Ugly Ghadam and his gang. Their resounding slogans pierced the sky as they advanced towards the farm and aqueduct, determined to seize them.

Imam Asghari and Haji Ghazanfar joined the crowd, riding their donkeys in tow. And no fight would be complete without the presence of Mard Ali, who, as usual, felt deeply wounded and rode on his wooden horse. His lamentations and arrogance echoed louder than ever as he took the lead, envisioning himself in a battle against Islam's nemesis, Shamar.

However, before Imam Asghari's army, led by Ghadam Baldy, could reach the hut at the silent beggar's farm, they encountered a large group of armed people from Tikken, equally prepared to fight and die. Rustam Khan, now advanced in age, remained composed, watching his men go to war from atop a horse on a hill. On the opposite hill, near the Village of Shourcheh, Imam Asghari, Haji Ghazanfar, and Kadkhoda observed the horrifying scene unfold, witnessing innocent lives being brutally taken.

Ugly Ghadam and his gang also patrolled the battlefield, forcefully pushing back anyone attempting to flee or show regret, forcing them back into the fray to be sacrificed for Imam Asghari's cause. Only Mard Ali remained safe, staying away from the commotion, his wooden sword slashing at an invisible enemy, Shamar. Unbeknownst to Mard Ali, he was unsure which side was Shamar's or Imam's; he simply fought his imagined foe.

Zulfiqar, having learned from Imam Asghari's teachings, distanced himself from the square and sought refuge in a room. He sat there, mimicking the silent beggar's stillness, his senses heightened as he awaited the outcome. Zulfiqar understood that he must remain neutral, refraining from aligning with any group until the victor emerged. Only then would he choose their side and engage in profitable business with them.

As the two villages engaged in a violent conflict, resulting in fatal beatings with shovels, pickaxes, sticks, and clubs, inflicting severe injuries to heads, faces, arms, and legs, a figure emerged from the distance—Shaykh Gonabadi. Residing in a modest, rundown hut on a small hill between Tikken and Shourcheh, Shaykh Gonabadi was known as a Tikkenian due to his closer proximity to the village of Tikken. Unlike other

Mullamen, he did not frequent the mosque. Shaykh Gonabadi favored simple attire, donning ordinary clothes and a plain black hat, rejecting the ostentatious Arabic garments worn by his counterparts. He staunchly believed that Islam forbade imitation and disapproved of associating Arabic clothing with the religion. His conviction was valid, as he argued that the robes and turbans of the Mulla served to create divisions and set them apart from the common people.

Shaykh Gonabadi held the view that the Mulla should not rely on the people for sustenance. He vehemently opposed receiving gifts or wages for providing Islamic guidance, considering it forbidden. Consequently, he refused to accept money or gifts as religious taxes, directing any funds brought to him directly to those in need. In addition to his spiritual duties, he engaged in farming during the day, working alongside the common folk. Despite his unorthodox approach, Shaykh Gonabadi earned the respect of individuals like the late Shaykh Ahmad from Village Shourcheh, who shared his beliefs but had disappeared, leaving his fate unknown.

The behavior of Shaykh Gonabadi, mirroring that of Shaykh Ahmad, often drew the ire of other Mulla/Clergyman, fueling their anger and frustration. However, Rustam Khan, influenced by his father's teachings, held a deep respect for individuals like Shaykh Gonabadi, viewing them as more genuine compared to other Mulla/Clergyman. Assad Khan, Rostam Khan, and Kal Abbas shared this sentiment, considering most Mulla/clergy men to be deceitful and dishonest, tarnishing the reputation of Islam by exploiting the religion for personal gain. Consequently, during their time, Mulla/clergy men were not granted the authority, power, or opportunity to manipulate and deceive the people.

However, just as the story of the quarrel and the brutal killings between the two villages reached its climax, Shaykh Gonabadi emerged from the distance, whispering to himself. Despite his old age, he walked with the aid of his cane, approaching from the side of Tikken village. He carelessly entered the chaotic scene, still engrossed in his murmurs. Amidst the turmoil, it seemed as though there was no space left for Shaykh Gonabadi to maneuver, yet he continued reciting prayers.

It was not merely the influence of the false Fatwa issued by Imam Asghari that fueled the animosity and violence between the villagers. Nonetheless, Shaykh Gonabadi, miraculously unharmed amidst the intense clashes, appeared as though he were invisible to the swinging wooden sticks, knives, punches, and kicks. Even amid the chaos, some individuals noticed his presence and gradually others followed suit. As Shaykh Gonabadi's influence grew, the number of people engaged in the fight dwindled.

However, Imam Asghari desired a relentless conflict and the demise of all his adversaries, which was not what unfolded. At that moment, the sound of gunshots echoed as the Law Men rode in on horseback, arriving at the battlefield. Upon their arrival, they struck the people with their rifles, feet, and horses, aiming to separate them. Slowly, the presence of the Law Men quelled the fighting, one person at a time. The entire crowd from both villages gazed upon Shaykh Gonabadi and the Law Men, who stood between the two groups. Positioned on their horses, rifles raised, the Law Men ensured that any potential rekindling of the conflict was promptly suppressed. Even they observed Shaykh Gonabadi attentively.

It became apparent to everyone that Shaykh Gonabadi was engaged in a conversation, seemingly with an invisible entity, or perhaps he was staging a performance to pacify the crowd. Nevertheless, only his side of the dialogue was audible, comprising responses and queries. The elders from both villages, along with the rest of the inhabitants and the Law Men, observed this peculiar scene.

Upon hearing the name Shaykh Gonabadi and the arrival of the Law Men, Zulfiqar finally emerged from the room. He made his way to the Shaykh, leaning on his trusty old cane, with his head held high and his ears more attentive than ever. Of course, Mard Ali couldn't resist joining in on the spectacle. He positioned himself between Shaykh and Zulfiqar, echoing the words of the Shaykh as he spoke.

Now, all eyes and ears were fixated on Shaykh Gonabadi, filled with silence and confusion, hoping to glean some meaning from his conversations with the invisible entity, if there was indeed one. However, the more people listened, the less they understood. Undeterred, Shaykh

Gonabadi strolled over to the mulberry tree, surveying it from both sides. He picked up two signs, one from the 'Noor Shrine' and the other from the village of 'Saleh the Payghambar'. These signs, plucked by villagers, had fallen to the ground, covered in dust and berries. Raising them up, Shaykh Gonabadi contemplated, "Alright, I shall inform them that this side represents the 'Noor Shrine' and the other side, 'The Saleh Payghambar'. Not a bad thought."

Meanwhile, Imam Asghari's patience had worn thin. He could no longer stay silent and approached Zulfiqar, whispering in his ear, "Do you know who Shaykh is speaking to?"

Zulfiqar replied, "Perhaps the silent beggar, not Kal Abbas... maybe even Sattar."

Haji Ghazanfar joined their conversation, adding, "I believe he's speaking with the silent beggar."

"The silent beggar?! The one who is deceased!? What are they saying?" Imam Asghari exclaimed.

Zulfiqar speculated, "Maybe with Kala Abbas..."

"With Kal Abbas?! Can you hear their voices?" Imam Asghari inquired.

As Shaykh Gonabadi continued his theatrical performance, he quietly listened to the conversation between Imam Asghari and Zulfiqar. Suddenly, he turned towards them, speaking louder to ensure their attention. "Certainly, the guardian of the shrine should be able to hear the voice of his master, even from beneath the grave. Otherwise, how can he be the rightful guardian? Can't you hear the voice, Zulfiqar?"

Startled by Shaykh Gonabadi's sudden address, Zulfiqar was momentarily taken aback. However, he quickly gathered himself, realizing Shaykh's intentions. A smile graced Zulfiqar's face, as a surge of excitement overcame him. In that instant, he became an active participant in Shaykh Gonabadi's play. Ignoring Imam Asghari, he broke away from him and approached Shaykh Gonabadi. With his head held even higher and his cane striking the ground with a newfound pride, Zulfiqar proclaimed, "Indeed, Shaykh, I could see them all—the silent beggar, Kal Abbas, Sattar Khan, and Asyeh."

Mard Ali also joined the scene, riding on his wooden horse, following Zulfiqar and Shaykh Gonabadi. He pretended to be one of the players in the play, repeating and translating their words. The people became even more confused, wondering how the silent beggar could communicate with Shaykh Gonabadi and how Shaykh Gonabadi could seemingly talk to the dead. Curiosity bloomed among the crowd, leaving them breathless. The blood that dripped from the heads and faces of Imam Asghari's soldiers, who were actually Imam Asghari himself in disguise, went unnoticed. All attention and focus shifted to Shaykh Gonabadi.

Shaykh Gonabadi could sense the fear that had engulfed the people's hearts, and he didn't want them to flee before the play was over. He was determined to finish the show, hoping it would resolve the long-standing issues between the two villages. This prospect would have displeased Imam Asghari greatly. Shaykh Gonabadi raised his voice, directing his words towards the elders of both villages. Even the Law Men, who sat silently on their horses, seemed somewhat intimidated, eagerly awaiting what would unfold.

Shaykh Gonabadi employed Zulfiqar as his ally, who played his role even better than Shaykh Gonabadi himself. "You are absolutely right, Kal Abbas, Sattar Khan, Asyeh Khanoum. I will convey your message. So, you wish to divide your farm and house between the two villages?" Shaykh Gonabadi asked. "No, I don't mean to divide it. I understand that it no longer belongs to you; it is an endowment and belongs to the religious institution, which means it belongs to everyone, regardless of their origin. So, you want this side of the mulberry tree to become the shrine of 'Saleh Payghambar.'"

Shaykh Gonabadi then walked towards the mulberry tree and placed the sign, reading 'Saleh Payghambar,' facing the northern part of the tree, which was towards the village of Tikken. He called upon the people for help in installing the sign. The people from Shourcheh, however, remained motionless. On the other hand, the people from Tikken, seeing their sign going up, hurried to Shaykh Gonabadi's aid and took the sign from him, placing it on the northern part of the mulberry tree. Joy and happiness filled the people of Tikken, while sadness, anger, and hatred were etched on the faces of Imam Asghari, Haji Ghazanfar, and all the people from Shourcheh. Imam Asghari, consumed by rage, was about to make a move to initiate a fight, but he was swiftly halted as the barrel of one of the Law Men's rifles was pressed against his chest, leaving him unsure of what to do next.

But the joy of the people of Tikken did not last long, nor did the sorrows and grief of the people of Shourcheh. They witnessed Shaykh Gonabadi picking up the sign that read 'the Noor Shrine' from the ground and placing it on another branch of the mulberry tree, facing towards the south and Village Shourcheh. He began installing it, and this time the people of Village Shourcheh rushed to help, while none from Tikken did. The entire population of Shourcheh was filled with joy and gladness, while sadness and sorrow engulfed the people of Tikken. The law enforcement authorities also cooperated with Shaykh Gonabadi, and anyone who attempted to protest or cause trouble was promptly dealt with by the authorities.

Then Shaykh Gonabadi turned to the people of Tikken and continued, "Sattar and Kal Abbas informed me that you can now consider this side of the mulberry tree as your shrine, where you can pray to your God and your righteous prophet."

He then addressed the people of Village Shourcheh, saying, "And this side is yours to claim as your shrine, where you can pray to your God and your righteous prophet."

Shaykh Gonabadi then turned his attention to Mr. Zulfiqar, involving him in the proceedings. "And both Sattar and Kal Abbas, along with Asyeh, told me that you, Mr. Zulfiqar, are the custodian of both shrines, with Mard Ali serving as the subordinate custodian under you."

He then addressed the people from both villages of Tikken and Shourcheh, saying, "Sattar and Kal Abbas also wish for you to have no conflict with each other and to refrain from harassing or harming one another. If you wish, you can go and pray at the other shrine, and no one can or should stop you. If you do so, your reward will be doubled. These are not my words, but the words of Asyeh Khanum, Sattar, and Kal

Abbas's spirits, who are speaking to me from the rooftop of the hunt. Majnoon the dog is also with them."

Now, as they heard the names Sattar, Asyeh, Kal Abbas, and Majnoon, the dog of Kal Abbas, and witnessed their apparitions on the rooftop of the hunt while conversing with Shaykh Gonabadi, confusion and bewilderment engulfed everyone. All eyes turned towards the rooftop, hoping to catch a glimpse of something, but alas, nothing was visible. Uncertainty gripped them, leaving them unsure of how to proceed or what to say. A profound silence enveloped the surroundings, yet from the expressions of Imam Asghari, it was evident that Rostam Khan maintained his silence to allow Shaykh Gonabadi to fulfill his duty. He placed his trust in the Shaykh's integrity, and the villagers of Tikken followed suit. Similarly, Mard Ali searched for Shaykh Gonabadi, growing silent himself. He ceased his performance and refrained from repeating the words of the Shaykh. His lips sealed shut as he fixated on the rooftop of the hunt, his countenance reflecting shock. For Mard Ali, everything had taken a drastic turn; he remained dissatisfied with the recent events. Instead, anger and animosity towards Shaykh Gonabadi consumed him. Eventually, his patience wore thin, and he raised his voice, addressing Haji Ghazanfar and the people of Shourcheh, who stood gathered behind him.

"Are you all blind or deaf? Can't you see the ungodly actions of this non-Muslim Shaykh? Have you not noticed how he has unjustly allocated half of what rightfully belongs to the people of Shourcheh to his own followers from Tikken? Yet here we stand in silence, witnessing the sacrilege of our beliefs and religion. Haji Ghazanfar, let's imagine that each village possesses its own shrine, but what about the aqueduct? What about the water that is crucial for our survival and the irrigation of our fields during this drought? Without it, we will all perish. Who truly owns these resources? Today, they have seized half of our land, and in due time, when the dust settles, they will take over the aqueduct and the entire farm, leaving us with nothing. Furthermore, Haji Ghazanfar, Kadkhoda, remember that if Asyeh and Kal Abbas were not from Shourcheh, if they had not arrived here before Sattar and established this farm and aqueduct, do you recall, Haji Ghazanfar? Someone informed me that you personally planted this mulberry tree by Aryeh's grave, seeking forgiveness on behalf of the people for any sins committed against her. Then who should rightfully be the legal owner of this farm and aqueduct, Haji? It should be you, not these ungodly people from Tikken."

Imam Asghari's words stirred Haji Ghazanfar, particularly when he mentioned the mulberry tree and implied Haji Ghazanfar's ownership of the farm. Even if there were uncertainties and potential falsehoods, Haji Ghazanfar felt a surge of confidence and stepped forward to echo Imam Asghari's sentiments.

"Well, indeed, by initiating the planting of a mulberry tree here, we, the people of Shourcheh, commenced this farm. They resided here and established the farm and the aqueduct. Therefore, after their passing, it is only customary and religiously just for the ownership of this land to remain with the people of Shourcheh."

Just then, as all eyes and ears were fixed on Imam Asghari and Haji Ghazanfar, Mard Ali's voice rose as if he were talking and playing with Majnoon, young Abbas's dog.

"Majnoon... are you back? Are you alive again? Do you remember me? We used to play together; we were friends. Remember me? Come, let's play again. It's the day to fight for truth and justice, to slay Shamar and open the water. Run, let's go and fight the enemies of Islam."

Mard Ali mounted his wooden horse, laughing and playing with Majnoon amidst the Law Men who had gathered in the center of the crowd. Their purpose was to prevent the two villages from attacking each other again, ensuring the people remained separate. However, despite careful observation, nobody could see the dog. Only Mard Ali was visible. The sound of Majnoon barking, albeit just twice, confused and shocked the crowd. Many recognized the unmistakable sound, remembering it as Majnoon's bark. Particularly, the elders recalled the incident when they had assaulted and killed the dog. Nevertheless, there was no sign of Majnoon. Mard Ali diverted their attention once more by imitating the dog's bark. "I can bark too... see?"

Mard Ali now occupied himself with barking and mimicking the dog's voice, but the onlookers found no dogs in sight. Ultimately, they concluded that either Mard Ali himself was producing the dog's voice or they had imagined hearing Majnoon. Meanwhile, Zulfiqar held his head high in the air, observing and listening attentively to avoid missing anything. However, Imam Asghari, realizing that the situation was spiraling out of control, raised his voice in protest once again.

"Haji Ghazanfar, Kadkhoda! Among all these Muslims and believers, only this deceitful Shaykh claims to see the souls of Sattar, Kal Abbas, and Asyeh, as well as this insane wanderer. Why don't you open your eyes and see that this Shaykh is playing games with us? Can't you see he's lulling you to sleep with his magic tricks, while he steals our rights, farms, and aqueduct that belong to the people of Shourcheh, handing them over to his own people in Tikken?"

Imam Asghari's speech and Ghadam Baldy's gang's provocations stirred up the people's emotions, leading to a gradual rise in their voices and protest movements from every corner. It was inevitable that the people of Tikken would not remain silent. Upon hearing Imam Asghari's words and witnessing his soldiers, led by Ghadam Baldy, as well as the escalating voices of the people, they too began to protest and prepare to fight against Imam Asghari's soldiers.

At that moment, Sergeant Bagher Khan fired a warning shot from his rifle into the air. The deafening sound resonated through the hills, freezing the people in their tracks as they looked around, contemplating their next move. Mounted on his horse, Sergeant Bagher Khan, the new head of the Law Men, raised his rifle in the air, fixing his gaze on Imam Asghari, his soldiers, and the people of Tikken, warning them not to make any sudden moves. The rest of the Law Men followed suit. Once Sergeant Bagher Khan sensed that the situation had calmed, he rode towards Shaykh Gonabadi, halted, turned, and regarded him as if he were his disciple, silently urging him to continue his actions. Once again, all eyes were fixed upon Shaykh Gonabadi.

But none of this had stopped Rostam Khan from forgetting the mention of Sattar's name by Shaykh Gonabadi. Determined, he reached out to Shaykh Gonabadi, seeking a suitable opportunity to inquire about Sattar's fate, whether he was alive or dead. However, Shaykh Gonabadi seemed so absorbed in his play that he appeared oblivious to Rostam Khan's presence, leaving his question unanswered. The rest of the crowd, including Rostam Khan, directed their attention back to Shaykh Gonabadi, noticing that he was fixated on the mulberry tree, seemingly speechless and surprised. It became evident that Shaykh Gonabadi was not the same person they had known and observed before; he seemed lost and detached. His face appeared pale, and his widened eyes and open mouth further revealed his astonishment. The spectators were not mistaken; Shaykh Gonabadi himself was now bewildered, struggling to comprehend what he was witnessing. He couldn't believe his eyes as he saw the spirits of Kal Abbas, Sattar, Asyeh, and Majnoon the dog standing by the mulberry tree, smiling at him. The reality of the situation began to dawn on him: the game he had initiated to foster peace among the people had now materialized. Simultaneously, doubts arose within him, questioning whether he was truly seeing their souls or if he was merely experiencing a hallucination.

"Hello, Master Kal Abbas, you've returned? So, you weren't imprisoned? The wicked people lied when they claimed you were shot and killed? Look, Asyeh Khanoum, hello... why do you still look so young? I have aged, but you remain youthful... Master, who is the man standing beside you? Sattar Khan?"

If Shaykh Gonabadi harbored any doubts about witnessing the souls of Sattar, Kal Abbas, and Asyeh, those doubts dissipated when he observed that Mard Ali also saw them and was conversing with them. Now, instead of addressing Kal Abbas, he responded to Mard Ali's query. "Yes, Mard Ali, he is Sattar... Assad Khan's younger son from Tikken, standing next to his beautiful wife, Asyeh."

Upon hearing the name "Sattar," Assad Khan's son known for his gun-wielding prowess, Mard Ali was suddenly flooded with memories of Assad Khan and the immense power he wielded. Fear gripped his soul, and he thought to himself, "Sattar!? Assad Khan's son, the one with the gun? Oh God, Assad Khan would shoot and kill all of us... It's time to run." Consequently, Mard Ali retreated and positioned himself behind the Law Men's horses. The bewildered crowd grew even more perplexed, with all eyes fixated on the mulberry tree in the hope of catching a glimpse of what

Shaykh Gonabadi and Mard Ali claimed to see. Yet, no one could perceive anything other than the tree. The situation evoked fear in many. However, Rostam Khan, whose patience and endurance had reached their limits, rode up to Shaykh Gonabadi and posed his question once more. "Shaykh, do you see Sattar? Is he alive or dead?"

"I see their souls," Shaykh replied.

"So, they are dead...!? Shaykh, ask him where he has spent all this time and where he is buried," Rostam Khan implored.

"All this time, he has been in the same place where he is standing now, alongside Asyeh and Kal Abbas. All three of them are buried here... beneath the mulberry tree... Asyeh's grave is in the middle," Shaykh responded.

Then Shaykh Gonabadi went to the graves and showed them to Rostam Khan. The more they watched and listened, the more people became confused and lost. A dead silence enveloped everyone and the hill. However, Imam Asghari, undeterred, raised his voice again and turned to his soldiers, calling for a loud prayer to regain their focus. "Let us recite a loud prayer for the blessings of God."

The commotion that Imam Asghari had stirred started to settle, but Ugly Ghadam and his gang began protesting, attempting to disrupt the proceedings. Sergeant Bagher Khan and the rest of the Law Men swiftly rode towards them, silencing their commotion forcefully this time. Then, Sergeant Bagher Khan turned to Shaykh Gonabadi. "Shaykh, since you have the ability to see their souls and communicate with them, can you ask them what should be done with this farm? Who should it be passed on to? Is there any documentation that indicates its ownership? And if there is, where can we find it?"

"Shaykh, tell Sergeant that you are our representative, and it is up to you to decide the fate of the farm and the distribution of the aqueduct's water. Let him know that whatever decision you make, we will accept it," Kal Abbas's spirit spoke to the Shaykh.

With the speeches of Sattar and Kal Abbas, the souls began to speak up. Shaykh Gonabadi found himself even more surprised and confused. It was something he never anticipated or expected to happen. He turned his gaze, scanning both sides and the Law Men, wondering if anyone else had heard the voices of Sattar and Kal Abbas. He saw no signs or felt that anyone else had. So, he turned back to the spirits, still dutiful but bewildered. Unbeknownst to him, he was conversing with the spirits. "Oh, Kal Abbas, Sattar, Asyeh Khanoum, when greed overtakes human hearts, even God cannot bring them to their senses. How am I, a mere servant of God, expected to make any sense to them? This is beyond my control."

"Yes, Shaykh is scared of Imam Asghari. He fears that Imam Asghari will issue a Fatwa to stone and kill him. He is afraid that Imam Asghari will turn him into stone with his miracle," Mard Ali's voice brought Shaykh back to his senses. With Mard Ali's words, laughter appeared on the faces of the three spirits. Mard Ali, who could see them, continued, pointing at the spirits. "They are laughing, as if the dead people could laugh too. Look, Shaykh, all three of them are laughing. Can dead people laugh?"

"You shouldn't worry, Shaykh. Shaykh Ahmad is here to help you. You are the representative of Village Tikken, and Shaykh Ahmad is the representative of the Village of Shourcheh, an honest and pious man, just like you," Sattar's soul spoke to Shaykh Gonabadi.

"Shaykh Ahmad!?" Shaykh Gonabadi responded.

"Yes, Shaykh. Don't worry, Shaykh Ahmad is on his way to assist you," Sattar assured him.

With Asyeh informing Shaykh Gonabadi about Shaykh Ahmad's imminent arrival to offer assistance, his eyes scanned the surroundings, searching for any sign of him, but to no avail. However, upon hearing Shaykh Ahmad's name, a wave of happiness swept over him. He was well acquainted with Shaykh Ahmad, who hailed from the city of Gonbad Kavoms but had wandered away and settled about eight hundred miles away. Shaykh Gonabadi himself had gained a wealth of knowledge from Shaykh Ahmad. He recalled how Sattar, like all the other students, used to secretly visit Shaykh Ahmad during the night, fearing the wrath of Mulla Mahmud, the village Mulla and a staunch adversary of Shaykh Ahmad due to his lack of religious understanding, akin to Imam Asghari's ignorance. It was during one of these clandestine visits that Sattar encountered Asyeh, who happened to be fetching drinking water from the creek at dawn. The rest, as they say, is history—they fell in love at first sight, unaware of the tragic events that awaited them. People, led by Mulla Mahmud, rose up against Asyeh solely because of his affection for their enemy's son. On their way to kill Asyeh, they stormed Shaykh Ahmad's house, intending to end his life as well. However, upon reaching him, he vanished, leaving everyone unsure of his fate. Some speculated that he had returned to his hometown, but all knew of Shaykh Ahmad's ability to separate his soul from his body and traverse different places. Shaykh Gonabadi was momentarily snapped out of his thoughts by the raised voice of Mar Ali. "Yes, Shaykh, do not worry. Look, Shaykh Ahmad is coming. Let me check if he has arrived or not." Confused and concerned, Shaykh Gonabadi and the rest of the people followed Mar Ali, who repeated the words uttered by the spirits. They moved closer to the village of Shourcheh, hoping for a clearer view of the road that led to the farm. Despite his gaze fixed on the path, Shaykh Gonabadi still couldn't spot Shaykh Ahmad. Silence enveloped the scene, and all eyes were on Shaykh Gonabadi. Zulfiqar, too, gazed upward, carefully observing Shaykh Gonabadi's every move. Determined not to be left behind, Zulfiqar raised his voice, pretending to hear the voices of the three spirits as well. "Shaykh, I didn't catch the last part. What did Kal Abbas say?" Before Shaykh Gonabadi could respond, Mard Ali's voice resonated once again. "Are you deaf? Kal Abbas didn't say anything. Mr. Sattar mentioned that Shaykh Ahmad is the representative of the people of Shourcheh and is now also representing the Village of Tikken. Look, if you are blind and can't see him approaching." Zulfiqar shouted back, "I heard everything until this point. I just didn't understand a part of it." Mard Ali swiftly put Zulfiqar in his place, remarking, "Well, if you didn't understand, then you must be dumb or deaf. Or sick, so perhaps you should visit a doctor."

It was then that Sergeant Bagher Khan felt a touch on his foot. He looked around but saw no one nearby. He wondered if it might be one of the spirits playing a prank on him. And he was not mistaken. Kal Abbas had indeed placed his hand on Sergeant Bagher Khan's foot. Although fear and apprehension rushed through him, the sergeant did not want to reveal his vulnerability to others. He cautiously and anxiously rested his hand on his foot, as if trying to touch the spirit's hand that was supposedly there. He glanced around, hoping to catch a glimpse of the person responsible, but to no avail. No one was seen, and his hand did not make contact with any other hand. Only Shaykh Gonabadi and Mard Ali had the ability to see spirits, but this incident erased any doubt Sergeant Bagher Khan had about their claims. He became a disciple of Shaykh Gonabadi, accepting his words, which was no easy task for Imam Asghari, who observed the scene. The jealousy and anger towards Shaykh Gonabadi grew in Imam Asghari, consuming him. However, he was under the watchful eye of a few lawmen who prevented him from taking any action. Imam Asghari's primary concern was that if Shaykh Gonabadi and Mard Ali could see the souls of Sattar, Kal Abbas, and Asyeh, they might also know the true identity of Imam Asghari and expose him to the lawmen, leading to his arrest and imprisonment. Lost in his thoughts about what to do, Imam Asghari was interrupted by Sergeant Bagher Khan's raised voice. "Well, Shaykh, now that you have been fortunate enough to witness their spirits, they have also acknowledged you. Shaykh Ahmad, tell us what to do. How should this situation be resolved? It seems that the fate of this mess rests in your hands... the thread and scissors are in your possession. Please guide us. And Shaykh, please remind the spirits not to touch our shoulders, as our hearts are fragile and weak." Sergeant Bagher Khan felt compelled to inject humor or deliver a message, but before Shaykh Gonabadi could respond, Mard Ali's voice resonated once again. "Oh, how blind we have been! We failed to notice that Shaykh Ahmad was standing at the edge of the water pond. How did they all manage to gather there simultaneously?"

When Mard Ali's voice resounded, Shaykh Gonabadi and the rest of the people shifted their gaze toward the pond. However, Shaykh Gonabadi was the sole observer of Shaykh Ahmad standing at the water's edge, accompanied by Sattar, Asyeh, and Kal Abbas, patiently waiting for him to join them. Mard Ali swiftly ran toward their gathering. Witnessing this, the Shaykh proceeded towards the pond, trailed by Sergeant Bagher Khan and the rest of the crowd. It didn't take long for everyone to converge at the water pond, where the aqueduct's water was collected for irrigation purposes.

Meanwhile, the people of Village Shourcheh and Tikken remained divided, with the Law Men positioned between them. All eyes were fixed on Shaykh Gonabadi, who displayed an unprecedented level of excitement and engagement. It was an entirely new demeanor for him, brought about by the presence of Shaykh Ahmad. Shaykh Ahmad, too, turned his attention to Shaykh Gonabadi, visibly sharing in his joy and seeking his opinion on dividing the farm and distributing the aqueduct's water.

Now standing side by side, the two Shaykhs gazed upon the descending hill that led to the two villages. In a sudden moment, their eyes met, revealing identical smiles on their faces. They were clearly contemplating the same idea, and words were unnecessary. Shaykh Ahmad glanced at Kal Abbas, Sattar, and Asyeh, and the smiles on their faces confirmed their agreement with their shared thoughts.

With no hesitation or exchange of words, Shaykh Gonabadi directed his gaze towards Sergeant Bagher Khan. "Sergeant, no matter what decision we make, there will always be a few individuals who protest and instigate conflict. They prioritize their own interests over the well-being of the people. They are not seeking peace, friendship, brotherhood, or equality. Therefore, Shaykh Ahmad, Kal Abbas, Sattar, Asyeh Khanoum, Majnoon the dog, and I have all agreed that we should open the pond and allow the water to lead us. We will follow its course and let it determine its path. If it chooses a direction, there will be no doubt or room for anyone to accuse us of favoring either side."

Upon hearing this, Sergeant Bagher Khan, the head of the Law Men, turned to address the villagers. He fired a warning shot to capture their attention and informed everyone of the decisions made by the two Shaykhs, emphasizing the need for obedience. Then, he turned to Shaykh Gonabadi and spoke. "Well, Shaykh, open the water."

"It is Shaykh Ahmad's right to open the water. He is the Shaykh for all," Shaykh Gonabadi replied.

"Well, tell Shaykh Ahmad to open the water," Sergeant Bagher Khan replied.

Mard Ali interjected, "If Shaykh Ahmad is deaf, he could hear you himself."

Meanwhile, Imam Asghari, growing impatient and exhausted, cleverly evaded the few Law Men who were watching him. He hurried to Sergeant Bagher Khan to voice his protest. "Oh, Sergeant, how do we know that these Shaykh Gonabadi and Shaykh Ahmad are not siding with the village of Tikken?"

He then turned to Haji Ghazanfar and the people of the Village of Shourcheh, continuing his argument. "Ah, Haji, what has happened to you all? Suddenly, has this Shaykh Gonabadi enchanted you with his magic? Has this magician put you all to sleep, blinded your eyes, and deafened your ears? How is it that this magician Shaykh went to sleep at night and woke up in the morning with a message from God to be our representative? Haji, Kadkhoda, why should only these two individuals, the deluded Mard Ali and the trickster Shaykh Gonabadi, be able to see spirits while none of us can? Haji, if you are not a man of God, why don't you see it? Haji, if you have forsaken your intellect, religion, and faith for a handful of atheistic magicians, I would swear on the holy book Quran that these two people have taken bribes from the village of Tikken."

Meanwhile, tension grew among the people of Tikken, and some of them, taking offense at Imam Asghari's words, began shouting curses at the people of Shourcheh, preparing for a fight. The conflict between the two villages was on the verge of resuming. However, Sergeant Bagher Khan knew he had to firmly confront Imam Asghari and silence him. With this in mind, he fired a warning shot into the air and rode with his men towards the people of Shourcheh, pushing Imam Asghari back as well. This allowed Shaykh Ahmad and Shaykh Gonabadi to commence their work. However, Imam Asghari refused to remain silent. He continued to move among his followers, encouraging them to fight and proclaiming it as God's will for them not to remain silent. He urged them to reclaim what rightfully belonged to them—the farm and the aqueduct. He once again issued a fatwa to support his call for action.

Of course, Ugly Ghadam and his gang did not sit idly by. At the instigation of Imam Asghari, one or two of them approached Shaykh

Gonabadi, and Ugly Ghadam aggressively pushed him, threatening him with further punishment if he persisted in his actions. As Shaykh Gonabadi was forcefully pushed, he stumbled back a few steps, leaving deep footprints on the edge of the pond before landing in the water.

Mard Ali immediately entered the water and helped the Shaykh rise. Unfazed by being pushed and landing in the water, Shaykh Gonabadi seemed to forget his soaked state and the presence of Mard Ali, who was assisting him. Despite some individuals on both sides attempting to clash again, the Law Men intervened and quickly silenced the fight. Throughout these events, Shaykh Gonabadi remained fixated on Shaykh Ahmad, Asyeh, Kal Abbas, Sattar, and Majnoon. His gaze was drawn to the two small, deep footprints he had left on the pond's edge before being immersed in the water.

Zulfiqar, Mard Ali, and the crowd watched Shaykh Gonabadi, bewildered by his focus on the footprints. They wondered why he wasn't upset by Ghadam Baldy's actions, seemingly finding delight in the situation. He now sported a smile while gazing at the depths of his footprints. Majnoon, who had been with Kal Abbas, Asyeh, and Sattar, positioned himself in front of Shaykh Gonabadi's feet and also fixed his gaze on the deep footprint. Occasionally, he glanced at Shaykh Gonabadi and Shaykh Ahmad, but his attention remained on the footprint at the pond's edge. Shaykh Gonabadi awaited Shaykh Ahmad's next move, seemingly detached from his surroundings. Zulfiqar raised his head inquisitively, hoping to glean some understanding from the unfolding events. Sergeant Bagher Khan noticed Shaykh Gonabadi and observed the filling of the footprint with water leaking from the pond. Soon, everyone was astonished to witness the soil on either side of the footprint being pushed aside without any interference, while water gradually seeped out of the pond.

The sound of people's prayers, now witnessing this miracle, resonated loudly, capturing the attention of those previously engaged in quarrels and bloodshed. Their focus shifted to the footprint and the falling soil. The thoughts of strife and discord were abandoned as everyone's gaze fixated on the footprint, leaving them breathless with anticipation. All eyes were locked on the footprint and the untouched soil being displaced. Prayers were offered and grew louder. Shaykh Ahmad and Shaykh Gonabadi watched with content smiles as Majnoon tirelessly pushed the soil away with his paws. Only Shaykh Gonabadi and Mard Ali recognized that it was Majnoon, the dog, responsible for this act. The spectators were astounded by the unfolding spectacle, enveloped in a stunned silence.

"Majnoon, do you need any assistance?"

Once again, it was Mard Ali who announced that Majnoon, the dog, was frantically digging around the footprint. He then turned towards the crowd and began shouting, resuming his chant. "The grip of Majnoon resembles Kola Abbas's shovel - observe how he moves the soil. Why do I even bother speaking to you? You are all blind and deaf."

Upon hearing Mard Ali's words, the people became not only confused but also frightened. A few individuals from the crowd started calling for prayer, their voices gradually growing louder. Eventually, the soil was cleared away from the footprint, and water began to seep out slowly, trickling down the hill. Majnoon stood before the water, with Mard Ali, Shaykh Ahmad, Shaykh Gonabadi, Kal Abbas, Asyeh, Sattar, Zulfiqar with his aged cane, Sergeant Gholi Khan, and his men, followed by the villagers from both sides, moving alongside the water, following Majnoon's lead. All eyes were fixed on the water, eager to see its destination. It became evident that when the water shifted towards the village of Tikken, the people from Shourcheh began to worry and feel uneasy, thinking the water had chosen Tikken. However, the flow of water, driven by Majnoon's movements, quickly changed course again and headed towards the village of Shourcheh. Instantly, restlessness and anxiety consumed the inhabitants of Tikken. It seemed that Majnoon and the water were toying with the people, playing their game.

A hush fell over the entire crowd, and no sound could be heard. It was as if everyone had fallen silent, incapable of predicting the outcome or the direction the water would ultimately choose or which village it would flow into. Imam Asghari was even more perplexed, moving through the crowd and desperately trying to persuade them to change their minds, urging them to incite a riot, all to break Shaykh Gonabadi's enchantment and alter the situation in his favor. However, the people were so enthralled by the running water that it seemed they either couldn't or didn't want to hear their Imam's voice.

Finally, Majnoon and the water reached the pinnacle of the last hill, where the water had to make its crucial decision—to flow towards Shourcheh or Tikken. Everyone knew that once it made its choice, there was no turning back. Water began filling a natural pit, while people stood and impatiently waited, their worry growing about what would happen next. Majnoon stood atop the hill, gazing at the two villages, as the pit filled with water. The moment of decision drew near. All eyes were fixated on the small pit, slowly filling up, and everyone waited anxiously. Silence pervaded the air, and even breathing seemed to cease. Eventually, the pit reached its brim, and the water flowed towards the village of Tikken. Observing this, the people of Shourcheh became furious and filled with rage, and Imam Asghari's voice rose once again. "Haji, Kadkhoda, didn't I tell you that this unscrupulous Shaykh Gonabadi accepted bribes from Tikken? Didn't I warn you that he would deceive us?"

But Imam Asghari's words were not yet over. Some people began to notice that, without any interference, the soil in the pit towards the village of Shourcheh started to shift, and water from the collected pit began to flow towards Shourcheh as well. However, only Mard Ali and Shaykh Gonabadi could see that it was Majnoon, the dog, who was removing the soil. With people's attention now diverted to the water flowing towards their village, Imam Asghari finally regained his composure and realized that the water was flowing evenly on both sides of Shourcheh and Tikken. Despite Imam Asghari's desire to manipulate the situation in his favor, he couldn't ignore the fact that Shaykh Gonabadi had gained numerous followers, potentially more than himself. This realization threatened Imam Asghari's power and position, which he refused to accept.

Imam Asghari was determined to remove Shaykh Gonabadi by any means necessary and regain control over the people. However, the water was now equally distributed between the two villages, and the authorities were satisfied that the issue had been resolved. The people on both sides also appeared content, except for Imam Asghari, whose mind continued to devise ways to create conflict and change the situation.

Imam Asghari began whispering to Haji Ghazanfar, "Haji, did you see how this ungodly Shaykh Gonabadi outmaneuvered us? He took half of our water today and gave it to his own people in Tikken. Soon, when everything settles down, he will play another one of his tricks and take even more, until we have no water left. Can't you see that the water going towards Tikken is more than what comes to us? Haji Ghazanfar, the people may be naive, blindly following this trickster, but what about us? We must make the people aware of what's happening. You are a man of God, a man of truth. It's our duty to act; the people are looking up to you, Haji. Remaining silent would be a betrayal of their trust. Look, the water flowing towards Tikken is much greater than what comes to us. We should at least try to redirect more water towards ourselves. If we don't act now, it will be too late. They will gain control of the water, and we will be powerless. And who will be held responsible, Haji? You, I, and Kadkhoda... We will be the ones who committed the sin by not fighting for our rights."

Imam Asghari continuously whispered in Haji Ghazanfar's ear, fueling his anger towards Shaykh Gonabadi. Eventually, Haji Ghazanfar succumbed to Imam Asghari's manipulation and began hurling curses at Shaykh Gonabadi, accusing him of betraying the people of Shourcheh and favoring his own followers in Tikken. Seizing the opportunity, Imam Asghari secretly orchestrated the intervention of his henchmen, led by Ghadam Baldy, who further encouraged Haji Ghazanfar by proclaiming him a man of God and the village leader. Haji Ghazanfar, consumed by arrogance, rallied the people of Shourcheh to defend their rights.

Imam Asghari exploited the situation by issuing a fatwa for Jihad, urging his followers to fight and die for their perceived rights. However, Imam Asghari's teachings had little to do with true Islam and were filled with falsehoods. Nevertheless, the misguided people blindly accepted his words. Imam Asghari himself was ignorant of the true meaning of Jihad, which is to struggle within oneself to overcome internal enemies and harmful thoughts. He did not understand that Islam prohibits killing and that the hijab signifies self-control, not merely covering one's hair.

Using Imam Asghari's fabricated orders, Ugly Ghadam and his men armed themselves with sticks, knives, and other weapons, spreading the message that they were fighting for Islam and their rights. Unaware of the deceit, some villagers joined Haji Ghazanfar and Imam Asghari, driven by fear of Hell or personal gain, and began insulting Shaykh Gonabadi. In response, a few individuals from Tikken diverted more water towards Shourcheh, provoking the Shourcheh villagers. This escalated into a violent clash, resulting in bloodshed and injuries.

Amidst the chaos, Imam Asghari reveled in his success, standing alongside Haji Ghazanfar and Kadkhoda, delighting in the sight of people being beaten and injured.

The Law Men, led by Sergeant Bagher Khan, were also present and actively engaged in their duties. They rode on horseback among the people, firing warning shots into the air and using their horses to push fighters to the ground, attempting to separate them. They resorted to beating them with their rifles in an effort to maintain order. However, it appeared that ensuring the safety of the people was not as significant as adhering to their Imam's mission, as assigned to them.

Meanwhile, Ugly Ghadam and a few of his gang members maneuvered through the battlefield and targeted Shaykh Gonabadi, launching an attack against him. Fortunately, Shaykh Gonabadi's supporters rushed to his aid and managed to rescue him from imminent danger, keeping him away from the enemies and the ongoing battle. As Shaykh Gonabadi turned his despairing gaze away from the chaotic scene, he noticed Shaykh Ahmad, Asyeh, Kal Abbas, Sattar, and Majnoon watching the clashes between the people from both villages. It was evident that they, too, were disheartened by their inability to reconcile the longstanding issues between the two villages, hoping for a peaceful coexistence. They recognized that the years of enmity had brought nothing but suffering and misery to both sides, yet they struggled to comprehend the true essence of peace. They pondered when the two villages would awaken to the desire for friendship and love.

It was clear that the presence of individuals like Imam Asghari and Haji Ghazanfar among the people only fueled these deep-rooted animosities. Their sole focus was their own personal interests, and they were willing to go to any lengths to safeguard them. Consequently, they seized every opportunity to achieve their desires, unconcerned about the well-being of the people or the principles of religion. They exhibited no regard or care for the impoverished and unfortunate individuals who suffered as a result. In fact, wherever such individuals existed, comfort, peace, and friendship were perpetually absent among the followers of religion. This problem extended to the villages of Tikken and Shourcheh, as their hatred and conflicts eventually culminated in the wrath of the earth, time, and God.

Several months later, the greed of the two villages consumed the hearts and minds of their inhabitants to such an extent that they were no longer satisfied with sharing or even possessing the majority of the water supply they coveted it all, regardless of the cost for each village. Bloodshed persisted, their struggle between good and evil endured, and no one truly grasped the underlying truth. They blindly followed their religious leaders and their emotions. The battle and the manipulation of water supply persisted, until one day both factions arrived at the pit to continue their struggle, only to find that there was no water left to fight over. The pit stood empty, devoid of the vital resource they had fiercely contested. Witnessing the dryness of the water did not quell their anger or hatred; instead, it ignited a blame game, with each side accusing the other of sabotage. Without hesitation, both groups raced to the aqueduct, determined to uncover the reason behind this sudden drought.

Amidst the dry creek, two groups seethed with rage and hatred, their sole purpose to finally settle their long-standing disputes. Armed with sticks, shovels, pickaxes, knives, and spears, they ascended the hill with tumultuous clamor, determined to uncover the cause of their strife. Even as they made their way, insults and curses continued to be hurled, resulting in a few skirmishes along the path.

And in the midst of it all stood Mard Ali, an indispensable presence armed with his wooden sword, chanting, and reciting as if preparing for a battle against evil. He traversed the dry creek alone, leading the way for both factions. It was Mard Ali who reached the hilltop and the pond first. However, his enthusiasm abruptly waned, and his sword fell silent, frozen in mid-air.

Soon, the people from both villages arrived at the hilltop, finding Mard Ali standing in a nearly empty pond, his perplexed gaze surveying the surroundings. They were astounded to witness the diminished water flow from the aqueduct, no longer gushing forth as it had before. Confusion reigned as they pondered the cause: What had transpired? Why had the water levels dwindled to the point where irrigation became a struggle? In the ensuing silence, Mard Ali's sword once again rose into the air, and his voice echoed towards the mouth of the aqueduct, its source. "Let us fight against those who obstruct the water, the enemies of God and Islam!"

Moved by Mard Ali's actions, the villagers from both sides, inexplicably drawn, began following him. It didn't take long for Mard Ali and his entourage to reach the opening of the aqueduct, a short distance away from the mulberry tree. A hush fell over the crowd, bewilderment painted on their faces. As if a veil had been drawn, their voices were muted, leaving them in a state of obliviousness. They stared in confusion, grappling with the sudden disappearance of the abundant water that once flowed freely through the aqueduct. There were no answers to be found. They pondered the mystery: Why had the water ceased to flow? Both villages now weighed this quandary, contemplating the wrath of a displeased God who had deprived them of water, a sign of their ungodliness.

Mard Ali broke the silence once again, speaking like a preacher who was not himself. It seemed he had finally provided an answer to their question. However, who would listen to or even hear Mard Ali? Who would make them understand that their behavior and greed had led them to be overwhelmed by the passage of time and creation, causing the water to recede? Now, who could convey the message and convince them that people could enjoy life within the bounds of their wisdom? Instead of learning from the drying aqueduct, each village came up with its own scapegoat, blaming others instead of themselves. In the village of Shourcheh, Imam Asghari's deceitful actions resumed, gaining even more followers. Together with Ugly Ghadam and his gang, they spread false news among the villagers, accusing the people of Tikken of the cause of the dried-up aqueduct. This sparked a thirst for revenge against the people of Tikken, deemed responsible for the disaster. Incited by Imam Asghari, fighting erupted once again between the two factions. As always, Imam Asghari, Haji Ghazanfar, and their gang watched from the sidelines, reveling in the bloodshed and malevolence of the people.

Meanwhile, the ghosts of Kal Abbas and his dog Majnoon, along with Sattar and Asyeh, sat on the rooftop of a hut, observing the madness with deep regret. Zulfiqar, as usual, remained silently in his room, contemplating, and worrying about his future. He continued to adhere to a policy of neutrality, hoping to find solace in the past.

* * * * *

Chapter 15
When, rage, hate, knives, sword and gun replace love, peace, and affection in religion

The weather was mild, and the hills were quiet, with a gentle breeze blowing. A jug of water emerged from the mouth of the farm's aqueduct, gracefully flowing between the earth and the air. Water droplets continued to slip and detach from the jar, falling to the ground. The jar rested in the hands of a woman, swaying as it lightly tapped against her colorful dress. As she approached the front of the hut and the platform, she raised her voice, breaking the silence.

"How long will you continue to sit here every day, gazing at the road and the hills? Eventually, it will drive you mad. Get up and do something, so you don't dwell on things I can't even fathom."

After addressing her husband, Zulfiqar, she entered the room. Despite being in her forties, she was much younger than Zulfiqar. It had been twenty years since the water supply diminished, yet nothing had changed. Animosity still lingered between the two villages. The rule of Imam Asghari remained intact and formidable, with the only notable difference being the increased number of his stick-wielding men who ruthlessly suppressed any opposition. Zulfiqar had adapted and settled down, no longer resorting to wandering and begging.

The naive people from nearby villages, believing that a divine light had truly descended upon the place and that it was blessed by God and the Imams, began to visit and partake in pilgrimage and prayers, making vows to seek healing and secure a place in Paradise. Gradually, the site transformed into a humble shrine, ultimately named 'SALEH PAYGHAMBAR.' Naturally, Zulfiqar became its trustee and guardian, living a contented life without the need to roam and beg. The generous donations received sustained both him and his wife, although a significant portion of these contributions found their way into the pockets of Imam Asghari.

But despite leading a quiet and well-cared-for life, Zulfiqar remained dissatisfied with his situation. He had grown accustomed to a nomadic lifestyle, constantly on the move, and now, as age and infirmity took hold, he found himself confined to one place. He had gotten married, but thoughts of death and the afterlife weighed heavily on his mind. This worried his wife, who observed him engaging in seemingly one-sided conversations with invisible individuals, referring to Kal Abbas, Sattar, Asyeh, and Kal Abbas' dog, Majnoon—entities he neither saw nor had knowledge of. Zulfiqar's wife, unfamiliar with the residents of Shourcheh and Tikken, where they resided, was unable to make sense of these apparitions or the conversations he had with them. She had accompanied an elderly man on a pilgrimage to the area, and it was he who confided in Zulfiqar about Fatima's tragic loss of her mother and her need for companionship. The old man had come to seek a suitable husband for Fatima, as he himself neared the end of his life. In a twist of fate, it seemed that the shrine—a mere mulberry tree surrounded by low walls—answered Fatima's prayers, leading to her marriage to Mr. Zulfiqar, after which they settled in that place.

However, finding himself alone with his wife in this new environment, Zulfiqar had ample time for introspection. His days were spent pondering his past, contemplating his choices and their consequences, and worrying about the afterlife, particularly concerning the fate of his wife after his own demise. Occasionally, he would be haunted by the thought that perhaps this was divine retribution, a consequence of his lies when he falsely claimed to have witnessed a shining light at the shrine, a fabrication he concocted to secure his place in the community and ensure their survival. Now, he feared that his falsehoods would be punished in the Hereafter. Regret gnawed at him, but he knew it was too late for remorse. On a few occasions, he had confided in Imam Asghari, sharing his thoughts and fears, only to be met with threats. The Imam warned him that speaking out would result in their deaths—Zulfiqar's own fate didn't concern him, but he was deeply troubled by the potential harm that could befall his wife, Fatima. Unfortunately, his condition deteriorated daily, and his regrets grew stronger. He questioned why he had ever divulged anything to Imam Asghari, fearing the consequences and the Imam's ruthlessness. His conversations with the unseen became a regular occurrence. Mard Ali, another elderly individual, would often visit them, spending most of his time at the mosque. Zulfiqar had engaged in conversations with the ethereal beings—Kal Abbas, Sattar Khan, and Asyeh Khanum—while Mard Ali was present. "Kal Abbas, Sattar Khan, Asyeh Khanum, I never harmed you, so why do you haunt me? If I wronged you, please forgive me. I was mistaken to deceive others about the fallen light. I am filled with shame before God, and I must confess my lies to everyone. But Imam Asghari warned that if I were to speak up, I would be killed, and my wife, Fatima, would suffer the same fate."

Mard Ali overheard Zulfiqar's conversation with unseen individuals, whispering and joking about it. Fatemeh, Zulfiqar's wife, grew worried upon hearing Mard Ali's voice and hastily left the room. She placed tea in front of both of them and sternly scolded Zulfiqar, demanding his silence. She then turned towards Mard Ali and threatened that if he continued sharing what he had heard from Zulfiqar, he would no longer be welcome in their presence. However, Mard Ali, who lived in his own world, unaffected by logic or threats, saw her words as a game and laughed it off before leaving for the village. Even days later, he continued to whisper and have fun with the information he had overheard from Zulfiqar.

Unbeknownst to Mard Ali, by repeating Zulfiqar's conversations with the unknown entities in the village of Shourcheh, he unwittingly signed Zulfiqar's death warrant. Mard Ali had no idea about the lies concocted by Imam Asghari to deceive people, nor did he realize the grave consequences of exposing the truth and jeopardizing the shrine's fraudulent practices. The majority of donations made to the shrine were funneled into Imam Asghari's pockets, a considerable sum that far exceeded the income of the entire village. With the increasing number of pilgrims each year, the Imam's share also grew. Therefore, Imam Asghari took immediate action and discreetly ordered Ugly Ghadam to eliminate Zulfiqar without delay.

On a dark, windy night, Zulfiqar and his wife were fast asleep when a knock on the door startled them awake. Groggy and bewildered, they stared at the door, wondering who could be visiting at such a late hour. Ghadam Baldy's voice was nearly drowned out by the howling wind outside, adding to the chaos of the moment. "Zulfiqar, you have a guest. Open the door," he called out.

After knocking persistently and receiving no response, Ghadam Baldy, growing impatient, forcefully slammed the door and began shouting at the top of his lungs. Fearful and trembling, Fatemeh reluctantly opened the door. Before the lock could fully disengage, Ugly Ghadam angrily shoved the door, knocking Fatemeh to the ground with a loud crash. Ugly Ghadam and his gang barged in, spewing curses and insults. "You are a shameless, stupid fool! Didn't we warn you to keep your mouth shut? Your voice should have been silenced, and you should have never spoken ill of the Imam. Did you think I was joking? Who do you think you are, you ignorant fool?"

In the blink of an eye, before Unfortunate Zulfiqar could even comprehend what was happening, he found himself overwhelmed and assaulted by Ugly Ghadam and his gang. The beating was merciless, rendering Zulfiqar unconscious within moments, lying motionless on the ground. Throughout the ordeal, his wife Fatima sought refuge in the corner of the room, trembling with fear and desperately pleading for mercy.

"Please, in the name of God, leave him be... He made a mistake and didn't say anything. Let him go, you're killing him," Fatima pleaded, her voice filled with terror.

However, her pleas fell on deaf ears. Ugly Ghadam, showing no mercy, turned his attention to Fatima while his gang continued to brutalize Zulfiqar. "Shut up... Shut up, you idiotic whore! If you don't stop, you'll suffer even more than him... Just shut up!" he barked angrily.

Fatima's voice was silenced, and she crouched in the corner, clutching her belly with her arms and legs, weeping silently for her unfortunate and defenseless husband, lying lifelessly in the center of the room, still being assaulted. Eventually, Fatima mustered the courage to speak again through her trembling voice. "Please, he's already dead. This is enough in the name of honor. He's dead."

Upon hearing her plea once more, Ugly Ghadam, consumed by anger and rage, turned his attention back to Fatima. "Shut up, you whore! I will defile this shrine that both you and your husband held sacred," he snarled.

Upon hearing Ugly Ghadam's voice, Fatima received a few harsh and painful kicks. She could only weep silently as she watched. Ugly Ghadam, determined to ensure Zulfiqar's demise, leaned over him and covered Zulfiqar's mouth and nose, pressing down until he was certain he had suffocated him. Fatima watched in agony and fear, her tears flowing silently. Ugly Ghadam then turned to Fatima again, as his gang members gestured to leave the room. "Why are you crying? Do you want this older blind man as your husband? I will take care of you myself. The Imam himself will make it lawful, and you will also go to heaven."

An hour later, as Ugly Ghadam pulled up his pants and put on his coat, he faced Fatima once more. "Remember, if you dare to reveal what happened here, you'll face the same fate... Just remember, you should tell everyone that people from Tikken stormed in, killed, and raped you... Do you understand?... Remember?"

Fatima, too afraid to speak, gestured her compliance. Just before Ugly Ghadam left, he turned to her for the final time. "You are now my woman. Don't worry, I will take care of you." And with that, he departed, leaving Fatima's gaze fixed on the door, filled with self-loathing and resentment toward the shrine and, undoubtedly, Ugly Ghadam, with her deceased husband lying between her and the exit.

*****

The wind relentlessly battered the branches and leaves of the mulberry tree, as Fatima sat beneath it, beside the graves. She engaged in a conversation, both spoken and through prayers, with the man interred in the shrine. Despite her lack of knowledge regarding his identity, Fatima wept profusely, her tears flowing like blood. She implored the shrine and the man within it for forgiveness, beseeching them not to condemn her to hell for the transgressions between her and Ghadam Baldy. Fatima pleaded fervently that if forgiveness was unattainable, at least the innocent child within her womb should be spared.

She conveyed to the shrine that she was not guilty, emphasizing that she had informed Ugly Ghadam of her pregnancy four months prior to his abhorrent act of rape. Driven by fear, she now referred to him as Haji, as Ugly Ghadam had suddenly transformed into a haji overnight, without even making the pilgrimage to Mecca. In a desperate attempt to be heard by the shrine and anyone who would listen, Fatima declared that Haji Ugly Ghadam had forcefully violated her.

Despite her heartfelt pleas, it seemed that Fatima's voice was drowned out by the howling wind, unheard by the shrine or anyone else around. Unbeknownst to Fatima, the buried soul within the shrine had failed to perceive her cries and supplications. Furthermore, she remained unaware that the spirits of Kala Abbas, Sattar, Asyeh, and even the dog stood by her side, intently listening to every word she uttered.

*****

The air was no longer dark, and the wind no longer whipped trees and people. The warm sunbathed everything in a radiant glow, infusing color and warmth into the surroundings. The old man quickened his pace, his footsteps echoing through the tranquil road and along the river, urging him to reach the mosque sooner. Passing through an alley, he finally caught sight of the mosque in the distance. A gathering of people stood in front and around it, indicating a significant event or unfortunate occurrence. Curiosity piqued, and the old man made his way through the crowd and entered the bustling courtyard, which was brimming with people.

Haji Ugly Ghadam and his group were scattered throughout the mosque, vigilantly observing the crowd to prevent any unwanted disturbances during Imam Asghari's speech. They also worked to invigorate the attendees before Imam Asghari took the pulpit. From time to time, they would shout "Prayer," interjecting it between Imam Asghari's words to express their reverence for the Imams. Imam Asghari's resounding voice echoed from the pulpit as he passionately spoke, his words reaching every corner.

"Zulfiqar, the hero of our religion and our village of Shourcheh, has become a martyr for our faith and our community. He bravely confronted the atheists and enemies of our religion until his last breath, sacrificing his life for us. We must erect a tomb for him beside the shrine so that the perpetrators who callously took his life are blinded by their own jealousy."

Mard Ali, seated at the foot of the pulpit, occasionally raised his voice to greet and praise Imam Asghari. However, his enthusiasm seemed to have waned, as his voice lacked its previous fervor and even, he struggled to hear himself amidst the bustling crowd. "Zulfiqar is our hero. He was brutally beaten to death."

Imam Asghari raised his voice even louder, determined to make himself heard over the clamor. "We have a religious, cultural, and moral obligation to ensure that the blood of our religious hero and martyr, Zulfiqar, is not trampled upon. This is what jihad means in our faith. It is for moments like this, for us to rise up and seek vengeance for his death."

Ugly Ghadam and his group called for several prayers, and the people responded in unison. Amidst the growing excitement, it took Imam Asghari a moment to calm the crowd and continue his speech from the elevated pulpit. "So, what does jihad mean? And when is the time for it? It is now, my friends. But we also have a religious duty to care for Fatima Khanum, Zulfiqar's innocent wife. Let us remember to support and protect her during these challenging times."

Fatemeh sat in the women's section, her heart heavy with sorrow. The people surrounding her offered comfort, unaware of the true reason behind her tears. They assumed she was grieving for her husband, Zulfiqar, and they were not entirely mistaken. Her anguish, however, stemmed not only from her husband's loss but also from the oppression she endured at the hands of the deceitful and hypocritical Imam on the pulpit. Despite his public praise of her and her husband, he was the source of her deep depression and resentment.

No matter how fervently Fatemeh cried out, begging God or anyone to hear her, it seemed that her pleas fell on deaf ears. Her pain went unnoticed, and she longed for someone to recognize her suffering and understand the true enemy—Imam Asghari and his cohorts. Yet, she could only scream silently within herself, afraid to speak out and reveal the truth. She remained silent about the abuse she endured, the beatings and rapes inflicted upon her by Ghadam Baldy, one of the Imam's men.

She wondered if God, the Imam, or the Prophet were even aware of her existence, of her presence in the mosque under the constant threat of Ghadam Baldy. It seemed as if her voice went unheard, her cries unanswered, and no one came to her aid.

Meanwhile, in the men's section, the attention shifted to Mard Ali, seated near the pulpit. He rose from his place, his eyes searching, scanning the surroundings with a smile on his face. Unbeknownst to others, Mard Ali was following the ethereal presence of Kal Abbas, who moved around Imam Asghari and the pulpit. Mard Ali couldn't contain his excitement and exclaimed, "Kal Abbas!? You're alive? You've returned!"

His laughter echoed through the mosque, causing disturbance, and attracting the attention of Haji Ghadam Baldy, who approached him and struck him forcefully on the head, attempting to silence him. However, the blow only fueled Mard Ali's excitement and anger. Especially when Kal Abbas's spirit began to communicate with him.

"He's not an Imam; he's an imposter, a fraud," Kal Abbas's spirit revealed. "He's Moharram Bogundo, masquerading as a Clergyman or an Imam. He even poisoned and killed Mullah Mahmoud. Mullah Mahmoud wanted you to inform the people that their supposed Imam is a fake. Ask the Imam to present his birth certificate. He doesn't possess one."

As Kal Abbas's spirit spoke, Mard Ali would passionately shout out and repeat his words, resonating loudly across the mosque's premises. He was trailed by Ugly Ghadam and his gang, but despite his older age, witnessing Kal Abbas's spirit seemed to infuse him with the energy and spirit of his youth. Skillfully evading them, Mard Ali moved with agility, brandishing his wooden sword in the air, directing it towards Imam Asghari, as if engaging in a battle against Islam's fiercest adversaries.

"Kal Abbas says he is Moharram Bogundo... Moharram, who set fire to Ghodrat and took his life... Zulfiqar also fell victim to Ugly Ghadam and his men last night, not the people of Tikken. Ugly Ghadam violated Fatima, Zulfiqar's wife... Why don't you ask Fatima about it? Kal Abbas is relaying this information to me... Are you all deaf or blind that you can't hear or see him yourselves? Look, he is standing beside Imam Asghar."

Gradually, Mard Ali's performance began to affect the crowd. Confusion and surprise enveloped them, particularly due to the repetition of Kal Abbas's spirit, speaking through Mard Ali, amidst his escape from Ugly Ghadam and his gang within the mosque. The commotion disrupted the proceedings of the parliament. People observed intently, regardless of how badly Mard Ali was beaten and the blood streaming from his head and face. He refused to surrender; on the contrary, his courage and determination grew. It was as if the blood reminded him of the Day of Ashura, the historic battle in Islam's ancient times, where Imam Hussein fought valiantly with only seventy-two men against an army of thousands, all of whom perished. In his mind, he had become Imam Hussein, the hero of that battle, ready to sacrifice himself.

As he fled, Mard Ali pulled down the curtain that divided the men and women sections, uniting them in one space. His unwavering resolve and bravery made Ugly Ghadam, and his gang hesitate and grow slightly nervous. Unbeknownst to them, Mard Ali perceived Imam Asghari as the embodiment of Shamer, the adversary who fought against Imam Hussein in the infamous battle and caused his demise. Mard Ali sought revenge for Imam Hussein's death, envisioning his wooden sword as Imam Hussein's and Imam Ali's. With resounding chants and tearful eyes, Mard Ali reached the pulpit from amidst the crowd, unexpectedly striking Imam Asghari on the head with his wooden sword, causing Imam Asghari's turban to fall. As one corner of the turban clung to the tip of Mard Ali's sword, the other end floated in the air, dancing among the people. Mard Ali continued running through the crowd, chanting, and combating the worst enemy of Islam—Imam Asghari. His shouts grew louder and louder. "Imam is a false Imam! He is not a true leader; he deceives all of you... He is Moharram!"

Hearing and seeing Mard Ali, people gradually began to feel sympathy for him, especially the younger ones and women whose voices had been silenced over time. Now, with the mosque in ruins and the Imam's enforcers like Ugly Ghadam and his gang unable to exert their power with sticks, knives, and clubs, people found their courage and started raising their voices in protest against Mard Ali's beating.

"Let him go, leave him alone," they cried out.

"What sin has he committed to deserve such punishment?"

"Do you not believe in religious and mercy?"

"And do you not believe in God?"

"What kind of Muslims are you?"

"What kind of person takes pleasure in beating a poor, wandering old man?"

"Do you want to see an old man bleed to death?"

"Perhaps he is not a true Imam after all."

"What kind of religion lacks mercy for a madman in his own mosque?"

As some people rushed to help Mard Ali, Fatima's brave voice, which had been silenced for so long, suddenly resonated throughout the mosque. "People, Ugly Ghadam came to our house last night in the middle of the night. He broke down our door, killed Zulfiqar, and disgraced me. What kind of religion is this? An Imam who kills people? He is not a real Imam. Mard Ali is right; he is a fake... he stole our religion. God is my witness... but it seems that God could not hear my voice. Perhaps you can?"

With the rise of Fatima and Mard Ali's voices, followed by many others, both women and men, gradually their minds overcame superstitions and fears. They regained their senses and joined the cause. Finally, people were no longer afraid of the Imam's bodyguards and hitmen, Ugly Ghadam and his gang, nor of Imam Asghari himself. Almost all the people, except for a few, began chanting that Imam Asghari was not the true Imam. They called him a cheater, an enemy of Islam. Clashes between the people and the Imam's bodyguards, Ghadam Baldy, and his gang ensued, while some loyal followers of the Imam fought back.

Imam Asghari realized that the situation was becoming dire and dangerous for him. He knew that the people would eventually reach him and discover that he was none other than Moharram, a liar and deceiver who had manipulated them all along. He attempted to escape, but there were too many people fighting around him. He understood that if he descended from the pulpit, he would be attacked as well.

While he searched for an escape route, he noticed a couple of candles still flickering near the pulpit. Seizing the opportunity, he slyly pushed the candles, causing them to topple onto the pulpit's green covering, igniting a fire. As the flames grew, they captivated the attention of the crowd, creating a diversion that allowed Imam Asghari to cleverly slip away. By the time people realized his absence, he had nearly reached the mosque's exit. However, the panicked and fearful mob, driven by the blazing fire, pursued Imam Asghari and his followers. In a matter of seconds, his men either fled or succumbed to the relentless assault of the furious crowd. Overwhelmed, they were beaten mercilessly, and their weapons—sticks, knives, and clubs—were wrested from their grasp and turned against them. The tide of anger and rage consumed both the crowd and the surroundings. In an act of vengeance, some individuals even set fire to the pulpit, which further fueled the chaos. Dark smoke billowed, flames engulfed the mosque, and the chant of "Imam is not a true Imam; he is a fraud" echoed through the air as the mob closed in on Imam Asghari.

Within a short span of time, the mosque emptied as people fled, leaving behind a blazing inferno. Imam Asghari and a few of his men fought for their lives amidst the flames, their cries mingling with the crackling fire and resounding through the mosque. It was reminiscent of the cries of Ghodrat, Haji Amir's son, who had met a similar fate at the hands of Imam Asghari. Now the tables had turned against him. The fire blazed through the mosque's doors and windows, while thick smoke billowed out and hung in the air like a shroud, casting a veil of darkness over the village. Imam Asghari's shouts pierced through the smoke, reverberating out of the mosque and reaching the ears of the villagers as they advanced, chanting, towards the cemetery. Led by Mard Ali, drenched in blood, the majority of the village's young men and women followed suit. The bloodlust had blinded them to any notions of religion or divinity. Finally awakened, they recognized Mullah Mahmud as the root cause and architect of their misfortunes, as well as the subsequent afflictions imposed upon their beliefs by Imam Asghari. Driven by this realization, they arrived at Mullah Mahmud's grave, now marked by a humble tomb, and armed with shovels, pickaxes, and hammers. In an instant, the graves were obliterated, and even Mullah Mahmud's corpse was exhumed and consumed by the flames, reducing it to ashes.

On the hill overlooking the cemetery, Kal Abbas, Asyeh, Sattar, and Majnoon the dog observed with hopeful gazes, contemplating whether the people had truly absorbed the lessons or if the passage of time would cause them to forget once more. Alas, history repeated itself, as another religious cleric emerged, attracting another wave of deceitful opportunists who blindly trailed behind.

* * * * *

Chapter 16
When uninformed and naive individuals amplify trivial matters. A century has come and gone, yet...

The majestic mountains of Shourcheh towered above, their peaks reaching the sky. Overturned tulips adorned the hills, accompanied by a vibrant array of wildflowers and thorny desert artichokes. The melody of crickets filled the air, blending harmoniously with the gentle breeze that caressed the face of a blind man strolling along a dirt road amidst the hills. Despite his lack of sight, clarity resonated within his mind. Even if his cane were to be taken away, he felt an unbroken connection leading him towards the shrine.

Mashhadi ABDOLLA, the blind man, perceived an unfamiliar sound echoing from the distance. Intrigued, he stood up, raised his head, and directed his gaze towards the source of the sound. As the volume intensified, curiosity, confusion, and concern gripped him. Abdullah's ears sharpened, recognizing that this sound was distinct from those he had grown accustomed to. He turned his head in the direction of the noise, witnessing a cloud of dust swirling on the hill. He pondered that it might be a car, yet unlike any he had heard before. The rumble was softer, distinct from its predecessors. Mashhadi Abdullah proceeded towards the shrine and the neighboring stone and lumber houses. Leaning against the front garden, he raised his head, honed his senses, and awaited the arrival of the car. Pilgrims wandered inside and outside the shrine, their presence discernible. Finally, the car, unfamiliar yet recognizable as a car, approached the shrine, applying the brakes and coming to a halt. Mashhadi Abdullah was enveloped by the dust cloud raised by the car.

Gradually, the dust settled, dissipating into the air. The car had not fully stopped when three or four children emerged, brimming with excitement. Soon after, their father ABBAS, a man in his fifties, also alighted. Abbas and his children gazed warmly as a petite woman, Abbas's wife and the mother of their children, stepped out of the car. Their urban attire hinted at their city origins.

Mashhadi Abdullah's attention remained suspended in the air, his senses alert, as if anticipating the voices of the newly arrived passengers, yearning to identify them. The sound of the car doors closing informed him that the passengers had disembarked, yet he awaited their identification. Abbas and his family observed the shrine and its surroundings in awe. They beheld an aged wooden shrine, its entrance adorned by a mulberry tree with two lofty branches reaching out in every direction. Above the door, a colorful sign displayed the words "Saleh Payghambar." A vibrant sign displayed the words "Saleh Payghambar," which translated to "Hello The Messenger." The trunk of the mulberry tree was enveloped in a kaleidoscope of green, red, and various other colored clothes. Sunflowers graced both sides of the platform leading to the inner room, nestled within two gardens. Kamal, still engrossed in his surroundings, questioned whether he had arrived at the correct place. His wife fixated her gaze on the elderly couple emerging from the shrine, mindful not to turn her back towards the graves inside, out of respect for the deceased. They exchanged kisses on either side of the door before entering the shrine. Finally, they departed from the shrine, approaching Abbas and his family. Along their path, they warmly greeted Mashhadi Abdullah, who remained by the platform, bewildered and longing for the voices of the newcomers to reach his ears, unveiling their identities. Upon reaching Abbas, they exchanged greetings, continuing their journey, as they reached the car, the elderly man paused, gazing at it for a moment before rejoining his wife, and together, they disappeared behind the hills.

Abbas, taken aback and somewhat confused by his surroundings, walked calmly towards Mashhadi Abdullah. He leaned on a nearby platform, mirroring Mashhadi Abdullah's position, and both of them fixed their gaze upon the shrine, waiting for someone to break the silence. Eventually, Mashhadi Abdullah's patience wore thin, and he spoke up, shattering the quietness.

"You must be a stranger, finding yourself here for the first time," Mashhadi Abdullah remarked.

"Yeah," Abbas replied.

"If you had come solely for pilgrimage, you would be inside the shrine, paying homage to the grave," Mashhadi Abdullah inquired.

"That's correct. I came to search for my great grandfather, to discover the place of his burial," Abbas responded.

Mashhadi Abdullah retrieved his handkerchief from his pocket, wiping his forehead and face, as he raised his voice again. "Why did you come here to find him?"

"I was told that he was a legendary figure, and he was likely buried here... It must have been over a hundred years ago. I was informed that he was once wealthy and influential, but he relinquished everything and turned to begging in pursuit of truth... His name was Kal Abbas, yet he was commonly known as the silent beggar," Abbas explained.

"The silent beggar!? Yes, I have heard tales from my grandmother too... It is said that in ancient times, a relative of Imam Ali fled from the infidels' army and sought refuge here. Despite relentless pursuit, he disappeared after entering the aqueducts. No matter how diligently they searched, he was never found. Then, during the night, people witnessed a radiant light shining down from the sky upon this very place, as though it were daylight. This led to the establishment of this shrine. Furthermore, I was informed that many years later, an elderly beggar known as 'The Silent Beggar' appeared. They say he was both mute and deaf. He fled from the ruthless tyrant of the Village of Rabat Karim and, while facing a snowstorm behind these mountains, he found himself here with the master. When Karim Khan's gunmen pursued him, they saw him enter the shrine. However, upon their entry, they found no trace of the silent beggar. It was as if he had vanished instantaneously. Yes, indeed, he had disappeared, leaving Karim

Khan's gunmen were terrified, prompting them to flee. Word of the silent beggar vanishing inside the shrine spread far and wide... The following day, people rushed here to witness the events for themselves.

They discovered that overnight, a grave had appeared next to another grave beneath the berry tree. On top of it rested a large tombstone, as if it had been there for ages. However, the most astonishing aspect was not the tombstone itself but the sudden appearance of this grave, two miracles occurring consecutively... After that, no further information was ever heard about the silent beggar. And yes, it is highly likely that he was the same silent beggar," Mashhadi Abdullah concluded and then fell silent.

Now, Abbas, listening to Mashhadi Abdullah, voiced his curiosity. "Who was the gentleman who disappeared? Where did he come from?"

Mashhadi Abdullah turned towards Abbas and, after a moment of reflection, raised his voice. "Sir, there have been several miracles that have occurred here. If you're referring to the man who fled from the infidels, it is said that he was one of the grandsons of Imam Asghari. He escaped from the infidels' army, who pursued him with the intention of capturing and killing him. Just as they were about to seize him, an army of Elves and fairies appeared out of nowhere, surrounding the infidels and eliminating them all. This event took place at night, accompanied by the ethereal sounds of the Elves. The villagers, awakened by the commotion, witnessed the desert suddenly bathed in an illuminating light from the sky. They hurried here, only to discover the majestic mulberry tree and the flowing aqueduct, which had appeared simultaneously with the radiant light. It is believed that God created the mulberry tree and concealed the man within its trunk, never to emerge again. Thus, the shrine came into existence. Nowadays, people who are ill come here seeking healing."

Mashhadi Abdullah's attention was momentarily diverted by the sound of another car approaching from the base of the hill. He turned his head towards the noise, awaiting the arrival of the car and preparing to share the shrine's history with the new travelers. He didn't have to wait long; the car arrived and parked beside Abbas's car. Once again, Mashhadi Abdullah, the guardian of the shrine, commenced recounting the shrine's story to the new visitors.

The shrine of "Saleh Payghambar," once a simple place of pilgrimage, had now transformed into a destination for both religious devotion and leisure. People from the surrounding areas would ascend the mountain, spend a few days there, complete their pilgrimages, and then return home.

* * * * *

The End.

Characters at Shourcheh's are:

Mullah Mahmoud - Is an unscrupulous fraud clergy who exploits religion to deceive innocent people, using it to serve his own interests. Despite his advanced age, he continues to engage in such manipulative practices.

Imam Asghari/Moharram - In his younger days, was Mulla Mahmoud's informant and also, his secret lover. He used to carry out Mulla Mahmoud's commands unquestioningly. After he killed Ghodrat, Hajji Amir's older son, he disappeared. In his old age, he returns to the village, assuming a different appearance and disguising his true identity by adopting an Arabic accent.

Kal Abbas - Was a lawman who later abandoned his position and turned to thievery. Eventually, he became a fugitive and went underground, hiding from the law by assuming the identity of the Silent Beggar.

Hajji Ghazanfar – He is Kadkhoda, the former village mayor and one of Mulla Mahmud's previous partners in crime. And after Kadkhoda's death, he inherited all his wealth and became Hajji consequently, Hajji Ghazanfar is now affluent.

Zulfiqar – Now in his sixties, he is a wandering homeless beggar who used to reside in the mosque.

Fatemeh - Is Zulfiqar's wife.

Crazy Mard Ali - Is a young man who lives with his widowed mother and works at various households to survive. He possesses wisdom in his own unique world.

Mashadi Hassan Gorkan - Is an older man whose profession involves digging graves for the deceased.

Kal Ahmad - Is an elderly gentleman who spends his time sitting in front of his house, which faces the graveyard. He engages in conversations with anyone entering or leaving the village.

Ugly Ghadam - Is an informant and enforcer for Imam Asghari, earned his nickname due to his complete baldness.

Sergeant Teymur Khan - Was Kal Abbas's best friend, who assisted him in joining law enforcement. Later, he became a sergeant and head of the law enforcement department.

Majnoon - Is the spirit of Abbas's deceased dog.

Shaykh Ahmad's spirit… - He was a holy man and spiritual teacher who vanished.

Asyeh Spirit.

Shaykh Gonabadi Spirit.

The Village of Tikken

Rostam Khan – IS Assad Khan's older son who is in charge after his father.

Sattar – Is one of the main characters in the three books, and Ghodrat's younger brother.

Goldokht Khanum – Assad Khan's daughter.

Borzoyeh Khanum – Assad Khan's Wife
Shaykh Gonabadi – Was a kind and nice Shaykh in the Village of Tikken.

www.ingramcontent.com/pod-product-compliance
Lightning Source LLC
Chambersburg PA
CBHW070437120726
47910CB00003B/822

* 9 7 8 1 0 8 8 2 0 5 6 5 5 *